THE COMPLETE IDIOT'S GUIDE®

Quinoa Cookbook

by Susan Irby, The Bikini Chef

ALPHA

A member of Penguin Group (USA) Inc.

I dedicate this book to all the people who strive to live a healthy lifestyle and enjoy healthy, flavorful foods. May this information and these recipes help you on your journey.

ALPHA BOOKS

Publisher: *Marie Butler-Knight*
Associate Publisher: *Mike Sanders*
Executive Managing Editor: *Billy Fields*
Senior Acquisitions Editor: *Tom Stevens*
Senior Development Editor: *Christy Wagner*
Senior Production Editor: *Janette Lynn*

Copy Editor: *Teresa Elsey*
Cover Designer: *William Thomas*
Book Designers: *William Thomas, Rebecca Batchelor*
Indexer: *Tonya Heard*
Layout: *Ayanna Lacey*
Proofreader: *John Etchison*

Contents

Introduction

Quinoa (pronounced *KEEN-wah*, not *quinn-OH-ah*) has been around for thousands of years—since the time of the Incas, in fact. Thought to be a grain but actually a seed, quinoa is loaded with nutritional benefits. It cooks quickly, and when combined with spices, vegetables, and other tasty ingredients, it can be wonderfully delicious.

If you're wondering how I wrote a whole cookbook about one seed, prepare to be very pleasantly surprised! In the following chapters, I give you a breakdown of what quinoa is, the numerous ways you can incorporate it into dishes, and more than 180 mouthwatering recipes—from breakfast to dessert—you can make and be proud to serve your family and friends—all with this one small superseed!

Within each recipe, I've provided nutritional information based on a single serving, so if you're following a specific diet plan or just want to know exactly how many calories and grams of fat, fiber, protein, and carbs you're consuming, you have all the information you need right at your fingertips.

It's my goal that by the end of this book, you can wow your friends and family with a dinner party filled with delicious, nutritious quinoa dishes and become the expert when everyone at the party asks, "*Quinn-oh-ah*—what's that?"

How to Use This Book

This book is divided into seven parts:

Part 1, Getting to Know Quinoa, serves as an introduction to this popular seed. I give you a nutritional breakdown of all of quinoa's amazing properties, including all the vitamins, minerals, protein, fiber, and other nutrients packed in each seed.

In **Part 2, Good-for-You Breakfasts,** I show you how easy it is to incorporate quinoa into your morning meals. From quick grab-and-go breakfasts for busy weekday mornings to more leisurely breakfasts you can prepare on a weekend or for a brunch, I give you tons of delicious ways to wake up with quinoa.

Part 3, Really Tasty Lunches, is chock-full of lunchbox-worthy recipes. With soups, salads, sandwiches, and more, you'll find plenty of quinoa-based midday dishes to wow your co-workers (and maybe make them a little jealous while they eat their fast-food drive-thru lunches).

When you want to impress your friends or need a light snack, turn to **Part 4, Easy Appetizers and Snacks.** The chapters in this part will have you dipping, spreading, snacking, and munching on finger-licking quinoa starters and light bites.

"What's for dinner?" You'll find plenty of answers to this age-old question in **Part 5, Delicious Dinners.** Whether you're vegetarian, vegan, or 100 percent carnivore, you'll love the pleasing quinoa main dishes in these chapters.

A meal isn't complete without tempting side dishes, and that's what **Part 6, Scrumptious Side Dishes,** is all about. You're sure to find plenty of quinoa-based sides to highlight any main dish.

Finally—and this is my editor's favorite part—**Part 7, Delectable Desserts,** will wow you with dozens of sweet and scrumptious desserts—all made with quinoa. Cookies, pies, cakes, custards—I've got plenty of options for satisfying your sweet tooth here.

At the back of the book, I've included a glossary of helpful terms plus a list of further resources you can use to learn more about quinoa.

Extras

Throughout the book, you'll also notice nuggets of extra information packaged in sidebars. Here's what to look for:

DEFINITION

These sidebars offer definitions and explanations of terms, ingredients, and cooking techniques.

KEEN ON QUINOA

For fun "seeds" of information, check out the Keen on Quinoa sidebars.

QUICK FIX

Check out these sidebars for quick tips and helpful hints.

WHOA!

Do heed these warning sidebars that help guide you on what to do or what not to do.

In addition to sidebars, you'll see this icon next to some recipes:

This icon indicates the recipe was contributed by a top restaurant chef or professional.

But Wait! There's More!

Have you logged on to idiotsguides.com lately? If you haven't, go there now! As a bonus to the book, we've included additional quinoa recipes you'll want to check out. Point your browser to idiotsguides.com/quinoacookbook, and enjoy!

Acknowledgments

I'd like to thank my editors, Tom Stevens, Christy Wagner, Karyn Gerhard, Janette Lynn, and the Alpha Books team who showed patience, kindness, support, and impeccable direction; my agent, Marilyn Allen; and my wonderful hair stylist, Eric Allen of Allen Somers Salon, for providing me with Wi-Fi and a comfortable place to write this book while getting beautified. Thanks to my husband, Christopher, and my daughter, Rachel, for their suggestions, love, and support on the days I had to pass on watching a movie or shopping at the mall; and to my parents, Melba and Dave, for giving me the gifts of cooking and writing as well as their never-ending love.

Thank you to each of the chefs and professionals who contributed their recipes to the book: Chef Chris Barnett, Chef Katy Clark, Chef Brendan Collins, Chef Mark Ellman, Denice Fladeboe, Kevin Fortun, Chef Jon Gibson, Chef Lee Gross, Chef Katsu Hanamure, Chef Dana Herbert, Chef Elizabeth Howes, Chef Ashley James, Hailey Kehoe, Chef Brock Kleweno, Chef Manfred Lassahn, Chef James McDonald, Chef Jessica Obie, Chef Keith Otter, Chef Serena Palumbo, Chef Bruno Serato, Chef Randal St. Clair, and Chef Giselle Wellman.

Special Thanks to the Technical Reviewer

The Complete Idiot's Guide Quinoa Cookbook was reviewed by an expert who double-checked the accuracy of what you'll learn here, to help us ensure that this book gives you everything you need to know about cooking delicious, nutritious meals with quinoa. Special thanks are extended to Rhonda Lerner.

Trademarks

All terms mentioned in this book that are known to be or are suspected of being trademarks or service marks have been appropriately capitalized. Alpha Books and Penguin Group (USA) Inc. cannot attest to the accuracy of this information. Use of a term in this book should not be regarded as affecting the validity of any trademark or service mark.

Getting to Know Quinoa

Quinoa (pronounced *KEEN-wah*, not *quinn-OH-ah*) has been around for thousands of years, but don't be surprised if your friends and family have never heard of it. They'll soon get to know and love quinoa and relish all the nutrients it provides.

Part 1 gives you the inside scoop on exactly what quinoa is (it's a seed, not a grain, as commonly thought), where it comes from, and where you can find it today.

Then, I shine a spotlight on just how healthy quinoa really is. Filled with the right proteins for a balanced diet, rich in fiber, and packed with nutrients, quinoa is truly deserving of its ancient Inca title, "the mother of all grains."

What Is Quinoa?

In This Chapter

- Quinoa 101
- Quinoa's many health benefits
- Where to find quinoa
- Quinoa preparation tips

If you're unfamiliar with quinoa, let me introduce you! Quinoa (pronounced *KEEN-wah*, not *quinn-OH-ah*) is a grainlike seed, much like rice, cornmeal, and oats. It perfectly blends a slightly crunchy texture with a hint of softness like white rice. Its naturally mild, nutty flavor goes well with citrus; cayenne, oregano, cumin, basil, dill, cilantro, rosemary, and other spices and herbs. Quinoa tastes great with virtually everything, including proteins such as beef, chicken, turkey, and fish, or solo with fresh roasted vegetables. And don't rule out sweets—quinoa works in those dishes, too!

Quinoa is not only a delicious alternative to rice and oat dishes, but it also often appeals to those who aren't huge fans of brown rice and other whole grains. Dishes with brown rice, oats, and barley often have an overwhelming earthy flavor and can make you feel heavy after consuming them. Refreshing quinoa is light both in flavor and texture. Although quinoa and grains such as rice, brown rice, and oats all contain fiber, quinoa is a seed, not a grain, so it's smaller than most grains, even when cooked, and it leaves you satisfied but not stuffed.

In this chapter, I introduce you to quinoa and give you a few ideas for the many wonderful ways you can use it whole and as a flour. In the following chapters, I share tips for cooking quinoa; using it for baking casseroles and breads; incorporating it into dips, salads, and side dishes; toasting and sautéing it; and so much more!

A Brief History of Quinoa

Quinoa isn't a new thing. Thousands of years ago, the Incas were among the first civilizations to embrace quinoa. The Incas revered quinoa as one of their staple crops, favoring it over both potatoes and corn. They believed it gave power and stamina to their warriors.

The Incas also used quinoa in their ceremonial rituals. They believed quinoa was a gift from the gods that contained spiritually enhancing properties. The first planting of the season was celebrated by the emperor, who ritually sowed the first seeds using a golden shovel. Considering it superior to all other grains and crops, the Incas called quinoa "the mother grain."

During the sixteenth century, the Spanish arrived in South America. In an effort to wipe out the Inca civilization, the Spanish outlawed the natives' use of quinoa, burning and destroying their fields. The Inca were forced to grow wheat; what quinoa survived became food for poor people and eating quinoa fell out of fashion.

KEEN ON QUINOA

In ancient times, quinoa was harvested by field workers who would cut and bundle the quinoa and carry it to a central location, where women would separate the seeds from the stalks. Today, a machine separates the seeds, which are then placed in an alkaline solution to remove *saponins,* the bitter, soapy toxic resins that protect the seeds while they grow. Commercially processed quinoa has had the saponins removed, but it's still a good idea to rinse the seeds before use.

It wasn't until the late 1970s that quinoa garnered even the slightest interest again. The rest, as they say, is history, as quinoa's nutritional values and culinary versatility have become a welcome addition to many dishes all over the world.

Today, quinoa is enjoyed in a grainlike manner in all sorts of dishes and also used as a flour in breakfast breads, delicious cakes, and other bakery-worthy items. You may also find quinoa pancake mix, quinoa crackers, and other baking or snack products made with quinoa. (See Appendix B for online outlets for these and other quinoa products.)

Quinoa greens are also edible. They have a spinachlike quality and can be eaten raw in salads or cooked just as you would spinach—sautéed with garlic, added to soups or pastas, etc. Spottings of quinoa greens are very far and few between, though, and you probably won't find them at your local grocery or health food store.

KEEN ON QUINOA

Quinoa grows naturally as white/ivory/tan, black, and red in color. Black and red quinoa have a stronger flavor than the white/ivory/tan variety but can be equally interchanged in recipes.

The Many Benefits of Quinoa

The Incas believed that quinoa enhanced strength and improved health. Quinoa was thought to improve endurance, heighten psychic abilities, and aid in meditation. The Incas also used quinoa to treat urinary tract infections, tuberculosis, appendicitis, liver problems, altitude sickness, and motion sickness. Both cooked and ground quinoa has been noted to be effective in drawing out pain and discoloration of bruises when used as a compress.

Andean natives contend that quinoa helps strengthen women during pregnancy and postpartum, and that it promotes healthier milk in nursing mothers. Because of its high calcium content, it was customary in Andean society to heal broken bones by eating quinoa and applying a plaster made of quinoa flour and water. This practice continues today.

I talk more about the nutritional qualities of quinoa in Chapter 2, but I think it's important to highlight some of quinoa's many health benefits here:

- Quinoa is high in protein, containing all the essential amino acids
- Quinoa is high in complex carbohydrates.
- Quinoa is low in saturated fat.
- Quinoa is rich in vitamins and minerals.

Each of these qualities can help reduce your risk of heart disease and other ailments, such as migraines, as well as improve overall endurance. Minerals such as magnesium, for example, help relax the blood vessels, thereby improving their elasticity.

Quinoa is also known to help with memory loss because of its high B vitamin content, which includes folate. Folate is required to make new cells in the body and also is connected to the improvement of brain function.

Buying and Storing Quinoa

You might find quinoa in your local supermarket, or look for it in your health food store, where it's often sold in packages in the organic grains section as well as in the bulk bins. Some farmers' markets in your area may sell quinoa, too. If all else fails, hop online, where it's readily available. (See Appendix B for some sources.)

Look for quinoa flour in the organic or health food section of your grocery store. Or again, shop online if you can't find local sources.

KEEN ON QUINOA

A little quinoa goes a long way. When cooked, quinoa increases to four times its size: 1 cup uncooked quinoa makes 4 cups cooked! With the average serving size at ½ cup, 1 cup uncooked quinoa can serve up to 8 people!

Store quinoa in an airtight plastic or glass container away from moisture. The best place is in your refrigerator. If you purchase quinoa flour, keep it in the original packaging, but place it in a plastic bag before refrigerating. Stored this way, your quinoa and quinoa flour can last for up to 6 months.

Cooking with Quinoa

Quinoa is a fast-cooking ingredient. As it cooks, the outer germ, or shell, breaks away from the grain and forms a little spiral-like flake, which adds to the texture and mouthfeel. You'll often use the same method of preparing quinoa for a recipe, and it's quick and easy. The following recipe shows the basic technique.

Quick-and-Easy Quinoa

Cooked quinoa bursts in your mouth with a light, beadlike texture and has a nutty, earthy flavor that embraces spices, citrus, fresh herbs, and virtually any other flavor.

Yield:	Prep time:	Cook time:	Serving size:
2 cups	1 minute	20 minutes	½ cup

Each serving has:			
86 calories	15.5 g carbohydrates	1.4 g fat	1.5 g fiber
3.0 g protein			

½ cup uncooked quinoa	1 cup water

1. Rinse and drain quinoa.

2. In a medium saucepan over high heat, combine water and quinoa. Bring to a boil, reduce heat to low, cover, and simmer for 15 minutes or until almost all liquid has been absorbed.

3. Turn off heat, and let stand, covered, for 5 minutes before using.

4. Give your cooked quinoa a taste test before serving. When properly cooked, it should have a slight crunch. You should be able to see uncooked white starch in the center, too.

QUICK FIX

Remember that quinoa seeds are coated with saponins. Most commercially harvested quinoa has the saponins removed, but it's still a good idea to rinse your quinoa before cooking it.

The Least You Need to Know

- Contrary to popular belief, quinoa is not a grain; it's an edible seed that's been around for thousands of years.

- Quinoa has many health benefits, because it's packed with fiber and nutrients.

- Quinoa is available at most supermarkets and natural food stores, and it's also easy to find online.

- Quinoa is easy to use, cooks quickly, and can be made ahead of time and used in a variety of recipes.

Quinoa Nutrition Basics

In This Chapter

- What makes quinoa so good for you?
- Protein and the plant-based diet
- Essential amino acids explained
- Gluten-free cooking with quinoa
- Nut allergies? No problem!

What is it about quinoa that makes it so good for you? In Chapter 1, I touched on some of quinoa's many nutritional benefits, but now let's really take a look at all the good-for-you vitamins, minerals, and so much more packed in each tiny quinoa seed, which make it the nutritional superstar it is.

Super Quinoa

You've probably heard of superfoods—those nutrient-rich foods like beans, broccoli, blueberries, and walnuts that give you the most vitamins, minerals, fiber, and other nutritional benefits per serving. These foods often also have properties that help prevent a variety of health problems. Plus, they're usually low in fat and calories, making them some of your best food options for living a healthy lifestyle. Quinoa is also a superfood!

> **KEEN ON QUINOA**
>
> Some of the top superfoods include apples, beets, black beans, blueberries, brussels sprouts, cayenne, cumin, quinoa, salmon, and walnuts. Work as many of these nutritional powerhouses into your daily diet as you can!

Because quinoa is naturally high in protein, it's a wonderful ingredient for vegetarians and vegans. A common misperception of these plant-based diets is that they lack key nutrients like protein, B vitamins, calcium, zinc, and iron, which are usually obtained by consuming animal proteins. Vegetarians and vegans must get these vital nutrients from nonanimal, plant-based foods such as nuts, seeds, legumes, vegetables, and grains. Quinoa's protein and nutrient-rich content makes it the perfect partner for a healthy plant-based diet.

Powerful Protein

Whether you're vegetarian, vegan, or omnivore, you need protein. And considering that many people don't meet the U.S. dietary reference intake (DRI) of protein each day—46 grams of protein for women and 56 grams for men—quinoa is an easy and delicious way to boost your protein intake.

As little as ½ cup of cooked quinoa contains more than 3 grams of protein. What's more, the protein in quinoa is a complete protein, meaning it contains all the *essential amino acids* necessary to meet your nutritional needs. Let's take a look at the essential amino acids found in quinoa to see why they're so important to your health:

> **DEFINITION**
>
> **Essential amino acids** are those that must be obtained from your diet; your body doesn't make them.

Lysine: Most grains lack lysine, so the fact that quinoa contains it makes it a complete protein. Lysine helps build muscle and collagen, promotes calcium absorption, and stimulates the production of hormones and antibodies.

Tryptophan: Present in most grains, tryptophan increases levels of serotonin in the brain, which can have a calming effect. Tryptophan has also been shown to aid in the treatment of depression.

Valine: Valine is needed for muscle coordination and tissue repair. It's also known to be helpful in treating liver and gallbladder diseases.

Methionine: Methionine is an antioxidant that promotes healthy hair, skin, and nails. It also helps break down fats, which contributes to healthy blood flow and circulation.

Threonine: Threonine helps maintain proper protein balance in the body and is important for the formation of collagen, elastin, and tooth enamel.

Phenylalanine: This essential amino acid promotes alertness and vitality, helps improve your mood, aids in learning, and is useful in pain relief, among other benefits.

Histidine: Histidine helps protect nerve cells and is used to treat arthritis, allergies, ulcers, and anemia, to name a few.

Isoleucine: Aiding in blood sugar regulation, isoleucine is an essential amino acid valuable to athletes because it helps heal and repair muscle tissue, skin, and bones.

Leucine: Leucine works to heal muscle tissue, skin, and bones and can aid in increasing the production of growth hormones.

As you can see, quinoa is an excellent source of protein and beneficial to your overall health.

More Vitamins and Minerals in Quinoa

Studies have shown that a diet rich in minerals and vitamins is essential for proper body function, and quinoa scores at the top of the list for minerals and vitamins. With high amounts of magnesium, phosphorous, manganese, copper, zinc, iron, potassium, and calcium, quinoa is worthy of its superfood status. When it comes to vitamins, thiamin, vitamin B_6, folate, riboflavin, and niacin round out the list.

Quinoa also is naturally high in fiber. Envision fiber as a friendly broom helping sweep out all the toxins and fats from your body. A diet rich in fiber helps prevent heart disease, diabetes, high blood pressure, arthritis, and numerous other ailments. Fiber is essential to a healthy diet and also helps break down proteins.

A Word About Carbohydrates

Look at the nutritional breakdown for 1 cup of cooked quinoa, and you might be alarmed by the number of carbs per serving—about 31.0 grams, or roughly 13 percent of the DRI in a serving.

Carbohydrates often get a bad rap. Diets frequently recommend cutting or limiting carbohydrates. In my experience, though, it's not carbohydrates as a whole that are to blame or that need to be cut down on or eliminated—it's the *type* of carbs. Your body needs some carbs to function. Carbs provide energy to get you through the day, are essential for brain function, and provide fuel for tired muscles.

Quinoa accounts for a substantial number of carbs per serving, but it's one of the good guys. Bite for bite, quinoa is a better option than other heavier, starchy carbs like baking potatoes; french fries and other fried carbs; and processed foods such as potato chips, tortilla chips, and store-bought snack foods. Even highly processed commercial salad dressings have carbs, as do cookies and other desserts.

The key to managing your carbohydrate intake is making healthier choices. Instead of "bad" carb foods, opt for fresh apples and bananas; greens such as spinach, broccoli, and asparagus; kidney, black, and other beans; and healthy grains and seeds—like quinoa!

Gluten-Free Quinoa

Quinoa is naturally gluten free, which is a blessing for those who have *celiac disease* or are wheat intolerant. Quinoa flour, which is made from ground quinoa seeds, can be used in baking cookies, breads, muffins, and cakes. (It can't be substituted for wheat flour in equal portions, though. I talk about this more in later chapters.)

DEFINITION

Celiac disease is a digestive disease causing damage to the small intestine and therefore interfering with the body's ability to absorb nutrients in foods.

Because of its mild nutty flavor, quinoa can be substituted for oatmeal; added to breakfast cereals such as muesli; and used to make granola-style breakfast and snack bars, pancakes, and other delicious foods that usually require wheat flour.

While you're shopping, check out the organic grains section of your grocery store or market. You might find other gluten-free quinoa-based mixes and snacks there.

No Nut Allergies Worries

Nuts can present a huge problem for those who are allergic. Although quinoa has a nutty flavor, quinoa is not a nut. Quinoa is a seed, remember, and is usually harmless to people with nut allergies. For this reason, quinoa is the perfect way to get a nutty flavor fix without fear of allergic reactions.

WHOA!

If you have questions or are unsure whether you might be allergic to quinoa, it's a good idea to consult your physician or nutritionist before trying it.

Considered a vegetable protein, quinoa is easy to digest and usually nonallergenic, making it a good option for those who can't eat other types of grains, are allergic to nuts, or are interested in exploring a raw food diet.

Quinoa provides a good foundation for any type of diet. It's versatile to cook with, has a delicious mild nutty flavor, and tastes incredible with almost any food. Plus it's packed with all the good nutrients, vitamins, minerals, protein, and fiber your body needs. In the next chapter, I share some recipes to get you started with this wonderful superfood. Let's get cooking!

The Least You Need to Know

- Quinoa is super good for you because it's packed with vitamins and minerals, including magnesium and folate.
- Quinoa is high in protein, making it the perfect nongrain grain for traditional diets as well as vegan and vegetarian diets.
- Quinoa contains all the essential amino acids your body needs.
- Quinoa is naturally gluten free, making it a preferred addition to gluten-intolerant diets.

Good-for-You Breakfasts

Breakfast is the key to beginning your day right. You might not make time for breakfast now, but after sampling some of the recipes in Part 2, you'll want to wake up early and *make* time for a quinoa-filled breakfast!

Part 2 explains why breakfast is so important to your day and to a healthy lifestyle, and how quinoa can play a key role in your healthy breakfast dishes. From eggs to breads to pancakes and more, I share plenty of quick, easy, and flavorful ways to enjoy healthful quinoa breakfasts. Quinoa is the perfect carb option—high in fiber and protein and naturally low in fat.

Making quinoa part of your morning routine sends you off on your day feeling satisfied, energized, and ready to take on the world!

Quick-Start Breakfasts

In This Chapter

- Making quinoa an essential part of your morning
- Healthy quinoa breakfasts
- Quick-and-easy quinoa breakfast treats

Breakfast is a key element of a healthy lifestyle—studies have proven it. Even if it's something as simple as yogurt and berries (my favorite), eating breakfast is essential to starting your day off right. Think about it: if you sleep 7 or 8 hours nightly and you skip breakfast, by the time lunch rolls around, you'll have gone 12 to 15 hours without giving your body fuel!

Plus, studies show that eating breakfast helps you lose weight. Food is needed to give your body fuel and nutrients. People who eat breakfast are less likely to snack on high-fat, high-sugar foods and are less likely to overeat during the day.

Quinoa is one of the best foods you can eat. Packed with fiber and essential vitamins and minerals—and naturally low in fat—it has everything you need to begin your day. One $\frac{1}{2}$ cup serving of quinoa contains 127 calories, 2 grams fat, and 15.5 grams carbohydrates, of which 2 grams (8 percent of the recommended daily allowance) come from fiber.

🍳 Mohawk Bend's Breakfast Quinoa

Pomegranate, almonds, pistachios, sweet orange, and maple syrup mix with quinoa in this delicious breakfast cereal by Chef Randal St. Clair, Executive Chef, Mohawk Bend (Los Angeles, CA).

Yield:	Prep time:	Serving size:
1 cup	15 minutes	$\frac{1}{2}$ cup

Each serving has:		
387 calories	59.5 g carbohydrates	14.5 g fat
6.9 g fiber	9.9 g protein	

1 cup Quick-and-Easy Quinoa (recipe in Chapter 1)	$\frac{1}{2}$ cup pomegranate seeds
3 TB. maple syrup or agave syrup	$\frac{1}{4}$ cup toasted sliced almonds
2 medium oranges, supremed, and juice reserved	$\frac{1}{4}$ cup chopped toasted pistachios
	$\frac{1}{4}$ cup freshly chopped mint leaves

1. In a medium bowl, toss Quick-and-Easy Quinoa with maple syrup and orange juice.

2. Add oranges, pomegranate seeds, almonds, pistachios, and mint, and toss.

Variation: If you have access to organic (unsprayed) rose petals, these are a great addition. Simply chiffonade the petals and fold in 2 tablespoons with the mint. Sprinkle a few whole petals on top for garnish.

KEEN ON QUINOA

Quinoa has been a favorite of mine for a while—it's great in soups (chicken, tomato, fennel with bouillabaisse seasonings), salads (tabbouleh), and fritters, and is the base for our vegan burger. I was eating some leftover asparagus quinoa tabbouleh one morning for breakfast and it got me to thinking, *Would this sell on a breakfast menu? Probably not.* But I thought it would be a lighter start to the morning than oatmeal, and so I thought of this—which is kind of a breakfast tabbouleh—substituting fruits for the vegetables.

—Chef Randal St. Clair

Quinoa with Cinnamon and Raisins

With the light, crunchy texture of quinoa, a little spice from the cinnamon, and the sweetness of raisins, this is a refreshing alternative to traditional breakfast oatmeal.

Yield:	Prep time:	Cook time:	Serving size:
4 cups	5 minutes	20 minutes	1 cup

Each serving has:			
358 calories	75.2 g carbohydrates	4.2 g fat	4.5 g fiber
9.4 g protein			

1 cup low-fat milk	½ tsp. ground cinnamon
1 cup water	1 cup raisins
1 cup uncooked quinoa, rinsed and drained	2 TB. honey or agave nectar

1. In a medium saucepan over high heat, combine low-fat milk, water, and quinoa. Bring to a boil, reduce heat to medium-low, cover, and simmer for 15 minutes or until almost all liquid is absorbed.

2. Turn off heat, and let stand, covered, for 5 minutes.

3. Stir in ground cinnamon and raisins.

4. Transfer to 4 serving bowls, and drizzle each with ½ tablespoon honey before serving.

Variation: For **Quinoa with Cinnamon, Cranberries, and Pecans,** substitute dried cranberries for the raisins and add ¼ cup chopped pecans with the cranberries.

Quinoa Muesli with Roasted Hazelnuts and Dried Apricots

The sweetness of the apricots will satisfy your morning sugar craving, and you'll love the crunch of the *hazelnuts*. If hazelnuts aren't your thing, feel free to use pecans or walnuts instead.

Yield:	Prep time:	Cook time:	Serving size:
3 cups	20 minutes	30 minutes	½ cup

Each serving has:			
250.8 calories	46.6 g carbohydrates	5.9 g fat	4.6 g fiber
7.6 g protein			

¼ cup coarsely chopped hazelnuts	1 cup dried apricot halves
½ cup uncooked quinoa, rinsed and drained	2 TB. brown sugar
¾ cup water	¾ cup nonfat vanilla yogurt
	Juice of ½ lemon

1. Preheat the oven to 300°F. Line a baking sheet with parchment paper.

2. Spread out hazelnuts evenly on the prepared baking sheet. Roast for 15 minutes.

3. Meanwhile, in a medium saucepan over medium-high heat, combine quinoa and water. Bring to a boil, reduce heat to low, cover, and let simmer for about 15 minutes or until almost all liquid is absorbed.

4. Turn off heat, and let stand, covered, for 5 minutes.

5. Remove hazelnuts from the oven, and set aside.

6. Stir apricot halves, brown sugar, nonfat vanilla yogurt, and lemon juice into quinoa. Stir in hazelnuts. Serve warm.

DEFINITION

A **hazelnut** is a round, brown, hard-shelled nut that's the edible fruit of the hazel tree. Hazelnuts are also referred to as *filberts* or *cob nuts*. They're rich in vitamins E and B and contain good fats and minerals that may help ward off cataracts and also improve circulation.

Quinoa with Apples, Almonds, and Honey

Nut lovers, rejoice! Nutty soy and almonds add to the already nutty flavor of quinoa, and sweet apples and honey balance out all the yummy nuttiness.

Yield:	Prep time:	Cook time:	Serving size:
6 cups	10 minutes	20 minutes	1 cup

Each serving has:			
380.7 calories	61.1 g carbohydrates	13.3 g fat	7.2 g fiber
14.9 g protein			

1½ cups uncooked quinoa, rinsed and drained	1 medium Granny Smith apple, cored and chopped
3 cups *soy milk*	3 TB. honey
1 cup coarsely chopped almonds	

1. In a large saucepan over high heat, combine quinoa and soy milk. Bring to a boil, reduce heat to medium-low, cover, and simmer for 15 minutes or until almost all liquid is absorbed.

2. Turn off heat, and let stand, covered, for 5 minutes.

3. Stir in almonds and Granny Smith apple.

4. Transfer to 6 serving bowls, and drizzle each with ½ tablespoon honey before serving.

DEFINITION

Soy milk is a nondairy product made by soaking soybeans in water, grinding them, and straining out any remaining granules. Soy milk can have a "beany" taste, so vanilla or chocolate flavoring is often added. Substitute almond milk, rice milk, or 1 ½ cups water and 1½ cups low-fat milk for soy milk if you prefer.

Quinoa Breakfast Parfait

Berries are packed full of antioxidants and flavor. Kick-start your morning with this festive berry-filled treat.

Yield:	Prep time:	Cook time:	Serving size:
4 parfaits	15 minutes	20 minutes	1 parfait

Each serving has:			
210.9 calories	37.1 g carbohydrates	1.7 g fat	6.5 g fiber
13.9 g protein			

$\frac{1}{2}$ cup uncooked quinoa, rinsed
  and drained

$\frac{1}{2}$ cup water

$\frac{1}{2}$ cup pineapple juice

2 cups low-fat Greek yogurt

$1\frac{1}{2}$ tsp. lemon zest

1 cup fresh blackberries

1 cup fresh raspberries

1 cup fresh blueberries

4 fresh mint leaves

1. In a medium saucepan over high heat, combine quinoa, water, and pineapple juice. Bring to a boil, reduce heat to medium-low, cover, and simmer for 15 minutes or until almost all liquid is absorbed.

2. Turn off heat, and let stand, covered, for 5 minutes.

3. Meanwhile, in a small bowl, combine Greek yogurt and lemon zest.

4. In a medium bowl, toss together blackberries, raspberries, and blueberries.

5. Using 4 parfait glasses or other tall glasses, spoon 2 tablespoons yogurt mixture into the bottom of each glass. Top with 2 tablespoons quinoa, followed by 2 tablespoons mixed berries. Repeat by adding 2 tablespoons yogurt, 2 tablespoons quinoa, and 2 tablespoons berries until the glasses are full.

6. Garnish each parfait with 1 mint leaf and serve immediately, or chill for up to 2 hours before serving.

Excellent Eggy Breakfasts

In This Chapter

- Quinoa-packed frittatas and omelets
- Punching up the protein
- The versatility of quinoa for breakfast

There's a reason why quinoa is one of the hottest nongrain grains around—it goes with everything! From cereal and oatmeal to frittatas to omelets, quinoa is so light in texture, it's the perfect way to add fiber, flavor, and a little extra protein to any breakfast!

Eggs taste great with pretty much everything, but if you're looking to maximize the protein in your diet, adding quinoa to an egg dish gives it a boost. One of the best protein sources for vegetarian diets, quinoa boasts about 3.0 grams protein per $\frac{1}{2}$ cup. Combine the tasty grain with an egg, and you get both your protein and your fiber in one tasty dish.

Omelets are a quick and easy eggy breakfast dish. When cooking an omelet, you'll want an omelet pan, a nonstick pan specifically designed for making omelets. When cooking a frittata, I suggest using an iron skillet. I have at least half a dozen of them, and they're generally nonstick and ovenproof. They're also easy to clean—just use water. Skip the soap, because the soap washes away the "seasoned" coating. (A "seasoned" iron skillet has soaked up oils from cooking and is easier to use.)

Quinoa Frittata with Fresh Vegetables

An easy, no-flip frittata is one of the simplest skillet breakfasts you can make. This recipe provides crisp, fresh veggie flavor with a hint of spice.

Yield:	Prep time:	Cook time:	Serving size:
1 (8-inch) frittata	10 minutes	8 minutes	1 slice

Each serving has:			
164.6 calories	9.0 g carbohydrates	9.4 g fat	1.0 g fiber
11.1 g protein			

10 large eggs

¼ cup nonfat milk

½ tsp. cayenne

½ tsp. sea salt

½ tsp. ground black pepper

1 TB. unsalted butter

¼ cup diced white onion

¼ cup diced red bell pepper

¼ cup chopped fresh asparagus tips

1 batch Quick-and-Easy Quinoa (recipe in Chapter 1)

¼ cup grated Parmesan cheese

1. Preheat the broiler to high.

2. In a large bowl, whisk together eggs, nonfat milk, cayenne, sea salt, and black pepper until well combined. Set aside.

3. In an 8-inch heavy ovenproof skillet over medium heat, melt unsalted butter.

4. Add egg mixture, and tilt the skillet slightly to spread egg mixture evenly around the pan.

5. Evenly sprinkle white onion, red bell pepper, asparagus tips, and Quick-and-Easy Quinoa over egg mixture. Cook for about 4 minutes or until edges are set (getting cooked).

6. Add Parmesan cheese to top of egg mixture.

7. Transfer the skillet to the broiler, and place directly under the broiler for 1 minute or until center of frittata is cooked.

8. Remove from the oven, slice as you would a pie into 8 equal pieces, and serve.

QUICK FIX

A frittata is an open-face omelet traditional to Italy. I prefer cooking frittatas to omelets because I don't have to worry about flipping half of the egg over the other half and still having it look good. I also don't have to worry about how much filling I put in my frittata. When cooking an omelet, it's easy to overstuff it, making it difficult to flip.

Spicy Quinoa Mushroom Crustless Quiche

Crimini, or button, mushrooms are generally the most common and most affordable mushrooms, but they don't pack a ton of flavor. Combining them with spices like cayenne brings both texture and flavor to this tasty quiche.

Yield:	Prep time:	Cook time:	Serving size:
1 (9-inch) quiche	10 minutes	45 to 55 minutes	1 slice

Each serving has:			
160.4 calories	11.7 g carbohydrates	9.3 g fat	2.0 g fiber
8.5 g protein			

2 TB. unsalted butter	3 cups fresh spinach leaves
1 clove garlic, chopped	$\frac{1}{2}$ tsp. cayenne
$\frac{1}{4}$ cup chopped yellow onion	4 large eggs, beaten
2 green onions, both white and green parts, chopped	1 batch Quick-and-Easy Quinoa (recipe in Chapter 1)
$1\frac{1}{2}$ cups sliced crimini mushrooms	$\frac{1}{2}$ cup goat cheese, crumbled

1. Preheat the oven to 350°F. Spray a 9-inch pie plate with nonstick cooking spray.

2. In a large, heavy saucepan over medium heat, melt unsalted butter. Add garlic, yellow onion, and green onions, and sauté for about 3 minutes.

3. Add crimini mushrooms and spinach leaves, and sauté for 2 more minutes. Add cayenne, and stir to combine.

4. In a large bowl, and using a wooden spoon, combine eggs and Quick-and-Easy Quinoa. Add goat cheese and mushroom mixture, and mix well.

5. Transfer entire mixture to the prepared pie plate, and bake for 40 to 50 minutes or until golden brown and cooked through. To test for doneness, insert a knife or long wooden skewer into center of quiche. If the knife or skewer comes out clean, quiche is done.

6. Slice as you would a pie into 8 pieces, and serve.

Quinoa Hash Browns with Poached Eggs

Typically, hash browns are potatoes and not much else. Here potatoes are spiced with jalapeño, onion, and quinoa—the best of a carbohydrate-driven breakfast enhanced by protein-rich eggs.

Yield:	Prep time:	Cook time:	Serving size:
4 cups	15 minutes	18 minutes	1 cup

Each serving has:			
285.1 calories	38.3 g carbohydrates	10.1 g fat	4.3 g fiber
12.1 g protein			

½ cup uncooked quinoa, rinsed and drained	2 medium jalapeños, seeded and diced
2 cups water	½ cup frozen kernel corn
1 TB. olive oil	½ tsp. sea salt
½ white onion, chopped	½ tsp. ground black pepper
1 large baked potato, cut into 1-in. cubes	4 large eggs

1. In a large saucepan over medium heat, combine quinoa and 1½ cups water. Bring to a boil, reduce heat to medium-low, cover, and simmer for about 15 minutes or until almost all liquid is absorbed. Remove from heat, and set aside.

2. In a large saucepan over medium heat, heat olive oil. Add white onion, and sauté for about 1 minute.

3. Add potatoes, jalapeño, kernel corn, sea salt, and black pepper, and stir until combined.

4. In a medium saucepan over medium heat, heat remaining $\frac{1}{2}$ cup water. Gently crack each egg into water, and spoon warm water over eggs for 2 or 3 minutes or until egg white is solid and center is still very soft. Transfer eggs to a plate, and set aside.

5. Gently stir quinoa into potato mixture until well combined. Transfer about 1 cup quinoa mixture to each of 4 serving plates. Place 1 poached egg atop each serving of quinoa mixture, and serve.

KEEN ON QUINOA

When it comes to poaching eggs, the fresher the egg, the better, because in fresh eggs the egg white tends to cling to the yolk.

Quinoa Eggs Benedict

Eggs Benedict doesn't have to be all about English muffins and traditional hollandaise. Although those are classics, nutty, crunchy quinoa cakes offer a whole new flavor that complements the turkey slices and a lighter version of hollandaise made with creamy yogurt, lemon, and mustard.

Yield:	Prep time:	Cook time:	Serving size:
6 eggs Benedict	10 minutes	20 minutes	1 eggs Benedict
Each serving has:			
292.9 calories	22.5 g carbohydrates	13.1 g fat	1.7 g fiber
20.8 g protein			

1 batch Quick-and-Easy Quinoa (recipe in Chapter 1)

$\frac{3}{4}$ cup plain breadcrumbs

$\frac{1}{4}$ cup chopped fresh cilantro leaves

9 large eggs

2 green onions, white and green parts, chopped

2 TB. grated Parmesan cheese

$\frac{1}{2}$ tsp. sea salt

$\frac{1}{2}$ tsp. ground black pepper

$\frac{1}{2}$ TB. olive oil

$\frac{1}{4}$ cup low-fat vanilla yogurt

$\frac{1}{4}$ cup low-fat sour cream

$\frac{1}{4}$ cup part-skim milk ricotta cheese

$\frac{1}{2}$ TB. fresh lemon juice

$\frac{1}{2}$ tsp. Dijon mustard

$\frac{1}{2}$ cup water

6 slices Canadian bacon–style turkey

2 TB. chopped fresh Italian flat-leaf parsley

1. In a medium bowl, combine Quick-and-Easy Quinoa, breadcrumbs, cilantro leaves, 3 eggs, green onions, Parmesan cheese, sea salt, and black pepper. Let rest for about 3 minutes.

2. Stir quinoa mixture again until well combined. Form into 6 patties.

3. In a large, heavy saucepan over medium-high heat, heat olive oil. Add quinoa patties, and cook for about 5 minutes or until browned. Flip over each patty, and cook for 5 more minutes or until browned on other side. Transfer to a plate, and set aside. Wipe out the saucepan using a paper towel.

4. In a small bowl, combine low-fat vanilla yogurt, low-fat sour cream, part-skim milk ricotta cheese, lemon juice, and Dijon mustard. Set aside.

5. In the same saucepan over medium heat, heat water. Gently crack 3 eggs into water, and spoon warm water over eggs for 2 or 3 minutes or until egg white is solid and center is still very soft. Transfer eggs to a plate, and set aside. Repeat with remaining 3 eggs, adding an additional $1/2$ cup water if necessary. Drain any remaining water from the saucepan.

6. Heat the same saucepan over medium heat, and add deli turkey slices. Cook for about 30 seconds to 1 minute or until warmed.

7. To serve, place 1 quinoa cake on a serving plate, top with 1 deli turkey ham slice, followed by 1 poached egg. Top with 1 or 2 tablespoons yogurt mixture, and finish with a pinch of chopped Italian flat-leaf parsley.

Quinoa, Pancetta, and Tomato Omelet

One of the main flavors in this recipe comes from pancetta (Italian bacon), a salt- and spice-cured unsmoked pork belly that's dried for several months. It really complements quinoa's crunch and nutty flavor.

Yield:	Prep time:	Cook time:	Serving size:
4 omelets	8 minutes	25 minutes	1 omelet

Each serving has:			
332.7 calories	18.1 g carbohydrates	18.8 g fat	2.1 g fiber
23.1 g protein			

½ cup chopped pancetta	12 large eggs
½ cup uncooked quinoa, rinsed and drained	1 tsp. smoked paprika
1 cup water	½ tsp. sea salt
3 medium tomatoes, seeded and chopped	½ tsp. ground white pepper
3 green onions, white and green parts, chopped	¼ cup chopped fresh mint leaves

1. In a medium skillet or sauté pan over medium heat, cook pancetta for about 2 minutes or until crisp. Remove from heat, transfer to a paper towel, and set aside.

2. In a medium saucepan over medium-high heat, combine quinoa and water. Bring to a boil, cover, reduce heat to medium-low, and simmer for 15 minutes or until almost all liquid is absorbed.

3. Turn off heat, and let stand, covered, for 5 minutes.

4. Add tomatoes and green onions to quinoa, and set aside.

5. In a large bowl, whisk together eggs, smoked paprika, sea salt, white pepper, and mint leaves.

6. In the medium skillet over medium heat, add ¼ egg mixture. Swirl egg mixture lightly to coat the bottom of the skillet, and cook for about 1 minute or until almost set.

7. Sprinkle ¼ of quinoa mixture onto ½ of eggs, and sprinkle ¼ of fresh mint leaves and ¼ of pancetta over quinoa mixture. Using a rubber spatula, gently fold ½ of omelet over the other ½, and cook for 30 more seconds to 1 minute.

8. Remove from heat, and transfer to a serving plate and cover with aluminum foil to keep warm. Repeat steps 6 and 7 with remaining ingredients.

QUICK FIX

Many recipes in this book call for repeating cooking steps to make individual servings. When you see such instructions, remember that the quantity divisions explained in the first steps carry over to the "repeat with" steps. So if ¼ cup quinoa mixture is used to create 1 serving, ¼ cup quinoa mixture is used for each subsequent serving.

Quinoa Egg White Omelet

Egg whites typically don't have a lot of flavor, but they don't have a lot of calories and fat either. Add flavor to this healthy recipe with slightly nutty flavored quinoa and metabolism-friendly crushed red pepper flakes.

Yield:	Prep time:	Cook time:	Serving size:
4 omelets	15 minutes	12 minutes	1 omelet

Each serving has:			
156.9 calories	6.3 g carbohydrates	6.7 g fat	1.2 g fiber
22.9 g protein			

½ TB. unsalted butter	1 tsp. sea salt
½ cup chopped white onion	1 tsp. ground black pepper
4 medium Roma tomatoes, seeded and diced	12 large egg whites
¼ cup chopped broccoli florets	½ cup Quick-and-Easy Quinoa (recipe in Chapter 1)
1 tsp. crushed red pepper flakes	½ cup shredded mozzarella cheese

1. In a medium saucepan over medium heat, melt unsalted butter. Add white onion and Roma tomatoes, and sauté for about 1 or 2 minutes.

2. Add broccoli florets, crushed red pepper flakes, ½ teaspoon sea salt, and ½ teaspoon black pepper, and sauté 1 or 2 more minutes. Transfer onion mixture to a small bowl, and set aside.

3. In a large bowl, whisk together egg whites, remaining $\frac{1}{2}$ teaspoon sea salt, and remaining $\frac{1}{2}$ teaspoon black pepper.

4. Spray a small nonstick skillet or omelet pan lightly with nonstick cooking spray, and set over medium heat. Add $\frac{1}{4}$ of egg whites to the skillet, and swirl eggs lightly to coat the bottom of the skillet. Cook for about 1 minute or until eggs are just set.

5. Sprinkle $\frac{1}{4}$ of onion mixture onto $\frac{1}{2}$ of egg whites, and top with $\frac{1}{4}$ of Quick-and-Easy Quinoa and $\frac{1}{4}$ of mozzarella cheese. Using a rubber spatula, gently fold $\frac{1}{2}$ of omelet over the other $\frac{1}{2}$, and cook for 30 more seconds to 1 minute or until just cooked through.

6. Remove from heat, and transfer to a serving plate and cover with aluminum foil to keep warm. Repeat with remaining ingredients.

Easy Quinoa Breakfast Soufflé

This soufflé is packed full of flavor—and nutrients—thanks to the coconut water and fresh berries. And quinoa has never tasted better!

Yield:	Prep time:	Cook time:	Serving size:
4 (4-ounce) soufflés	10 minutes	35 minutes	1 soufflé

Each serving has:			
332.7 calories 23.1 g protein	18.1 g carbohydrates	18.8 g fat	2.1 fiber

$\frac{1}{2}$ cup uncooked quinoa, rinsed and drained

1 cup coconut water

4 large egg whites

1 cup fresh raspberries

1 cup fresh blackberries

4 TB. honey

1. Preheat the oven to 400°F. Spray 4 (4-ounce) ramekins with nonstick cooking spray.

2. In a medium saucepan over medium-high heat, combine quinoa and coconut water. Bring to a boil, reduce heat to medium-low, cover, and simmer for about 15 minutes or until almost all liquid is absorbed. Turn off heat, and let rest for 5 minutes.

3. Meanwhile, place egg whites in a medium bowl. Using an electric mixer on high, beat egg whites until stiff peaks form.

4. Gently fold egg whites into cooked quinoa, and divide quinoa mixture equally among the 4 ramekins.

5. Bake for 15 minutes or until quinoa is lightly browned and puffed up.

6. Meanwhile, in a medium bowl, gently combine raspberries and blueberries.

7. Top each soufflé with $\frac{1}{4}$ of mixed berries, drizzle with 1 tablespoon honey, and serve in the ramekins.

Breakfast Breads

In This Chapter

- Easy baking with quinoa
- A look at good carbs
- Delicious quinoa cakes, muffins, and more

Baking with quinoa couldn't be easier, especially if you use quinoa flour. If you've never worked with quinoa flour before, don't let that intimidate you. Quinoa flour is simply ground quinoa seeds. It's cream-colored, is slightly coarser than traditional wheat flours, and provides a somewhat strong, nutty flavor. It can be used in all kinds of recipes, from pastas to breads, to cakes and cookies. What's more, both cooked quinoa seeds and quinoa flour are gluten free.

In this chapter, I give you a dozen delicious, nutritious breakfast breads. Let's get baking!

Baking with Quinoa

Quinoa flour works well for many types of baking, including flat breads such as tortillas, pancakes, and even waffles. It doesn't yield as good results in baked products that need yeast to rise, however, such as most breads and some cakes. To work some nutritious quinoa into your yeast-based baked goods, you can still substitute quinoa flour for a portion—between 20 and 50 percent—of the all-purpose or other flour called for in a recipe.

If you eat a gluten-free diet, some flours are out, so you can mix naturally gluten-free quinoa flour with other nongluten flours such as almond flour, buckwheat flour, tapioca, and soy flour. Quinoa flour manufacturers also produce naturally gluten-free quinoa baking mixes for such items as pizza crust, vanilla cake, chocolate chip cookies, brownies, and more. Look for these products at your local health food store, in the organic/health food section of your grocery store, and online to discover other quinoa-based baking items.

A New Perspective on Carbs

Carbohydrates are often perceived as bad news. Mention the word *carbohydrate*, and most people visualize rich, starchy foods like potatoes, pasta, and bread, and heavy dishes like potatoes au gratin or fettuccine Alfredo. Because of this, you've probably seen numerous cautions to avoid overloading on carbs.

Yet carbs are present in lots of foods we eat, not just breads, pasta, and potatoes. You'll find them in fruits like apples, bananas, and figs, and in vegetables like bell peppers, onions, and corn. In this chapter—and throughout this book—I share recipes that present a healthy way to enjoy carbs, have a positive impact on your diet, and help keep you slim and trim.

Quinoa Coffee Cake

Rich-tasting orange zest and dark brown sugar add to the flavorful complexity of this delicious coffee cake.

Yield:	Prep time:	Cook time:	Serving size:
1 (9-inch-square) cake	20 minutes	25 minutes	1 square

Each serving has:			
242.2 calories 4.3 g protein	34.2 g carbohydrates	14.3 g fat	2.1 g fiber

1½ cups plus 1 TB. quinoa flour

2 tsp. baking powder

½ tsp. salt

⅓ cup plus ½ cup dark brown sugar, firmly packed

¼ cup plus 2 TB. unsalted butter, softened

½ cup hazelnut or almond milk

2 large eggs

1 TB. fine orange zest

1 tsp. coconut extract

1 cup chopped toasted hazelnuts

1 tsp. ground cinnamon

1. Preheat the oven to 350°F. Coat a 9-inch-square casserole dish with 1 tablespoon unsalted butter.

2. In a large bowl, combine 1½ cups quinoa flour, baking powder, salt, and ⅓ cup dark brown sugar. Add ¼ cup unsalted butter, hazelnut milk, eggs, orange zest, and coconut extract, and blend until smooth.

3. In a separate large bowl, combine remaining 2 tablespoons unsalted butter, remaining ½ cup dark brown sugar, hazelnuts, remaining 1 tablespoon quinoa flour, and cinnamon. Mix using a fork until mixture is crumbly.

4. Pour ½ of quinoa flour–hazelnut milk mixture into the prepared casserole dish. Top with ½ of crumbly quinoa flour–cinnamon mixture, add remaining ½ of quinoa flour–hazelnut milk mixture, and finish with remaining ½ of quinoa flour–cinnamon mixture.

5. Bake for about 25 minutes or until cake is slightly browned. Allow to cool for about 10 minutes before cutting into 9 squares and serving.

QUICK FIX

This gluten-free recipe uses hazelnut milk, which you can find at most grocery stores and health food stores. If you can't find hazelnut milk, use an equal amount of almond or soy milk.

Banana Nut Quinoa Muffins

Don't throw out those ripe bananas! Their intense flavor is delicious in breads and muffins. Walnuts add nutty depth to these muffins that get another flavor lift from brown sugar, yogurt, and orange zest.

Yield:	Prep time:	Cook time:	Serving size:
12 muffins	15 minutes	20 minutes	1 muffin

Each serving has:			
330.0 calories	41.5 g carbohydrates	18.9 g fat	3.1 g fiber
6.1 g protein			

½ cup quinoa flour	2 large eggs
½ cup all-purpose flour	⅓ cup low-fat Greek yogurt
½ cup whole-wheat flour	1 tsp. pure vanilla extract
1 TB. baking powder	1 tsp. fine orange zest
1 stick salted butter, cut into pieces	1½ cups walnuts, toasted and chopped
½ cup brown sugar, firmly packed	
½ cup granulated sugar	
3 large ripe bananas, peeled and lightly mashed	

1. Preheat the oven to 350°F. Spray a 12-cup muffin tin with nonstick cooking spray, or use paper liners.

2. In a large bowl, sift together quinoa flour, all-purpose flour, whole-wheat flour, and baking powder.

3. In another large bowl, and using an electric mixer on medium, cream together salted butter, brown sugar, and granulated sugar. Add bananas, and mix to combine. Add eggs, Greek yogurt, and vanilla extract, and mix to combine.

4. Add flour mixture, and mix until just combined.

5. Stir in orange zest and walnuts just until well combined.

6. Spoon batter equally into 12 muffin cups, filling each about ½ to ¾ full. Bake for about 15 to 18 minutes or until a toothpick inserted into center of muffin comes out clean.

7. Cool muffins on a wire rack for about 10 minutes before serving.

QUICK FIX

Greek yogurt not only provides flavor to this recipe but also moisture, replacing the oil many muffin recipes call for. Using Greek yogurt keeps this muffin recipe lower in fat and calories.

Blackberry Quinoa Muffins

Tart blackberries are delicious for breakfast. This easy blackberry muffin is perfect with honey or your favorite berry jam.

Yield:	Prep time:	Cook time:	Serving size:
6 muffins	18 minutes	20 minutes	1 muffin
Each serving has:			
443.1 calories	63.5 g carbohydrates	20.5 g fat	4.7 g fiber
7.1 g protein			

1 cup all-purpose flour

1 cup quinoa flour

$\frac{1}{2}$ cup granulated sugar

$\frac{1}{4}$ cup brown sugar, firmly packed

1 tsp. baking soda

1 cup nonfat milk

$\frac{1}{2}$ cup canola oil

2 large eggs

$1\frac{1}{3}$ cups fresh blackberries

1. Preheat the oven to 400°F. Spray a 6-cup muffin tin with nonstick cooking spray, or use paper liners.

2. In a medium bowl, combine all-purpose flour, quinoa flour, granulated sugar, brown sugar, and baking soda.

3. In a small bowl, whisk together nonfat milk, canola oil, and eggs until well combined.

4. Gradually add milk mixture to flour mixture, being careful not to overmix. Stir in blackberries.

5. Spoon batter equally into 6 muffin cups, and bake for about 20 minutes or until a toothpick inserted into center of muffin comes out clean. Allow to cool for 5 to 10 minutes before serving.

Carrot Quinoa Muffins

A hint of spice, a bit of sweet, and lots of crunchy carrots shine in this breakfast muffin that's so good it could be dessert.

Yield:	Prep time:	Cook time:	Serving size:
18 muffins	25 minutes	25 minutes	1 muffin

Each serving has:			
263.6 calories	32.1 g carbohydrates	15.7 g fat	1.8 g fiber
3.9 g protein			

1½ cups all-purpose flour	1 tsp. ground nutmeg
½ cup quinoa flour	4 large eggs
1 TB. baking powder	1 cup canola oil
2 tsp. baking soda	¾ cup brown sugar, firmly packed
1 tsp. salt	1 cup golden raisins
1 tsp. ground cinnamon	½ cup chopped walnuts

1. Preheat the oven to 350°F. Spray 18 muffin cups with nonstick cooking spray, or use paper liners.

2. In a large bowl, sift together all-purpose flour, quinoa flour, baking powder, baking soda, salt, cinnamon, and nutmeg.

3. In a small bowl, whisk together eggs, canola oil, and brown sugar until well combined.

4. Gradually add egg mixture to flour mixture until just combined, being careful not to overmix. Add golden raisins, carrots, and walnuts.

5. Spoon batter into 18 muffin cups, and bake for 20 to 30 minutes or until a toothpick inserted into center of muffin comes out clean.

6. Cool muffins on a wire rack for about 10 minutes before serving with honey or your favorite jam.

KEEN ON QUINOA

Walnuts are one of the healthiest nuts you can eat. High in protein and rich in fiber, walnuts are also a good source of B vitamins, antioxidants like vitamin E, and omega-3 fatty acids, which are good for your heart and your skin. Walnuts are also known to aid in breast cancer prevention.

Savory Rosemary Quinoa Breakfast Scones

Rosemary is my favorite herb. It goes with everything from soup to dessert to prime rib to breakfast. Try these rosemary quinoa scones with a simple orange marmalade.

Yield:	Prep time:	Cook time:	Serving size:
14 scones	15 minutes	20 minutes	1 scone

Each serving has:			
167.8 calories	27.4 g carbohydrates	5.5 g fat	0.8 g fiber
2.7 g protein			

$\frac{1}{2}$ cup Quick-and-Easy Quinoa (recipe in Chapter 1)	6 TB. unsalted butter, cut into pieces
1$\frac{1}{2}$ cups all-purpose flour	$\frac{1}{2}$ cup heavy cream
$\frac{1}{2}$ cup sugar	$\frac{1}{2}$ cup nonfat sour cream
2 tsp. baking powder	$\frac{1}{3}$ cup orange marmalade (or your favorite jam)
1 TB. finely chopped fresh rosemary leaves	
$\frac{1}{4}$ tsp. sea salt	

1. Preheat the oven to 375°F. Line a baking sheet with parchment paper.

2. In a food processor fitted with a chopping blade, pulse together Quick-and-Easy Quinoa, all-purpose flour, sugar, baking powder, rosemary, sea salt, and unsalted butter until mixture forms a coarse meal. Transfer mixture to a medium bowl.

3. Gradually stir in heavy cream and sour cream until just combined and mixture begins to form dough.

4. On a lightly floured work surface, and using a rolling pin, gently roll out dough to about $\frac{1}{2}$ inch thick. Using a 3-inch heart cookie cutter (or your favorite cookie cutter) cut out heart-shaped pieces of dough, and place on the baking sheet.

5. Bake for about 20 minutes or until edges are golden brown. Let cool on a wire rack for about 20 minutes before serving with orange marmalade.

Lemon Poppy Seed Quinoa Biscuits

Lemon and poppy seeds are wonderful for breakfast. The poppy seeds provides a slight crunch and the tart lemon wakes up your taste buds. The quinoa's light nutty flavor adds another tasty dimension.

Yield:	Prep time:	Cook time:	Serving size:
30 biscuits	45 minutes	10 minutes	2 biscuits

Each serving has:			
258.9 calories	33.7 g carbohydrates	13.1 g fat	0.7 g fiber
2.6 g protein			

¼ cup fresh lemon juice	½ tsp. salt
2 sticks unsalted butter	1½ cups sugar
1½ cups all-purpose flour	1 large egg
½ cup quinoa flour	2 tsp. pure vanilla extract
1 tsp. baking powder	1 TB. poppy seeds

1. Preheat the oven to 375°F. Line a baking sheet with parchment paper.

2. In a small saucepan over medium heat, bring lemon juice to a simmer, and cook for about 10 minutes or until reduced by half. Add 1 stick unsalted butter, and stir until melted. Turn off heat.

3. In a medium bowl, whisk together all-purpose flour, quinoa flour, baking powder, and salt.

4. In a large bowl, and using an electric mixer on medium speed, cream together remaining 1 stick unsalted butter and 1 cup sugar. Add egg and lemon-butter mixture, and mix well for about 3 minutes or until pale in color.

5. Add vanilla extract and ½ of lemon zest to egg mixture, and mix until well combined. Gradually add in flour mixture until just combined. Add poppy seeds. Refrigerate for about 20 to 25 minutes.

6. Meanwhile, in a small bowl, stir together remaining ½ cup sugar and remaining lemon zest.

7. Form dough into about 30 balls, and roll in sugar-lemon mixture. Place on the baking sheet, and bake for about 10 minutes or until lightly browned. Serve immediately, or let cool and store in an airtight container for about 1 week.

KEEN ON QUINOA

Zesting is the act of peeling or grating off the rind of a lemon, lime, or other citrus fruit. Zesting can be done using a traditional cheese grater, or for a finer zest, with a zester. Be sure to grate only the colored part of the rind; don't use the bitter-tasting white pith.

Zucchini Quinoa Nut Bread

Zucchini has a mild squashy flavor that blends well with cinnamon, nutmeg, and pecans. Applesauce, yogurt, and maple syrup also add flavor and moisture to this breakfast bread.

Yield:	Prep time:	Cook time:	Serving size:
1 (8-inch) loaf	15 minutes	60 minutes	1 (1-inch-thick) slice

Each serving has:			
218.0 calories 4.3 g protein	26.8 g carbohydrates	11.4 g fat	2.7 g fiber

½ cup all-purpose flour	¼ cup canola oil
½ cup quinoa flour	½ cup unsweetened applesauce
½ cup whole-wheat flour	2 TB. plain yogurt
½ tsp. salt	¼ cup sugar
½ tsp. baking soda	¼ cup maple syrup (light okay)
½ tsp. baking powder	2 tsp. pure vanilla extract
1 tsp. ground cinnamon	1 medium zucchini, skin on and grated (1 cup)
½ tsp. ground nutmeg	⅓ cup chopped pecans
1 large egg	

1. Preheat the oven to 325°F. Spray an 8-inch loaf pan with nonstick cooking spray.

2. In a large bowl, sift together all-purpose flour, quinoa flour, whole-wheat flour, salt, baking soda, baking powder, cinnamon, and nutmeg. Mix well.

3. In a small bowl, combine egg, canola oil, unsweetened applesauce, yogurt, sugar, maple syrup, and pure vanilla extract.

4. Gradually mix flour mixture to egg mixture, and stir until just combined. Fold in zucchini and pecans until just combined.

5. Pour batter into the prepared loaf pan, and bake for 50 to 60 minutes or until toothpick inserted into the center comes out clean. Cool on a wire rack for about 30 minutes, turn out onto a cutting board, slice, and serve.

Variation: If zucchini isn't your thing, you could substitute 1 cup canned pumpkin, 1 cup grated carrots, or 1 cup mashed ripe banana for it.

Fresh from the Griddle

In This Chapter

* Making the perfect pancake
* Having fun with toppings
* Mouthwatering quinoa pancakes, waffles, and crepes

Everyone loves a good griddle breakfast—stacks of pancakes short and tall, waffles in all shapes and sizes, or thinner and more sophisticated crepes. There are tricks to the trade in making these tasty, hearty dishes, and in this chapter, I share helpful hints for each.

Toppings and fillings are the key to variety in these recipes. Savory ingredients like fresh rosemary, fresh crisp vegetables, and sweet-tart wild berries give dimension to traditional syrup.

The Perfect Pancake

The perfect pancake begins with perfect batter. One of the biggest mistakes people make when mixing pancake batter is overmixing it. You don't need to stir and stir and stir. A simple combining of ingredients is just right.

A hot griddle is also essential. When little droplets of water bounce right off and evaporate as soon as they touch the surface, your griddle is ready. If you don't have a griddle, and don't want to invest in one, a large nonstick skillet suffices.

Next, lightly butter your heated griddle, and measure the pancake batter in ¼ cups. Pour the batter quickly onto the hot griddle because the batter cooks fast—3 or four minutes tops. When the edges look a little dry and bubbly, you know it's time to flip. Use a long spatula to flip your pancake so you get good leverage. Flip all in one motion—don't be scared! Cook the pancake another 1 or 2 minutes, and boom, you're done!

Tasty Toppings

Maple syrup isn't the only breakfast topping. Pancakes, waffles, and even crepes taste delicious with all sorts of toppings. For pancakes, try a berry syrup like raspberry or strawberry or a little boysenberry jam. Waffles are incredible dusted with confectioners' sugar and topped with fresh strawberry or mango slices. When it comes to crepes, my favorite breakfast crepe is a combination of sautéed spinach and mushrooms topped with a simple sour cream sauce. I use nonfat sour cream to keep it on the lighter side.

Quinoa Pancakes

Not your traditional pancake in flavor or nutritional value, these pancakes have a sweetly nutty flavor accented by a hint of lemon.

Yield:	Prep time:	Cook time:	Serving size:
8 pancakes	10 minutes	15 minutes	1 pancake
Each serving has:			
334.5 calories	54.2 g carbohydrates	10.5 g fat	3.2 g fiber
7.1 g protein			

½ cup *almond flour*

⅛ cup coconut oil

2 cups warm water

1 tsp. pure vanilla extract

1 tsp. fresh lemon juice

1 tsp. maple syrup

2 cups quinoa flour

2 TB. baking powder

¼ tsp. baking soda

2 TB. unsalted butter

8 TB. strawberry jam

1. In a large bowl, combine almond flour, coconut oil, warm water, vanilla extract, lemon juice, and maple syrup. Mix until just combined. Do not overmix.

2. In a small bowl, combine quinoa flour, baking powder, and baking soda.

3. Working in batches, add quinoa flour mixture to almond flour mixture, $\frac{1}{3}$ at a time.

4. In a nonstick pancake griddle or cast-iron skillet over medium heat, melt $\frac{1}{2}$ tablespoon unsalted butter. Spoon about $\frac{1}{4}$ cup batter onto the hot griddle, and cook for about 1 minute or until edges begin to bubble. Flip over pancake, and cook on other side for about 45 to 60 seconds or until edges are set.

5. Remove pancake to a serving plate, and repeat with remaining batter, adding additional unsalted butter, if needed.

6. To serve, place 1 pancake on a plate, and top with 1 tablespoon strawberry jam or your favorite.

DEFINITION

Almond flour, or *almond meal,* is simply ground almonds. It's naturally gluten free, like quinoa and quinoa flour. Many stores sell almond flour in the health food section, or you can find it at health foods and specialty stores. You can also find almond flour online, including at many of the same sites that sell quinoa flour (see Appendix B).

Blueberry Quinoa Pancakes with Wild Berry Maple Compote

Fresh, sweet blueberries complement nutty quinoa and traditional maple syrup, all enhanced by a sweet wild berry compote of raspberries, blackberries, and strawberries, and lemon and orange zests.

Yield:	Prep time:	Cook time:	Serving size:
8 pancakes	15 minutes	25 minutes	1 pancake with 3 table-spoons compote

Each serving has:			
347.1 calories	66.1 g carbohydrates	8.1 g fat	5.2 g fiber
5.8 g protein			

1 cup fresh raspberries	4 tsp. baking powder
1 cup fresh blackberries	$\frac{1}{4}$ tsp. sea salt
1 cup fresh sliced strawberries, green tops removed	2 large eggs
$1\frac{1}{2}$ cups plus $1\frac{1}{2}$ TB. maple syrup	$1\frac{1}{2}$ cups low-fat milk
$\frac{1}{2}$ TB. fine lemon zest	$1\frac{1}{4}$ cups water
$\frac{1}{4}$ TB. fine orange zest	1 tsp. pure vanilla extract
$1\frac{1}{4}$ cups quinoa flour	2 TB. unsalted butter, melted
1 cup whole-wheat flour	2 cups fresh blueberries
	2 TB. unsalted butter

1. In a medium saucepan over medium heat, heat raspberries, blackberries, strawberries, $1\frac{1}{2}$ cups maple syrup, lemon zest, and orange zest. Bring to a gentle boil, reduce heat to low, and simmer for about 10 minutes. Remove from heat, and set aside.

2. In a large bowl, combine quinoa flour, whole-wheat flour, baking powder, and sea salt.

3. In a medium bowl, whisk together remaining $1\frac{1}{2}$ tablespoons maple syrup, eggs, low-fat milk, water, and vanilla extract. Mix well and then whisk in melted unsalted butter.

4. Gradually add quinoa mixture to egg mixture, and mix until just combined. Fold in blueberries.

5. In a medium nonstick skillet or pancake griddle, melt ½ tablespoon unsalted butter. Pour ¼ cup batter onto the hot griddle, and cook for about 1 minute or until edges begin to bubble. Flip over pancake, and cook on other side for 1 minute or until golden brown.

6. Remove pancake to a serving plate, and repeat with remaining batter, adding additional unsalted butter, if needed.

7. Serve pancakes with 2 or 3 tablespoons wild berry compote.

Traditional Quinoa Waffles

These gluten-free waffles will have you begging for more. Sweet apple and cinnamon spice give these waffles a delicious twist.

Yield:	Prep time:	Cook time:	Serving size:
8 waffles	12 minutes	20 minutes	1 waffle

Each serving has:			
118.4 calories	15.2 g carbohydrates	5.2 g fat	1.5 g fiber
3.1 g protein			

¾ cup quinoa flour	2 TB. vegetable oil
1 tsp. baking powder	1 TB. honey
1 tsp. ground cinnamon	1 large egg
½ tsp. sea salt	1 large Fuji apple, grated
½ cup apple juice	

1. In a large bowl, stir together quinoa flour, baking powder, ground cinnamon, and sea salt.

2. In a medium saucepan over low heat, stir together apple juice, vegetable oil, and honey just until warmed. Remove from heat, and set aside.

3. Quickly whisk egg into apple juice mixture, and add grated apple. Pour into quinoa mixture, and whisk to combine. Do not overmix.

4. If batter is a little stiff, add a little bit more apple juice, about 2 tablespoons at a time.

5. Heat a waffle iron to medium-high, and lightly coat with nonstick cooking spray. Pour batter into the waffle iron in $\frac{1}{4}$ cup increments or enough to cover the waffle iron completely. Close the waffle iron, and cook until golden brown or until your waffle iron indicator light comes on.

6. Repeat with remaining batter, and serve with maple syrup or your favorite jam.

KEEN ON QUINOA

If you don't have a waffle iron, consider investing in one! These tasty waffles are a great break from traditional waffles and are healthier for you. Top with syrup; add fresh sliced strawberries; or sauté 1 or 2 cups fresh apple slices with 1 tablespoon unsalted butter, $\frac{1}{2}$ teaspoon ground cinnamon, and $\frac{1}{4}$ teaspoon ground nutmeg for topping.

Quinoa Waffles with Orange Maple Syrup

Healthy waffles have never been so tasty, especially when they're topped off with a simple orange maple syrup.

Yield:	Prep time:	Cook time:	Serving size:
10 waffles	20 minutes	25 minutes	1 waffle with 2 table-spoons orange maple syrup

Each serving has:			
408.5 calories 6.3 g protein	102.4 g carbohydrates	5.6 g fat	2.8 g fiber

$\frac{3}{4}$ cup maple syrup

2 cups brown sugar, firmly packed

$\frac{1}{2}$ cup orange juice

$\frac{1}{2}$ cup water

1 TB. fine orange zest

2 tsp. pure vanilla extract

1 cup whole-wheat flour

$\frac{1}{2}$ cup all-purpose flour

$\frac{1}{2}$ cup quinoa flour

1 tsp. ground cinnamon

$1\frac{1}{2}$ tsp. baking powder

$\frac{1}{4}$ tsp. sea salt

$1\frac{1}{2}$ cups low-fat milk

2 large eggs

2 TB. canola oil

1 very ripe banana, peeled and mashed

1. In a small saucepan over medium heat, heat maple syrup, brown sugar, orange juice, water, orange zest, and 1 teaspoon vanilla extract. Simmer for about 5 minutes or until sugar is dissolved and liquid is reduced by $\frac{1}{3}$. Set aside.

2. In a large bowl, whisk together whole-wheat flour, all-purpose flour, and quinoa flour. Add ground cinnamon, baking powder, and sea salt, and stir to combine.

3. In a medium bowl, whisk together low-fat milk, eggs, canola oil, and remaining 1 teaspoon vanilla extract until well combined. Pour into flour mixture, add mashed banana, and stir until just combined. Do not overmix.

4. Heat a waffle iron to medium-high, and lightly coat with nonstick cooking spray. Pour batter into the waffle iron in $\frac{1}{4}$ cup increments or enough to cover the waffle iron completely. Close the waffle iron, and cook until golden brown or until your waffle iron indicator light comes on.

5. Repeat with remaining batter, and serve with orange maple syrup or any flavor syrup you like.

QUICK FIX

If bananas aren't your favorite, you could substitute 1 or 2 tablespoons raisins, golden raisins, or chocolate chips. Or give your waffles a more savory flavor by adding 1 tablespoon chopped fresh rosemary leaves in place of the banana. The waffles won't be quite as moist, so you may want to increase the oil by $\frac{1}{2}$ tablespoon.

Quinoa Crepes with Fresh Berries

Crepes are usually filled with berries and some sort of whipped cream, as these delicious quinoa crepes are. Sweetness comes from not only the fruit inside the crepe but from the honey in the batter.

Yield:	Prep time:	Cook time:	Serving size:
8 to 10 crepes	15 minutes	20 minutes	1 crepe

Each serving has:			
198.7 calories	24.2 g carbohydrates	9.6 g fat	1.3 g fiber
4.2 g protein			

1 large egg	1½ cups all-purpose flour
1 cup water	1½ tsp. baking powder
½ cup apple juice	½ tsp. sea salt
4 TB. canola oil	½ cup sliced fresh strawberries, green tops removed
1 TB. honey	½ cup fresh blueberries
1½ cups Quick-and-Easy Quinoa (recipe in Chapter 1)	1 cup low-fat sour cream (optional)

1. In a large bowl, whisk together egg, water, apple juice, canola oil, and honey.

2. In a medium bowl, stir together Quick-and-Easy Quinoa, all-purpose flour, baking powder, and sea salt.

3. Add egg mixture to flour mixture, and mix well to combine.

4. Heat a flat nonstick or cast-iron skillet over medium heat, and lightly coat with nonstick cooking spray. Pour about ¼ cup batter onto the hot skillet, swirling to spread batter in a thin layer across the skillet. Cook for about 30 seconds or until bubbles have evenly formed on top of crepe. Using a flat spatula, flip over crepe, and cook for about 20 more seconds or until cooked through.

5. Transfer crepe to a serving plate, and fill with 2 tablespoons strawberries and 2 tablespoons blueberries. Fold sides of crepe into the center, and top with a dollop (about 1 or 2 tablespoons) sour cream.

DEFINITION

Crepes are a thin, pancake-style pastry originating from France. Usually made from wheat flour, crepes are served with a variety of fillings, including fruit and sugary fillings and savory fillings with rich sauces.

Savory Quinoa Breakfast Crepes with Rosemary

Rosemary has a pleasing, fresh flavor that enhances the foods it's paired with, whether breakfast, lunch, or dinner. Here, rosemary is paired with a hint of lemon and slightly earthy spinach.

Yield:	Prep time:	Cook time:	Serving size:
10 crepes	20 minutes	25 minutes	1 crepe

Each serving has:			
257.0 calories	27.3 g carbohydrates	13.3 g fat	1.9 g fiber
7.9 g protein			

2 slices bacon	$^2/_3$ cup chicken broth
$^1/_2$ lb. fresh crimini mushrooms, sliced	3 large eggs
3 TB. unsalted butter	$^1/_2$ cup lemon juice
$1^3/_4$ cups all-purpose flour	$^1/_2$ cup low-fat sour cream
1 cup low-fat milk	1 cup water
1 (10-oz.) pkg. frozen chopped spinach, thawed and drained	$^1/_2$ cup orange juice
1 TB. chopped fresh Italian flat-leaf parsley leaves	4 TB. canola oil
	$^1/_2$ TB. *agave nectar*
2 TB. grated Parmesan cheese	1 TB. finely chopped fresh rosemary leaves
$2^1/_2$ tsp. sea salt	$1^1/_2$ cups Quick-and-Easy Quinoa (recipe in Chapter 1)
2 tsp. ground black pepper	$1^1/_2$ tsp. baking powder

1. In a large skillet over medium-high heat, cook bacon for about 2 or 3 minutes or until crisp and browned. Using tongs, transfer bacon to a paper towel to drain. When cooled, crumble and set aside.

2. To the skillet, add crimini mushrooms, and sauté for about 2 minutes.

3. In a medium saucepan over medium heat, melt unsalted butter. Whisk in $^1/_4$ cup all-purpose flour, stirring constantly, until a smooth paste forms. Gradually whisk in milk, stirring constantly until combined and smooth.

4. Add bacon, mushrooms, spinach, parsley, Parmesan cheese, 1 teaspoon sea salt, and 1 teaspoon black pepper, and cook, stirring frequently, for about 10 minutes. Remove from heat, and set aside.

5. In a small saucepan over medium-high heat, bring chicken broth to a boil. Turn off heat.

6. In a small bowl, whisk together 2 eggs and lemon juice. Whisking constantly so eggs don't scramble, add $\frac{1}{3}$ of chicken broth to eggs. Whisk in $\frac{1}{2}$ of remaining chicken broth, and then whisk in remaining chicken broth.

7. Add low-fat sour cream, and whisk until well combined. Add 1 teaspoon sea salt and 1 teaspoon black pepper, and whisk to combine. Set aside.

8. In a large bowl, whisk together remaining 1 egg, water, orange juice, canola oil, and agave nectar.

9. In a medium bowl, stir together rosemary, Quick-and-Easy Quinoa, remaining $1\frac{1}{2}$ cups all-purpose flour, baking powder, and remaining $\frac{1}{2}$ teaspoon sea salt.

10. Add orange juice mixture to quinoa flour mixture, and mix well to combine.

11. Spray a flat nonstick or cast-iron skillet with nonstick cooking spray, and heat over medium heat. Pour about $\frac{1}{4}$ cup batter onto the hot skillet, swirling to spread batter in a thin layer across the skillet. Cook about 30 seconds or until bubbles have evenly formed on top of crepe. Using a flat spatula, flip over crepe, and cook for about 20 more seconds or until cooked through.

12. Transfer crepe to serving plate, and fill with 2 or 3 tablespoons spinach-bacon filling. Starting at one side of crepe, roll crepe over filling into a roll. Top with warm sour cream sauce.

Variation: You can skip the sour cream sauce and use plain sour cream only. A dollop, or 1 or 2 tablespoons, on top of your finished crepe will do.

DEFINITION

Agave nectar (pronounced *ah-GAH-vay*) is the sap of the agave plant, native to southern Mexico. It's used as a natural sweetener, like honey, and can be substituted for sugar in many recipes, including desserts, sauces, salad dressings, and drinks.

Quinoa Crepes with Eggs and Cheese

These lighter quinoa crepes are sweetened with a little honey to balance the eggs, ricotta, and sharp cheddar cheese.

Yield:	Prep time:	Cook time:	Serving size:
10 crepes	15 minutes	20 minutes	1 crepe

Each serving has:			
296.5 calories	22.9 g carbohydrates	16.5 g fat	1.0 g fiber
14.0 g protein			

12 large eggs	1½ tsp. baking powder
1 cup water	1½ tsp. sea salt
½ cup apple juice	¼ cup low-fat milk
4 TB. canola oil	¼ cup part-skim ricotta cheese
1 TB. honey	1 tsp. ground black pepper
1½ cups Quick-and-Easy Quinoa (recipe in Chapter 1)	1 cup grated sharp cheddar cheese
1½ cups all-purpose flour	

1. Preheat the oven to 400°F. Lightly coat a 9-inch rectangular casserole dish with nonstick cooking spray.

2. In a large bowl, whisk together 1 egg, water, apple juice, canola oil, and honey.

3. In a medium bowl, stir together Quick-and-Easy Quinoa, all-purpose flour, baking powder, and ½ teaspoon sea salt.

4. Add egg mixture to flour mixture, and mix well to combine.

5. Heat a flat nonstick or cast-iron skillet over medium heat, and lightly coat with nonstick cooking spray. Pour about ¼ cup batter onto the hot skillet, swirling to spread batter in a thin layer across the skillet. Cook for about 30 seconds or until bubbles have evenly formed on top of crepe. Using a flat spatula, flip over crepe, and continue cooking for about 20 more seconds or until cooked through.

6. Transfer crepes to a serving plate, and cover with foil to keep warm.

7. In the large clean bowl, whisk together remaining 11 eggs, low-fat milk, part-skim ricotta cheese, remaining 1 teaspoon sea salt, and ground black pepper.

8. Heat a large skillet over medium heat, and lightly coat with nonstick cooking spray. Add egg mixture, and cook, stirring with a wooden spoon or spatula to scramble, for 30 to 45 seconds or until eggs are just done. Do not overcook.

9. Spoon about 3 or 4 tablespoons egg mixture into each crepe, and beginning at one side, roll crepe over mixture. Transfer rolled crepes to the prepared casserole dish. Repeat until all crepes have been filled. Evenly sprinkle cheddar cheese over crepes, and bake for about 5 minutes, or until cheese is melted.

Really Tasty Lunches

The key to lunch is to have a balanced meal that doesn't weigh you down and make you feel sleepy afterward—and can be fit into the hour many of us get for lunch. Luckily, nutritious, delicious quinoa cooks fast—give it 15 minutes, and you'll be ready for a healthy lunch.

The chapters in Part 3 give you dozens of quick and flavorful lunches that fuel your body and mind and get you through the second half of your day. These recipes focus on fiber, protein, and energizing carbohydrates and should provide you with energy to power you through until dinner.

Vegetarian Salads

In This Chapter

- Versatile vegetarian dishes
- Protein-boosting quinoa
- Pointers for super salads
- Delicious and nutritious plant-based salads

As a vegetarian—someone who doesn't eat meat, fish, or poultry—you might lament the sometimes-sparse animal-free options for you when dining out, with family and friends, or even in the supermarket. No more! You can enjoy a delicious, nutritious plant-based diet thanks to the meat-free, veggie-friendly recipes in this chapter.

Quinoa is a natural ingredient to pair with veggie dishes. It's a complete protein, meaning it has all the amino acids needed for a healthy diet. That's especially true for vegetarians, who can sometimes struggle with consuming enough protein because of the lack of animal-based protein sources in their diets.

Successful Salads

You'll be peeling and chopping, slicing and dicing for these salad recipes. But before you begin, I'd like to share a few tips I've learned over the years.

First, always begin with a sharp chef's knife. If you don't own a chef's knife, get one. You can get a good-quality chef's knife in the home section of department stores or at specialty kitchen stores.

Seeding tomatoes is key to many salad recipes and pretty much any recipe that isn't a soup where you need the extra liquid.

♟ Chef James McDonald's Quinoa Super Salad

Fresh arugula, heirloom carrots, watermelon radish, passion fruit purée, and fresh mint are the stars in this recipe by Chef James McDonald, Executive Chef/Owner, I'o Restaurant, Pacific'o Restaurant, The Feast at Lele, Aina Gourmet Market, Honua Kai Resort, O'o Farm (Maui, Hawaii).

Yield:	**Prep time:**	**Serving size:**
6 cups	15 minutes, plus 3 hours steep time	1½ cups

Each serving has:		
1,315.6 calories	24.3 g carbohydrates	136.8 g fat
5.0 g fiber	4.2 g protein	

2 cups fresh mint leaves	2 cups purslane
1 cup canola oil	½ lb. fresh arugula
½ cup passion fruit purée	2 cups sliced heirloom carrots
2 TB. honey	2 cups sliced watermelon radish
½ cup rice wine vinegar	1 cup Quick-and-Easy Quinoa (recipe in Chapter 1)
1½ cups olive oil	1 cup crumbled feta cheese
3 dashes hot sauce	1 tsp. ground black pepper
1½ tsp. sea salt	

1. In a food processor fitted with a chopping blade or a blender, purée mint and canola oil for 30 seconds or until smooth. Allow to steep for 3 hours, strain through a cheesecloth, and set aside.

2. In the food processor or the blender, purée passion fruit purée, honey, rice wine vinegar, olive oil, hot sauce, and ½ teaspoon sea salt for 30 seconds or until well combined and smooth. Refrigerate until ready to use.

3. In a large bowl, combine purslane, arugula, carrots, watermelon radish, Quick-and-Easy Quinoa, and feta cheese. Add remaining 1 teaspoon sea salt and 1 teaspoon black pepper, and toss well.

4. Drizzle purslane mixture with passion fruit mixture, and toss well to combine. Place about 1½ cups mixture onto a serving plate, and drizzle with 1 or 2 teaspoons mint oil.

Roasted Vegetable Quinoa Salad

Grilling vegetables brings out their natural sugars and therefore depth of flavor. The slight acidity of the balsamic vinegar rounds out the roasted heartiness in this salad.

Yield:	Prep time:	Cook time:	Serving size:
4 to 6 cups	10 minutes	10 minutes	¾ cup

Each serving has:			
245.8 calories	24.2 g carbohydrates	15.3 g fat	4.1 g fiber
5.4 g protein			

1 medium fresh red bell pepper, ribs and seeds removed, and chopped	1 tsp. sea salt
	1 tsp. ground black pepper
1 medium *shallot,* peeled and diced	2 TB. balsamic vinegar
	1 TB. chopped fresh rosemary leaves
1 cup chopped fresh broccoli florets	½ cup fresh corn kernels
4 medium fresh asparagus spears, chopped	1 batch Quick-and-Easy Quinoa (recipe in Chapter 1)
4 TB. olive oil	

1. In a large mixing bowl, toss together red bell pepper, shallot, broccoli, and asparagus. Drizzle 2 tablespoons olive oil over vegetables, and toss to coat.

2. In a large sauté pan or cast-iron grill pan over medium-high heat, cook red bell pepper mixture for about 5 minutes or until tender.

3. In a large bowl, whisk together remaining 2 tablespoons olive oil, sea salt, black pepper, balsamic vinegar, and rosemary. Add corn, red bell pepper mixture, and Quick-and-Easy Quinoa. Toss well to coat evenly, and serve.

Variation: For **Roasted Vegetable Quinoa Salad with Mixed Greens,** add 4 cups mixed greens when adding the quinoa, and toss all to coat.

DEFINITION

Although different from onions, **shallots** are in the onion family. They have a brownish skin and resemble a large garlic clove in shape. Shallots have a sweet onion-and-garlic flavor and can be used interchangeably with onions.

Quinoa Salad with Tomatoes, Red Onion, and Feta

Rich kalamata olives, mild cucumbers, spicy mustard, and sweet tomatoes give you all the balance and flavor you need for this quinoa favorite that rounds out with spicy heat of pepperoncini mellowed by tart feta cheese.

Yield:	Prep time:	Serving size
6 cups	18 minutes	1 cup

Each serving has:		
201.1 calories	16.6 g carbohydrates	13.3 g fat
1.7 g fiber	4.4 g protein	

1 batch Quick-and-Easy Quinoa (recipe in Chapter 1)

½ TB. ground dry mustard

2 medium Roma tomatoes, seeded and diced

1 medium cucumber, peeled, seeds removed, and diced

½ cup chopped pitted kalamata olives

¼ cup chopped pepperoncini

½ medium red onion, chopped

½ cup crumbled feta cheese

2 TB. extra-virgin olive oil

1 tsp. sea salt

1 tsp. ground black pepper

1. In a large bowl, toss together Quick-and-Easy Quinoa, dry mustard, Roma tomatoes, cucumber, kalamata olives, pepperoncini, red onion, and feta cheese.

2. Drizzle olive oil over top, and add sea salt and black pepper. Toss well to coat, and serve.

Pomegranate Apple Quinoa Salad

Fresh pomegranate, Granny Smith apple, celery, walnuts, lemon, and fresh mint combine with quinoa to make one delicious salad that's finished with a pomegranate vinaigrette.

Yield:	Prep time:	Serving size:
6 cups	20 minutes	1 cup

Each serving has:		
294.2 calories	35.9 g carbohydrates	15.7 g fat
4.5 g fiber	6.0 g protein	

¼ cup pomegranate juice

2 TB. white wine vinegar

3 TB. extra-virgin olive oil

½ tsp. sea salt

½ tsp. ground black pepper

1 cup fresh pomegranate seeds

2 medium Granny Smith apples, cored and diced

3 medium celery stalks, diced

4 cups Quick-and-Easy Quinoa (recipe in Chapter 1)

½ cup chopped toasted walnuts

2 TB. chopped fresh mint leaves

1. In a small bowl, whisk together pomegranate juice, white wine vinegar, extra-virgin olive oil, sea salt, and black pepper.

2. In a large bowl, toss together pomegranate seeds, Granny Smith apples, celery, Quick-and-Easy Quinoa, walnuts, and mint leaves. Drizzle pomegranate vinaigrette over quinoa mixture, toss to combine, and serve.

Variation: If you can't find fresh pomegranates, substitute an equal amount of dried cranberries.

QUICK FIX

To release the seeds from a fresh pomegranate, split pomegranate in ½ and hold pomegranate under water in a large bowl. The pith will float to the top, making it easy to scoop up the seeds, discard the pith, and drain any excess water from the seeds.

♧ Chef Jon Gibson's Quinoa Palermo Salad

Infusing flavors from his experience as a chef in Sicily, Italy, Chef Jon Gibson, executive chef of The Beachcomber Café (Newport Beach, CA), uses quinoa as a base for this refreshing salad of cucumber, red onion, lemon, and fresh herbs, tossed with a white balsamic vinaigrette.

Yield:	Prep time:	Cook time:	Serving size:
6 cups	15 minutes	25 minutes	1 cup

Each serving has:			
349.1 calories	4.6 g carbohydrates	37.3 g fat	1.1 g fiber
0.7 g protein			

2 cups vegetable broth	1 medium red onion, diced
2 cloves garlic, minced	1 medium orange bell pepper, ribs and seeds removed, and diced
1 cup uncooked red quinoa, rinsed and drained	½ cup kalamata olives, pitted and chopped
1 cup extra-virgin olive oil	1 cup grape tomatoes, halved
1 TB. white balsamic vinegar	1 cup Italian flat-leaf parsley
Juice of 1 lemon	¼ TB. minced chives
1 tsp. minced fresh oregano leaves	Zest of 1 lemon
1 tsp. kosher salt	
1 tsp. ground black pepper	
1 medium cucumber, peeled and diced	

1. In a medium saucepan over medium heat, bring vegetable broth and garlic to a boil. Stir in red quinoa, reduce heat to medium-low, cover, and simmer for about 15 to 20 minutes or until quinoa is tender and liquid is almost all absorbed. If quinoa isn't tender, add a little more vegetable broth.

2. Meanwhile, in a large bowl, whisk together extra-virgin olive oil, white balsamic vinegar, lemon juice, oregano, kosher salt, and black pepper.

3. Using a rubber spatula, carefully transfer quinoa to olive oil mixture, and gently fold in.

4. Fold in cucumber, red onion, orange bell pepper, kalamata olives, grape tomatoes, Italian flat-leaf parsley, chives, and lemon zest until thoroughly mixed.

5. Serve warm or place in the refrigerator and serve cold.

KEEN ON QUINOA

[This salad] reminds me of when I lived in Sicily, and even though I love risotto, I wanted something lighter—and quinoa is a lot healthier for you, too!

—Chef Jon Gibson

Roasted Cherry Tomato Quinoa Salad

Flavorful and tender roasted tomatoes star alongside fresh thyme leaves and give this salad an earthy flavor that's then balanced by my favorite ingredient, lemon.

Yield:	Prep time:	Cook time:	Serving size:
4 cups	20 minutes	40 minutes	1 cup
Each serving has:			
225.0 calories	36.0 g carbohydrates	6.4 g fat	3.8 g fiber
6.6 g protein			

1 pt. fresh cherry tomatoes

1 TB. olive oil

1 tsp. fresh thyme leaves

2 or 3 fresh thyme sprigs

2 cups vegetable broth

1 cup uncooked quinoa, rinsed and drained

1 tsp. sea salt

1 tsp. ground black pepper

Fine zest of 1 lemon

1. Preheat the oven to 290°F. Line a baking sheet with parchment paper.

2. In a small bowl, toss cherry tomatoes with olive oil, thyme leaves, and thyme sprigs. Transfer mixture to the baking sheet, and roast for about 30 minutes. Remove thyme sprigs.

3. Meanwhile, in a medium saucepan over medium-high heat, combine vegetable broth and quinoa. Bring to a boil, cover, reduce heat to low, and simmer for about 15 minutes or until all liquid is absorbed.

4. In a medium bowl, toss together quinoa and roasted tomatoes. Add sea salt, black pepper, and lemon zest, and toss to coat. Serve warm.

Jalapeño Quinoa Salad with Monterey Jack

Crisp, fresh cucumber cools down the hot jalapeño in this energizing lunch salad. Green bell pepper, tomatoes, and red onion round out the flavors.

Yield:	Prep time:	Cook time:	Serving size:
6 cups	20 minutes	15 minutes	1 cup

Each serving has:			
249.7 calories	23.7 g carbohydrates	13.1 g fat	2.4 g fiber
9.7 g protein			

2 cups vegetable broth

1 cup uncooked quinoa, rinsed and drained

$\frac{1}{2}$ cup seeded and diced cucumber

$\frac{1}{2}$ cup seeded and diced tomato

$\frac{1}{2}$ cup diced green bell pepper

$\frac{1}{2}$ cup diced red onion

$\frac{1}{4}$ cup chopped fresh cilantro leaves

1 medium jalapeño, seeds removed, and diced

$\frac{1}{4}$ cup fresh lime juice

2 TB. extra-virgin olive oil

1 tsp. sea salt

1 tsp. ground white pepper

$\frac{3}{4}$ cup grated Monterey Jack cheese

1. In a medium saucepan over medium-high heat, bring vegetable broth and quinoa to a boil. Cover, reduce heat to low, and simmer for 15 minutes or until almost all liquid has been absorbed. Remove from heat and set aside.

2. In a large bowl, toss together cucumber, tomato, green bell pepper, red onion, and cilantro.

3. In a small bowl, whisk together jalapeño, lime juice, extra-virgin olive oil, sea salt, and white pepper.

4. Add quinoa to cucumber mixture, and toss to combine. Add jalapeño mixture to quinoa-cucumber mixture, and toss well to coat.

5. Place salad in 6 serving bowls, and top each with 1 or 2 tablespoons Monterey Jack cheese.

🍴 Farmers' Market Quinoa Salad with Pistachio-Lemon Vinaigrette

Fluffy, protein-dense quinoa is tossed with the freshest seasonal vegetables and luscious pistachio-lemon vinaigrette in this hearty spring salad by Chef Elizabeth Howes, owner, Saffron Lane (San Francisco, CA).

Yield:	Prep time:	Cook time:	Serving size:
4 cups	15 minutes	55 minutes	1 cup
Each serving has:			
504.4 calories	44.6 g carbohydrates	33.4 g fat	7.0 g fiber
9.6 g protein			

6 red baby beets	5 French breakfast radishes or traditional radishes, thinly sliced
6 golden baby beets	3 TB. raw unsalted pistachios
1 TB. plus $\frac{1}{2}$ cup olive oil	1 small clove garlic
1 tsp. sea salt	Juice of 2 lemons
1 tsp. ground black pepper	3 TB. water
4 cups Quick-and-Easy Quinoa (recipe in Chapter 1), cooled	1 TB. champagne or white wine vinegar
$\frac{1}{2}$ cup broccoli rabe, roughly chopped	$\frac{1}{2}$ tsp. honey

1. Preheat the oven to 400°F.

2. Remove greens from red baby beets and golden baby beets, and reserve greens for another use. Rinse beets and remove outer skin using a vegetable peeler or a sharp paring knife. Slice each beet in $\frac{1}{2}$ and place on a parchment paper–lined baking sheet.

3. Drizzle 1 tablespoon olive oil over beets, and sprinkle with $\frac{3}{4}$ teaspoon sea salt and $\frac{3}{4}$ teaspoon black pepper. Toss to coat, and roast for about 20 to 30 minutes or until fork-tender. Set aside to cool.

4. In a large bowl, combine Quick-and-Easy Quinoa, beets, broccoli rabe, and French breakfast radishes.

5. In a food processor fitted with a chopping blade or a blender, combine pistachios, garlic, lemon juice, filtered water, champagne vinegar, and honey. Pulse to combine and break up pistachios. Slowly drizzle in remaining $\frac{1}{2}$ cup olive oil, and purée until smooth. Season with $\frac{1}{4}$ teaspoon sea salt and $\frac{1}{4}$ teaspoon black pepper.

6. Toss quinoa and vegetables with pistachio mixture, and serve chilled or at room temperature.

KEEN ON QUINOA

Quinoa is, without a doubt, one of nature's most perfect foods. Since many of my clients gravitate toward a vegetarian diet, I use quinoa often because I know this humble seed provides the essential amino acids our bodies crave and require for long-term sustainability. It also has this irresistible nutty flavor and pillowy and slightly crunchy texture, which is the perfect base for countless healthy and satisfying dishes.

—Chef Elizabeth Howes

Carrot Cucumber Quinoa Salad

Sesame oil, ginger, *tamarind paste*, and rice vinegar give this salad an Asian twist, complemented by spicy nutty flavors.

Yield:	Prep time:	Serving size:
4 cups	20 minutes	1 cup

Each serving has:		
134.5 calories	20.8 g carbohydrates	4.4 g fat
3.0 g fiber	3.8 g protein	

2 tsp. sesame oil

1 TB. peeled and finely chopped fresh ginger

2 cloves garlic, finely chopped

2 tsp. tamarind paste

2 TB. rice vinegar

2 TB. water

1 cup shredded carrots

1 cup seeded and diced cucumber

2 tsp. sesame seeds

$\frac{1}{4}$ cup chopped green onion, white and green parts

1 tsp. crushed red pepper flakes

1 batch Quick-and-Easy Quinoa (recipe in Chapter 1)

1 tsp. sea salt

1 tsp. ground black pepper

1. In a small bowl, whisk together sesame oil, ginger, garlic, tamarind paste, rice vinegar, and water.

2. In a large bowl, combine carrots, cucumber, sesame seeds, green onion, crushed red pepper flakes, Quick-and-Easy Quinoa, sea salt, and black pepper. Toss well.

3. Pour sesame oil mixture over quinoa mixture, toss well to coat, and serve.

DEFINITION

Tamarind paste is ground pulp from the tamarind fruit. It's sour in flavor. Primarily used in Indian and Thai cuisines, it's also found in Asian, Latin American, and Mediterranean dishes. Tamarind paste is usually sold in the Asian section of your grocery store. If you can't find it there, look for an Indian or Asian market, or purchase it online.

Mediterranean Quinoa Salad

Spaghetti squash is the twist in this recipe. Its slightly sweet and nutty flavor goes great with sour olives, crunchy quinoa, and crisp cucumber.

Yield:	Prep time:	Cook time:	Serving size:
8 cups	20 minutes	55 to 60 minutes	1 cup
Each serving has:			
166.9 calories	26.1 g carbohydrates	5.6 g fat	3.4 g fiber
4.1 g protein			

1 medium spaghetti squash, cut in $\frac{1}{2}$	1 medium cucumber, peeled, seeded, and diced
2 cups vegetable broth	$\frac{1}{2}$ cup chopped pitted kalamata olives
1 cup uncooked quinoa, rinsed and drained	1 bunch green onions, white and green parts, chopped
3 medium tomatoes, seeded and diced	$1\frac{1}{2}$ tsp. sea salt
1 medium red bell pepper, ribs and seeds removed, and diced	$1\frac{1}{2}$ tsp. ground black pepper

1. Preheat the oven to 400°F. Line a baking sheet with parchment paper.

2. Place spaghetti squash cut side up on the parchment paper, and bake for about 40 minutes or until tender. Remove from the oven, and allow to cool.

3. Meanwhile, in a medium saucepan over medium-high heat, bring vegetable broth and quinoa to a boil. Cover, reduce heat to low, and simmer for 15 minutes or until almost all liquid has been absorbed. Remove from heat, and set aside.

4. In a large bowl, toss together tomatoes, red bell pepper, cucumber, kalamata olives, green onions, sea salt, and black pepper.

5. Using a large spoon, scoop out spaghetti squash from rind. Then, using a fork or your fingers, separate the strands a little bit. Add to tomato mixture, followed by quinoa, and toss well to coat. Serve immediately, or chill before serving.

Spinach and Strawberry Quinoa Salad

Here, fresh beets, sweet strawberries, and earthy spinach greens are topped with a fresh citrus vinaigrette.

Yield:	Prep time:	Cook time:	Serving size:
6 cups	15 minutes	20 minutes	1 cup
Each serving has:			
164.0 calories	20.6 g carbohydrates	8.3 g fat	3.7 g fiber
4.2 g protein			

4 medium red or yellow beets, or combination of	1 TB. honey
4 cups fresh spinach leaves, washed and dried	1 TB. fresh orange juice
1 cup sliced strawberries, green tops removed	1 TB. fresh lemon juice
½ cup chopped pecans	1 tsp. sea salt
2 TB. white wine vinegar	1 tsp. ground black pepper
	1 batch Quick-and-Easy Quinoa (recipe in Chapter 1)

1. Peel beets, and chop into 1- or 2-inch chunks.

2. Fill a medium saucepan ¾ with water, and set over medium-high heat. Add beets, bring to a boil, and cook for about 15 to 20 minutes or until beets are fork-tender. Drain, and set aside to cool.

3. In a large bowl, toss together spinach, strawberries, and pecans.

4. In a small bowl, whisk together white wine vinegar, honey, orange juice, lemon juice, sea salt, and black pepper.

5. Add Quick-and-Easy Quinoa and beets to spinach mixture, and toss to combine.

6. Pour white wine vinegar mixture over spinach-quinoa mixture, toss to coat evenly, and serve.

Southwestern Quinoa Salad

Tomatillos have a sweet flavor and are a great match for black beans and spicy jalape-ños. Quinoa provides a nutty crunch and solid protein base for this delicious salad.

Yield:	Prep time:	Serving size:
6 cups	20 minutes	1 cup

Each serving has:		
252.0 calories	36.7 g carbohydrates	8.5 g fat
8.7 g fiber	9.5 g protein	

4 medium tomatillos, peeled and finely chopped

2 large tomatoes, seeded and diced

1/2 medium red onion, thinly sliced

1 medium jalapeño, seeded and minced

1/2 cup mild fresh tomato salsa

1/4 cup chopped fresh cilantro leaves

1 (15-oz.) can black beans, rinsed and drained well

1/2 cup fresh corn kernels

1 batch Quick-and-Easy Quinoa (recipe in Chapter 1)

1/2 cup nonfat mayonnaise

1 tsp. fine lemon zest

1 tsp. sea salt

1 tsp. ground black pepper

4 cups mixed greens

1. In a large bowl, combine tomatillos, tomatoes, red onion, jalapeño, tomato salsa, cilantro leaves, black beans, corn kernels, and Quick-and-Easy Quinoa.

2. In a small bowl, whisk together nonfat mayonnaise, lemon zest, sea salt, and black pepper. Spoon over tomatillo mixture, and toss well to coat.

3. Evenly divide mixed greens among 6 serving bowls. Place 1 cup tomatillo mixture on top, and serve.

Variation: Change up this delicious salad by adding crushed tortilla chips for extra crunch. Or switch out the mixed greens for radicchio cups. If you can't find tomatillos, use 2 additional tomatoes and 1 green bell pepper.

Buffalo Wing Quinoa Salad

Tahini, barbecue sauce, hot sauce, and distilled vinegar combine to create an amazing buffalo wing flavor. Tossed as a vinaigrette with beans, corn, olives, tomatoes, cilantro, and more make this the perfect salad for your family or for parties.

Yield:	Prep time:	Serving size:
6 cups	15 minutes	1 cup

Each serving has:		
332.3 calories	47.4 g carbohydrates	11.2 g fat
11.8 g fiber	12.8 g protein	

1½ cups canned chickpeas, rinsed and drained, ½ cup original liquid reserved

2 cloves garlic

¼ cup tahini

¼ cup fresh lemon juice

1½ tsp. paprika

2 TB. barbecue sauce

2 TB. hot sauce

1 TB. distilled white vinegar

1 tsp. sea salt

1 (14-oz.) can red kidney beans, rinsed and drained well

½ cup sliced black olives

1 (8-oz.) can kernel corn, drained

½ medium red onion, chopped

1 TB. chopped fresh cilantro leaves

4 medium cucumbers, peeled, seeded, and diced

2 medium tomatoes, seeded and diced

1 batch Quick-and-Easy Quinoa (recipe in Chapter 1)

1. In a food processor fitted with a chopping blade or a blender, process chickpeas, garlic, tahini, lemon juice, paprika, barbecue sauce, hot sauce, distilled white vinegar, sea salt, and reserved chickpea liquid until smooth. Set aside.

2. In a large bowl, combine red kidney beans, black olives, kernel corn, red onion, cilantro leaves, cucumbers, tomatoes, and Quick-and-Easy Quinoa. Toss well.

3. Place kidney bean mixture on serving plates or in bowls, and top each with 1 or 2 tablespoons puréed chickpea mixture.

DEFINITION

Tahini is a paste made from sesame seeds. It's a fundamental ingredient in hummus and is high in nutrients like calcium and omega-3 fatty acids. Tahini is usually sold in the Asian or ethnic food section of your local grocery store. If you can't find it, you can substitute an equal amount of peanut butter.

Quinoa Salad with Yellow Squash and Zucchini

By itself, squash doesn't have tons of flavor, but pair it with ingredients like paprika, cayenne, and lemon, and ... well ... the results are delicious, as you'll find in this yummy salad.

Yield:	Prep time:	Serving size:
4 cups	15 minutes	1 cup

Each serving has:		
216.9 calories	40.4 g carbohydrates	1.9 g fat
9.7 g fiber	11.1 g protein	

1 cup chopped fresh yellow squash

1 cup chopped fresh zucchini

¼ cup chopped white onion

1 (15-oz.) can lima beans, rinsed and drained well

2 TB. chopped fresh Italian flat-leaf parsley leaves

1 batch Quick-and-Easy Quinoa (recipe in Chapter 1)

1 tsp. sweet Hungarian paprika

1 tsp. cayenne

2 tsp. fine lemon zest

1 tsp. ground black pepper

1 tsp. sea salt

1. In a large bowl, combine yellow squash, zucchini, white onion, lima beans, Italian flat-leaf parsley leaves, Quick-and-Easy Quinoa, sweet Hungarian paprika, cayenne, lemon zest, black pepper, and sea salt.

2. Toss well, and serve.

Quinoa-Stuffed Tomatoes

Cucumber, cilantro, and tomatoes make for a flavorful, healthy lunch. Using low-fat yogurt instead of mayonnaise keeps it light, and cayenne adds spice sure to wake up your taste buds.

Yield:	Prep time:	Serving size:
4 stuffed tomatoes	15 minutes	1 stuffed tomato

Each serving has:		
132.2 calories	24.4 g carbohydrates	2.1 g fat
4.5 g fiber	6.1 g protein	

4 medium cucumbers, peeled, seeded, and diced	1 tsp. sea salt
$\frac{1}{2}$ medium red onion, diced	1 tsp. ground black pepper
$\frac{1}{2}$ cup low-fat vanilla yogurt	$\frac{1}{2}$ tsp. cayenne
1 TB. fine lemon zest	1 cup Quick-and-Easy Quinoa (recipe in Chapter 1)
2 TB. chopped fresh cilantro leaves	4 large tomatoes

1. In a large bowl, combine cucumbers, red onion, low-fat vanilla yogurt, lemon zest, cilantro, sea salt, black pepper, cayenne, and Quick-and-Easy Quinoa.

2. Using a spiked tomato scooper or a paring knife, cut out top of tomatoes. Using a melon baller or a spoon, scoop out and discard seeds and membranes from inside tomatoes, being careful not to puncture tomato skin.

3. Spoon equal parts of cucumber salad into tomatoes, and serve.

Quinoa-Stuffed Bell Peppers

Stuffed bell peppers make terrific lunch dishes. (They're also great for dinner.) This recipe is all about flavors from spices such as cumin and chili powder, combined with citrus.

Yield:	Prep time:	Cook time:	Serving size:
4 stuffed peppers	15 minutes	35 minutes	1 stuffed pepper

Each serving has:			
176.6 calories 6.0 g protein	28.3 g carbohydrates	5.1 g fat	5.4 g fiber

1 batch Quick-and-Easy Quinoa (recipe in Chapter 1)	1/2 tsp. cumin
1 TB. fine lemon zest	1/2 tsp. chili powder
1 TB. fresh lemon juice	1 tsp. sea salt
1 cup frozen peas	1 tsp. ground black pepper
2 TB. chopped green onion, white and green parts	4 medium red bell peppers
1 TB. chopped fresh Italian flat-leaf parsley leaves	2 TB. olive oil

1. Preheat the oven to 375°F.

2. In a large mixing bowl, combine Quick-and-Easy Quinoa, lemon zest, lemon juice, peas, green onion, Italian flat-leaf parsley, cumin, chili powder, sea salt, and black pepper.

3. Slice tops off red bell peppers, and using your fingertips, pull out and discard seeds and membranes from inside bell peppers.

4. Evenly divide quinoa mixture among bell peppers, packing if necessary, to use all quinoa mixture.

5. Place stuffed peppers in an 8-inch-square or similar baking dish. Drizzle olive oil over peppers, and place tops back on each bell pepper.

6. Bake for about 35 minutes or until peppers are slightly tender yet still firm and holding together.

Meaty Salads

In This Chapter

- Time-saving lunch ideas
- Energizing lunches
- Light and healthy lunch salads

Think you're too busy to prepare a healthy, delicious lunch ahead of time? Think again! Gearing up for lunchtime success isn't difficult with ingredients that can be made ahead and used all week—like quinoa!—and the delicious meat-based salads in this chapter.

Planning Ahead

You've probably heard that you should plan your week's worth of meals ahead of time. That includes lunches! Whether it's preparing for a week's worth of dinners or your daily office lunches, preplanning on Sunday afternoon makes it easier on you during the busy week. Once you've thought out some meals for the week, browse through your favorite cookbooks and magazines for menu inspiration. Pay particular attention to items like quinoa that can be prepared ahead of time!

Cooked quinoa can be frozen, making it a real time-saver for preparing future meals. Simply plan a few meals for the next two weeks, cook the amount of quinoa you need, drop it in the freezer, and it'll be ready when you are. Freeze foods in individual portions, and clearly label the packaging so you remember what they are. When you're ready for a quick lunch or dinner, pull out your protein and quinoa, and let it thaw in cold water (or if you have time, set it in the sink to thaw). Better yet, take it out of the freezer the night before so it has time to thaw overnight in the refrigerator.

Choosing Your Fuel

Remember to think of food as fuel for your body, not just something to satisfy your rumbling tummy. Keep your fuel efficient by choosing flavorful foods that are high in fiber, provide good protein, and contain easily digestible carbohydrates. Hmm. That sounds like quinoa to me!

And keep it light when you can. The heavier the food, the more your body has to work to digest it. That means your metabolism slows down, and by mid-afternoon, if not sooner, you're ready for a nap. Keep your energy with light wholesome foods such as quinoa, and be alert the whole day through.

Blackened Chicken Quinoa Salad with Roasted Corn

Blackened seasonings are incredible for cooking all kinds of dishes. I love it with the chicken in this salad. It gives the dish a spicy flavor nicely offset by the sweet corn.

Yield:	Prep time:	Cook time:	Serving size:
2 cups quinoa salad plus 2 chicken breasts	20 minutes	25 minutes	½ cup quinoa salad plus ½ chicken breast
Each serving has:			
316.1 calories 31.7 g protein	24.6 g carbohydrates	10.1 g fat	3.1 g fiber

2 (6-oz.) boneless, skinless chicken breasts

2 TB. olive oil

4 TB. blackened seasoning

1 batch Quick-and-Easy Quinoa (recipe in Chapter 1)

1 medium red bell pepper, ribs and seeds removed, and diced

1 cup fresh kernel corn

1 tsp. paprika

1 tsp. cayenne

1 tsp. sea salt

1 tsp. ground black pepper

1. Preheat the oven to 375°F.

2. Coat both sides of chicken breasts with 1 tablespoon olive oil. Then, coat both sides of chicken with 2 tablespoons each blackened seasoning.

3. In heavy, ovenproof skillet over medium heat, heat remaining 1 tablespoon olive oil. Add chicken, and cook for about 4 minutes. Turn over chicken, and cook for about 4 more minutes. Place the skillet in the oven, and bake for about 17 minutes or until cooked through (depending on thickness of chicken breasts). Let cool for about 5 minutes.

4. Meanwhile, in a large bowl, combine Quick-and-Easy Quinoa, red bell pepper, kernel corn, paprika, cayenne, sea salt, and black pepper.

5. Place ½ cup quinoa salad on each of 4 serving plates and top each with ½ cooked chicken breast.

Chicken and Apple Quinoa Salad with Waldorf Vinaigrette

Lemon, yogurt, apples, pecans, green grapes, and orange are just a few of the delicious flavors you'll enjoy in this traditional dish with a quinoa twist that's perfect for your mid-week lunch or a weekend brunch.

Yield:	Prep time:	Cook time:	Serving size:
6 cups	20 minutes	15 minutes	1 cup

Each serving has:			
428.0 calories	24.4 g carbohydrates	26.9 g fat	3.7 g fiber
24.3 g protein			

¾ cup nonfat plain yogurt

½ cup nonfat mayonnaise

½ cup orange juice

Juice of ½ lemon

1 TB. poppy seeds

1½ TB. olive oil

2 (6-oz.) boneless, skinless chicken breasts

2 TB. water

1 cup halved green grapes

1 medium Granny Smith apple, cored and roughly chopped

1 cup chopped pecans

1 cup diced red onion

½ cup diced celery

1 tsp. sea salt

1 tsp. ground white pepper

1 batch Quick-and-Easy Quinoa (recipe in Chapter 1)

1. In a medium bowl, whisk together nonfat yogurt, nonfat mayonnaise, orange juice, lemon juice, and poppy seeds until well combined. Cover the bowl with plastic wrap, and refrigerate for at least 20 minutes or until ready to use.

2. In a medium sauté pan over medium heat, heat olive oil. Add chicken, cover, and cook for 5 to 7 minutes. Turn over chicken, and cook for about 5 to 7 more minutes, replacing the lid after turning. Add water (if needed) to prevent burning. When chicken is cooked through, remove from heat and set aside to cool.

3. In a large bowl, combine green grapes, Granny Smith apple, pecans, red onion, celery, sea salt, white pepper, and Quick-and-Easy Quinoa.

4. Chop chicken into 1- or 2-inch cubes, add to grape mixture, and toss to mix.

5. Remove yogurt–poppy seed dressing from the refrigerator, add to chicken mixture, toss well to coat, and serve.

Thai Chicken Quinoa Salad

Thai cuisine is filled with spicy peppers, peanuts, and other delicious spices like cumin. This salad blends all those flavors and infuses them with quinoa.

Yield:	Prep time:	Cook time:	Serving size:
4 cups	20 minutes	15 minutes	1 cup

Each serving has:			
328.6 calories	34.9 g carbohydrates	10.2 g fat	3.4 g fiber
24.5 g protein			

½ cup chicken broth

1½ tsp. cornstarch

1½ TB. creamy peanut butter

1 tsp. hot chili oil

½ TB. molasses

1½ tsp. seasoned rice vinegar

1 TB. *tamari*

¼ tsp. cumin

1 TB. peanut oil

1 lb. chicken tenders, chopped into 1- or 2-in. cubes

4 cups Quick-and-Easy Quinoa (recipe in Chapter 1)

1. In a small bowl, whisk together chicken broth and cornstarch until cornstarch is dissolved. Add peanut butter, hot chili oil, molasses, seasoned rice vinegar, tamari, and cumin. Set aside.

2. In a heavy skillet over medium heat, heat peanut oil. Add chicken, and cook, stirring frequently, for about 8 minutes or until cooked through.

3. Pour peanut butter mixture over chicken, reduce heat to medium-low, and cook, stirring to coat chicken, for about 2 minutes.

4. In a large bowl, place Quick-and-Easy Quinoa. Pour chicken mixture over quinoa, toss well to coat, and serve.

DEFINITION

Tamari is a type of soy sauce that's primarily used for cooking because of its dark and rich consistency and flavor. Regular soy sauce is primarily used as a dipping sauce, although it can be used in cooking, too.

Teriyaki Quinoa Salad with Beef

Teriyaki sauce is available at any grocery store, but in this salad, you make your own using sherry, rice vinegar, and soy sauce. With that, marinated beef is tossed with mushrooms, ginger, and quinoa for a delicious lunch with Asian flair.

Yield:	Prep time:	Cook time:	Serving size:
4 cups	20 minutes	10 minutes	1 cup
Each serving has:			
410.1 calories	39.2 g carbohydrates	16.4 g fat	4.5 g fiber
26.3 g protein			

3 TB. soy sauce

2 TB. seasoned rice vinegar

1½ TB. dry sherry wine

¾ lb. flank steak

1 garlic clove, minced

2 tsp. peeled and chopped fresh ginger

2 TB. canola oil

1½ cups sliced crimini mushrooms

¼ cup chopped green onions, green parts only

1 cup fresh bean sprouts

2 TB. water

2 cups fresh spinach leaves

½ cup seeded and chopped cucumber

4 cups Quick-and-Easy Quinoa (recipe in Chapter 1)

1. In a small bowl, stir together soy sauce, seasoned rice vinegar, and dry sherry wine.

2. In a medium bowl, toss flank steak with garlic, ginger, and 2 tablespoons soy sauce mixture. Set aside to marinate.

3. In a large nonstick skillet over medium-high heat, heat 1 tablespoon canola oil until hot but not smoking. Add steak, and cook for about 3 minutes on each side. Remove steak from the skillet, and set aside to cool for 5 minutes. Slice steak into $\frac{1}{4}$- to $\frac{1}{2}$-inch-thick strips.

4. Add remaining 1 tablespoon canola oil to the skillet. Add crimini mushrooms, green onions, and bean sprouts, and cook for 1 minute. Remove the skillet from heat, and add steak, remaining soy sauce mixture, and water.

5. In a large bowl, combine spinach, cucumber, Quick-and-Easy Quinoa, and steak mixture, and serve.

Spicy Sausage Quinoa Salad

Italian sausage, fresh basil, lemon, and quinoa combine in a salad your friends will want you to share!

Yield:	Prep time:	Cook time:	Serving size
6 cups	10 minutes	20 minutes	1 cup
Each serving has:			
248.7 calories	21.3 g carbohydrates	13.8 g fat	2.0 g fiber
9.7 g protein			

$\frac{1}{2}$ lb. spicy Italian sausage links	$\frac{1}{2}$ medium white onion, chopped
2 to 4 TB. water	$\frac{1}{2}$ TB. fine lemon zest
2 cups chicken broth	$\frac{1}{2}$ cup chopped fresh basil leaves
1 cup uncooked quinoa, rinsed and drained	

1. In a heavy skillet over medium heat, cook Italian sausage for about 15 minutes or until completely cooked. Add water in 2 tablespoon increments, if needed, to prevent burning.

2. In a medium saucepan over medium-high heat, combine chicken broth, quinoa, white onion, and lemon zest. Bring to a boil, cover, reduce heat to low, and simmer for 15 minutes or until almost all liquid has been absorbed. Remove from heat, and set aside.

3. Slice cooked Italian sausage into ½-inch-thick slices or dice, if preferred.

4. Transfer quinoa to a large bowl, and toss with sliced sausage. Add basil, stir to combine, and serve.

Variation: If you prefer less spice, opt for the mild version of Italian sausage. Or replace the sausage with cooked chicken breast, ground turkey, or even ground beef.

Shrimp Salad with Quinoa and Mango

Mango has a lusciousness that complements flavors like onion, lime, bell pepper, and shrimp. This easy salad will have you craving more.

Yield:	Prep time:	Cook time:	Serving size:
4 cups	20 minutes	20 minutes	1 cup

Each serving has:			
383.9 calories	47.9 g carbohydrates	8.0 g fat	5.7 g fiber
31.2 g protein			

2 cups chicken broth

1 cup uncooked quinoa, rinsed and drained

½ cup chopped white onion

1 lb. (30 to 35) large shrimp, peeled and deveined

1 TB. olive oil

1 medium mango, peeled, seeded, and chopped

2 medium tangerines, peeled and chopped

½ cup chopped red bell pepper

½ medium red onion, chopped

3 cloves garlic, chopped

1 medium jalapeño, seeded and diced

2 TB. fresh lime juice

½ tsp. sea salt

½ tsp. ground black pepper

3 TB. chopped fresh cilantro leaves

1. In a medium saucepan over medium-high heat, combine chicken broth, quinoa, and white onion. Bring to a boil, cover, reduce heat to low, and simmer for 15 minutes or until liquid is absorbed.

2. Meanwhile, in a medium bowl, toss shrimp with olive oil.

3. In a sauté pan over medium heat, cook shrimp for about 3 minutes or until they just turn pink on each side.

4. In a separate medium bowl, combine mango, tangerines, red bell pepper, red onion, garlic, jalapeño, lime juice, sea salt, black pepper, and cilantro. Mix well.

5. Evenly divide quinoa among 4 serving plates, top each with $\frac{1}{4}$ shrimp and $\frac{1}{4}$ mango salsa, and serve.

QUICK FIX

Mangoes have a large seed in the center that you can't really cut out. To remove it, use a chef's knife to slice through the mango on each side of the seed. Place the mango halves fruit side up, skin side down on a cutting board. Using a paring knife, slice lines lengthwise across the fruit. Then slice crosswise through the fruit, making a grid. Carefully slice along the skin of the mango underneath the grid to loosen the fruit from the seed.

Sensational Sandwiches and Wraps

Chapter

9

In This Chapter

- Planning ahead for lunch
- More flavor for fewer calories
- Tasty lunch sandwiches and wraps

Having fast and flavorful lunches available is essential to eating healthy. Quick-cooking quinoa can help fill out a menu of delicious, nutritious, on-the-go lunches.

That's all good for salads, but quinoa on sandwiches? You bet! In this chapter, I share more than a dozen tasty recipes for lunchbox-worthy sandwiches and wraps that feature quinoa.

Time-Saving Tips

When preparing your sandwich or wrap, be sure you have all the ingredients at your fingertips. Searching for ingredients wastes time, and during your office lunch hour, time is of the essence.

Use precooked chicken breasts, deli meats, and leftover roasted vegetables and proteins in your sandwiches and wraps. Not only do they save time, they save you money, too!

And when it comes to sandwiches and wraps, think outside the bread. Sandwiches can be built on hamburger buns, mini slider buns, tortillas, pita pockets, Italian breads, French breads, or even lettuce cups or leaves.

Adding Flavor Without Adding Calories

It's a common misconception that healthy foods such as quinoa don't taste good. I hear this over and over, and not just about quinoa. If you feel healthier foods in general don't have the flavor you're after, you can easily add flavor and still keep your lunch lean and healthy.

I'll bet you've never thought of quinoa as a condiment for a sandwich, but it works! Quinoa adds fabulous flavor and texture, making your simple sandwich feel like a meal. Dressing up your usual sandwich is as easy as adding cooked quinoa with a drizzle of balsamic vinegar, a spicy grain mustard, a simple homemade lemon basil aioli (from the Roasted Vegetable Quinoa Panini recipe later in this chapter), or your own black bean quinoa hummus (from the Black Bean Quinoa Pita Pockets recipe later in this chapter).

Add a tablespoon or two of chopped fresh herbs like cilantro, basil, dill, thyme, or rosemary for a boost of flavor. Chop the leaves only, and discard the stems.

Spice things up! A little cayenne goes a long way, so add it in small increments such as $\frac{1}{4}$ to $\frac{1}{2}$ teaspoon per $\frac{1}{4}$ to $\frac{1}{2}$ cup so you don't overspice your foods. Other great spices include blackened seasoning, white pepper, and ground mustard.

Meatball Quinoa Sandwich

With the combination of ground beef and ground sausage, these meatballs have so much flavor you won't need anything else. Yet provolone cheese and marinara sauce are the perfect finishing touches.

Yield:	Prep time:	Cook time:	Serving size
12 meatballs, 6 sandwiches	15 minutes	25 minutes	1 meatball sandwich with 2 meatballs
Each serving has:			
1,063.3 calories 45.1 g protein	131.7 g carbohydrates	37.8 g fat	9.3 g fiber

1 lb. lean ground beef

8 oz. mild or hot ground sausage

$\frac{1}{4}$ cup Quick-and-Easy Quinoa (recipe in Chapter 1)

1 tsp. sea salt

1 tsp. ground black pepper

1 (28-oz.) jar marinara sauce

1 clove garlic, chopped

6 (6-in.) sourdough loaves, sliced in $\frac{1}{2}$

6 slices provolone cheese

1. In a large bowl, combine ground beef, ground sausage, Quick-and-Easy Quinoa, sea salt, and black pepper. Form mixture into 12 (1½-inch) balls.

2. In a heavy skillet over medium heat, cook meatballs for about 10 to 15 minutes or until browned.

3. Pour out grease from the skillet, and add marinara sauce and garlic to meatballs. Reduce heat to medium-low, cover, and simmer for about 15 minutes or until meatballs are cooked through.

4. Spoon 2 meatballs and about ¼ cup sauce onto each sourdough loaf half. Top with 1 slice provolone cheese, and add remaining loaf half, along with any remaining sauce, if desired.

Pan-Grilled Vegetable Quinoa Panini

Balsamic vinegar provides both sweet and sour flavor to pan-grilled red bell peppers, broccoli, asparagus, and corn, which are all lightly coated with lemon basil *aioli*.

Yield:	Prep time:	Cook time:	Serving size:
4 panini	20 minutes	20 minutes	1 panino

Each serving has:			
436.8 calories	44.0 g carbohydrates	25.8 g fat	4.6 g fiber
8.1 g protein			

1 TB. olive oil

2 medium red bell peppers, ribs and seeds removed, and chopped

1 medium shallot, peeled and diced

1 cup chopped fresh broccoli florets

4 medium fresh asparagus spears, chopped

½ cup fresh corn kernels

1 tsp. sea salt

1 tsp. ground black pepper

1 cup fresh basil leaves

1 clove garlic

½ TB. fine lemon zest

1 cup nonfat mayonnaise

8 slices thick Italian bread such as ciabatta

½ cup Quick-and-Easy Quinoa (recipe in Chapter 1)

2 TB. balsamic vinegar

1. In a heavy skillet over medium heat, heat olive oil. Add red bell peppers, shallot, broccoli, asparagus, corn, sea salt, and black pepper. Cook, stirring occasionally, for about 5 minutes or until vegetables are tender.

2. In a food processor fitted with a chopping blade or a blender, purée basil, garlic, lemon zest, and nonfat mayonnaise until smooth.

3. Spread 1 tablespoon lemon basil aioli onto each bread slice. Top each of 4 bread slices with ¼ vegetable mixture, followed by 2 tablespoons Quick-and-Easy Quinoa. Drizzle ½ tablespoon balsamic vinegar over quinoa, and top with remaining bread slices.

DEFINITION

Traditionally, **aioli** is a garlic mayonnaise made by emulsifying garlic, olive oil, and egg. There are as many variations as the mind can imagine. This one features two of my favorites: lemon and basil.

Chicken Breast Panini with Quinoa

Italian flat-leaf parsley, lemon, and garlic are the secrets to this delicious sandwich filled with protein-rich grilled chicken and topped with melted mozzarella cheese.

Yield:	Prep time:	Cook time:	Serving size:
4 chicken panini	10 minutes	20 minutes	1 chicken panino

Each serving has:			
586.8 calories 29.9 g protein	37.1 g carbohydrates	35.1 g fat	2.4 g fiber

¼ cup chopped fresh Italian flat-leaf parsley

2 TB. fine lemon zest

1 TB. chopped fresh garlic

1½ tsp. dried Italian seasoning

1 tsp. sea salt

1 tsp. ground black pepper

8 TB. olive oil

¼ cup fresh lemon juice

4 (6-oz.) boneless, skinless chicken breasts

1 cup Quick-and-Easy Quinoa (recipe in Chapter 1)

8 slices ciabatta or other similar bread, toasted

4 slices part-skim mozzarella cheese

1. Preheat the broiler to high.

2. In a small bowl, combine Italian flat-leaf parsley, lemon zest, garlic, Italian seasoning, sea salt, and black pepper. Stir in 6 tablespoons olive oil, and set aside.

3. Drizzle lemon juice over chicken breasts.

4. In a sauté pan over medium heat, heat remaining 2 tablespoons olive oil. Add chicken, cover, and cook for about 10 minutes. Turn over chicken, cover, and cook for 10 more minutes or until cooked through.

5. Add Quick-and-Easy Quinoa to parsley mixture, and stir to coat.

6. Top 4 ciabatta slices with 1 or 2 tablespoons aioli. Place 1 chicken breast on each. Top chicken with $\frac{1}{4}$ cup quinoa mixture, and finish with 1 slice part-skim mozzarella cheese.

7. Place prepared ciabatta halves on a baking sheet, and broil for 30 seconds or until cheese melts. Don't leave under broiler too long.

8. Remove from the broiler, top each half panino with remaining ciabatta slice, and serve.

Variation: To add more flavor to this already delicious panino, brush each ciabatta slice with olive oil. Or add 1 tablespoon lemon basil aioli from the Roasted Vegetable Quinoa Panini recipe earlier in this chapter.

Black Bean Quinoa Pita Pockets

Black beans make a nontraditional hummus in these pita pockets. Cayenne adds spice, and fresh thyme balances out the spice with a slightly minty, earthy flavor. Roasted red bell peppers and fresh cilantro leaves add the finishing touch.

Yield:	Prep time:	Serving size:
8 pita pocket halves	15 minutes	1 pita pocket half

Each serving has:		
201.1 calories	36.1 g carbohydrates	3.1 g fat
7.1 g fiber	8.8 g protein	

1 (15-oz.) can black beans, drained and liquid reserved	½ tsp. cayenne
1 clove garlic	8 (5-in.) pita pocket halves
½ TB. fine lemon zest	8 small green leaf lettuce leaves
1 TB. fresh lemon juice	1½ cups Quick-and-Easy Quinoa (recipe in Chapter 1)
½ TB. fresh thyme leaves	¾ cup chopped roasted red bell peppers
1½ TB. tahini or creamy peanut butter	4 TB. chopped fresh cilantro leaves
½ tsp. sea salt	Hot sauce (optional)

1. In a food processor fitted with a chopping blade or a blender, pulse black beans, garlic, lemon zest, lemon juice, thyme leaves, tahini, sea salt, and cayenne twice to combine.

2. Add ¼ cup reserved black bean liquid, and purée until smooth.

3. Open pita pocket halves, and line each with 1 green leaf lettuce leaf. Top with 2 or 3 tablespoons black bean hummus, 2 or 3 tablespoons Quick-and-Easy Quinoa, 1 tablespoon roasted red bell peppers, and ½ tablespoon cilantro leaves. Serve as is or with a dash of hot sauce.

KEEN ON QUINOA

Roasting red bell peppers is easy. Just place a pepper over an open flame and burn it until it's black on all sides. Place the charred pepper in a paper bag and seal the bag, or place it in a mixing bowl and cover with plastic wrap. After about 15 minutes, remove the pepper and use your fingers to rub off the blackened outer skin. *Do not rinse the pepper!* If you don't have time to roast the peppers, buy a jar of roasted red bell peppers and drain the liquid before using.

Quinoa Sun-Dried Tomato Hummus on Pitas

Sun-dried tomatoes are rich in flavor and add a smoky flavor to these lunch pitas filled with quinoa, tahini, and creamy avocado.

Yield:	Prep time:	Serving size:
1 cup hummus and 5 pita halves	20 minutes	2 or 3 tablespoons hummus plus 1 pita half

Each serving has:		
313.9 calories	45.4 g carbohydrates	11.9 g fat
9.6 g fiber	10.5 g protein	

1 (15-oz.) can chickpeas, drained, with 2 TB. liquid reserved (optional)

$\frac{1}{2}$ cup sun-dried tomatoes

2 cloves garlic

$\frac{1}{4}$ cup tahini

2 TB. fresh Italian flat-leaf parsley leaves

2 TB. fresh lemon juice

$1\frac{1}{2}$ tsp. cumin

$\frac{1}{2}$ tsp. sea salt

$\frac{1}{2}$ tsp. ground black pepper

6 small green leaf lettuce leaves

6 (5-in.) pita pocket halves

1 medium avocado, peeled, pitted, and diced

$\frac{1}{2}$ cup Quick-and-Easy Quinoa (recipe in Chapter 1)

1. In a food processor fitted with a chopping blade or a blender, purée chickpeas, sun-dried tomatoes, garlic, tahini, Italian flat-leaf parsley, lemon juice, cumin, sea salt, and black pepper. Add reserved chickpea liquid, if needed, for thinner hummus.

2. Place 1 green leaf lettuce leaf in each pita pocket half. Add 2 tablespoons sun-dried tomato hummus, top with $\frac{1}{4}$ avocado and 2 tablespoons Quick-and-Easy Quinoa, and serve.

Variation: For **Quinoa Sun-Dried Tomato Hummus Pita with Grilled Chicken,** add 2 tablespoons chopped grilled chicken breast to each pita pocket before adding the sun-dried tomato hummus.

Grilled Shrimp Quinoa Pita

Delicious avocado, green apple, lemon juice, and mayonnaise are just a few of the flavors you'll enjoy in this tasty pita.

Yield:	Prep time:	Cook time:	Serving size
8 pita pocket halves with 4 cups grilled shrimp salad	10 minutes	8 minutes	1 pita pocket half with ½ cup grilled shrimp salad
Each serving has:			
343.7 calories 9.3 g protein	40.7 g carbohydrates	17.3 g fat	7.3 g fiber

2 medium ripe avocados, peeled, pitted, and diced

1 medium green apple, peeled, cored, and diced

1 TB. fresh lemon juice

½ lb. (15 to 20) large shrimp, peeled, deveined, and tails removed

2 TB. olive oil

1 batch Quick-and-Easy Quinoa (recipe in Chapter 1)

1 tsp. curry powder

1 tsp. sea salt

1 tsp. ground black pepper

½ cup nonfat mayonnaise

8 (5-in.) whole-wheat pita pocket halves

1. In a small bowl, toss avocado and green apple with lemon juice.

2. In a separate small bowl, toss shrimp with 1 tablespoon olive oil.

3. In a heavy grill pan or skillet over medium heat, heat remaining 1 tablespoon olive oil. Add shrimp, and cook for about 3 minutes or until just pink. Remove from heat, transfer shrimp to a cutting board, and chop into ½-inch pieces.

4. In a large bowl, combine Quick-and-Easy Quinoa, avocado-apple mixture, curry powder, sea salt, and black pepper. Add mayonnaise and shrimp, and toss again to coat.

5. Stuff each pita pocket half with about ½ cup quinoa mixture, adding more if you have some left over.

KEEN ON QUINOA

This recipe is also delicious stuffed in tomatoes or in iceberg lettuce cups. Or place the filling on green or red leaf lettuce and roll up as a wrap.

Quinoa Shrimp Po'boys

In this po'boy, shrimp is tossed with crushed red pepper flakes and cilantro for a spicy kick.

Yield:	Prep time:	Cook time:	Serving size:
4 po'boys	15 minutes	3 minutes	1 po'boy

Each serving has:			
753.3 calories	76.3 g carbohydrates	26.9 g fat	4.8 g fiber
48.4 g protein			

¾ cup nonfat mayonnaise

2 TB. chopped sweet pickles

2 TB. chopped red onion

1½ tsp. fresh lemon juice

1 clove garlic, chopped

1 tsp. crushed red pepper flakes

2 TB. chopped fresh cilantro leaves

1 tsp. sea salt

½ tsp. ground black pepper

1½ lb. (about 45) large shrimp, peeled, deveined, and tails removed

2 TB. olive oil

4 TB. unsalted butter

2 (10- to 12-in.) loaves French bread, sliced in half lengthwise, sliced again crosswise

4 small green leaf lettuce leaves

1½ cups Quick-and-Easy Quinoa (recipe in Chapter 1)

1. In a medium bowl, combine nonfat mayonnaise, sweet pickles, red onion, lemon juice, garlic, crushed red pepper flakes, cilantro, sea salt, and black pepper.

2. In a small bowl, toss shrimp with 1 tablespoon olive oil.

3. In a sauté pan over medium heat, heat remaining 1 tablespoon olive oil until hot but not smoking. Add shrimp, and cook for about 3 minutes or until just pink. Remove from heat, transfer shrimp to a cutting board, and chop into 1-inch pieces.

4. Add shrimp to mayonnaise mixture, and mix well.

5. Spread ½ tablespoon unsalted butter onto each French bread quarter.

6. Set the skillet over medium-high heat, and toast bread, butter side down, for about 1 minute.

7. Place each bottom slice of bread onto a serving plate, and top with 1 lettuce leaf. Add ¼ of shrimp mixture and ¼ of Quick-and-Easy Quinoa, cover with top half of bread, and serve.

Chicken Quinoa Lettuce Wraps

Curry, mango *chutney*, golden raisins, and dried cranberries are just a few of the fantastic flavors you'll enjoy wrapped up in a crisp lettuce leaf. This mixture is also terrific on a sandwich or used in stuffed tomatoes.

Yield:	Prep time:	Serving size	
4 lettuce wraps and 2 cups chicken salad	10 minutes	1 lettuce wrap with $\frac{1}{2}$ cup chicken salad	

Each serving has:			
537.8 calories 29.4 g protein	32.0 g carbohydrates	32.7 g fat	3.0 g fiber

$\frac{3}{4}$ cup nonfat mayonnaise	$\frac{1}{4}$ cup chopped red onion
$\frac{1}{4}$ cup mango chutney	2 TB. golden raisins
1 TB. apple cider vinegar	2 TB. dried cranberries
2 TB. curry powder	$\frac{1}{2}$ tsp. sea salt
$\frac{1}{8}$ tsp. cumin	$\frac{1}{2}$ tsp. ground black pepper
2 cups cooked diced chicken breast	4 medium red leaf lettuce leaves
$\frac{1}{4}$ cup chopped celery	$\frac{1}{2}$ cup Quick-and-Easy Quinoa (recipe in Chapter 1)
$\frac{3}{4}$ cup chopped pecans	

1. In a medium bowl, combine nonfat mayonnaise, mango chutney, apple cider vinegar, curry powder, cumin, chicken, celery, pecans, red onion, golden raisins, cranberries, sea salt, and black pepper.

2. Place $\frac{1}{2}$ cup chicken mixture in center of 1 red lettuce leaf, top with 2 table-spoons Quick-and-Easy Quinoa, fold in leaves to make a wrap, and serve.

DEFINITION

Chutney is a condiment that consists of fruit, vinegar, sugar, and a variety of spices. Originating in India, chutney is widely popular today. It's available in most grocery stores, and you can find a variety of flavor combinations, including tomato, apple, berry, peach, and more.

Quinoa Turkey Wraps

These wraps are everything a traditional Cobb salad should be, but rolled! Delicious deli turkey, avocado, fresh spinach leaves, cheddar cheese, eggs, and bacon are tossed with ranch dressing and wrapped in a flour tortilla.

Yield:	Prep time:	Serving size
4 turkey wraps	20 minutes	1 turkey wrap

Each serving has:		
956.2 calories	60.6 g carbohydrates	63.8 g fat
9.9 g fiber	34.6 g protein	

8 slices bacon

4 (10-in.) flour tortillas

2 cups fresh baby spinach leaves

8 oz. thinly sliced deli turkey

$\frac{1}{2}$ cup Quick-and-Easy Quinoa (recipe in Chapter 1)

2 medium tomatoes, thinly sliced

2 medium ripe avocados, peeled, pitted, and sliced

1 cup shredded sharp cheddar cheese

2 large hard-boiled eggs, peeled and thinly sliced

1 cup ranch dressing

$\frac{1}{2}$ tsp. sea salt

$\frac{1}{2}$ tsp. ground black pepper

1. In a heavy skillet over medium heat, cook bacon for about 4 minutes or until crisp. Transfer to paper towel to drain. When cooled, crumble into pieces.

2. Place tortillas on a flat work surface. Place $\frac{1}{2}$ cup spinach leaves in the center of each, top with 2 ounces deli turkey, and add 2 tablespoons Quick-and-Easy Quinoa. Evenly distribute tomatoes, avocado, cheddar cheese, hard-boiled egg slices, and crumbled bacon on tortillas. Top with $\frac{1}{4}$ cup ranch dressing, and finish with a little sea salt and black pepper. Beginning at one side of tortilla, roll up to make a wrap, and serve.

Quinoa Roast Beef Wraps with Caramelized Onions and Blue Cheese

Deli roast beef is transformed into a delicious wrap with mustard aioli and onions that have a sweet, smoky flavor, all accented with blue cheese and basil.

Yield:	Prep time:	Cook time:	Serving size:
4 wraps	10 minutes	35 minutes	1 roast beef wrap

Each serving has:			
646.0 calories	49.4 g carbohydrates	29.4 g fat	3.4 g fiber
44.2 g protein			

1 TB. unsalted butter	1 tsp. cayenne
2 medium white onions, thinly sliced	4 (8-in.) flour tortillas
½ TB. sugar	1 lb. sliced deli roast beef
½ tsp. sea salt	½ cup Quick-and-Easy Quinoa (recipe in Chapter 1)
2 TB. prepared mustard	4 TB. chopped fresh basil leaves
½ cup nonfat mayonnaise	½ cup crumbled blue cheese

1. In a heavy skillet over medium-low heat, melt unsalted butter. Add white onions, sugar, and sea salt, cover, and simmer, stirring occasionally, for about 20 minutes.

2. Uncover and continue to cook, stirring frequently, for about 15 minutes or until onions are lightly browned. Remove from heat, and set aside.

3. Meanwhile, in a small bowl, stir together mustard, nonfat mayonnaise, and cayenne.

4. Place tortillas on a flat work surface. Place ¼ roast beef down the center of each tortilla. Top with 2 tablespoons Quick-and-Easy Quinoa, 2 tablespoons mustard mixture, 2 tablespoons onion, 1 tablespoon fresh basil, and 2 tablespoons blue cheese. Beginning on one side, roll tortilla into a wrap, and serve.

Salmon, Spinach, and Goat Cheese Quinoa Wraps

Naturally salty smoked salmon and sour goat cheese paired with bitter spinach greens give this wrap a yummy, creamy depth of flavor.

Yield:	Prep time:	Serving size	
4 wraps	15 minutes	1 wrap	
Each serving has:			
443.3 calories	32.4 g carbohydrates	22.2 g fat	2.3 g fiber
27.7 g protein			

1 (11-oz.) log goat cheese	6 oz. smoked salmon, cut into thin strips
1 tsp. fine lemon zest	$\frac{1}{2}$ cup Quick-and-Easy Quinoa (recipe in Chapter 1)
1 tsp. fine orange zest	
4 (8-in.) flour tortillas	
2 cups fresh spinach leaves	

1. In a small bowl, combine goat cheese, lemon zest, and orange zest.

2. Place tortillas on a flat work surface. Spread each with equal parts goat cheese mixture, about 2 tablespoons per tortilla. Arrange spinach leaves liberally down center of each tortilla, top with $1\frac{1}{2}$ ounces smoked salmon, and finish with 2 tablespoons Quick-and-Easy Quinoa. Beginning at one side of tortilla, gently roll up tortilla. Serve.

KEEN ON QUINOA

Goat cheese is lower in fat than cow's milk cheeses such as blue cheese and Brie. Goat cheese has a distinct, strong flavor some people don't like. If you're not a fan of goat cheese, use cream cheese instead.

Stupendous Soups, Stews, and Chilies

In This Chapter

- Easy ways to use quinoa in soups
- Tips on adding flavor to your bowl
- Using dried and fresh herbs

Nothing says "comfort" like a bowl of warm soup or chili. Soups, stews, and chilies are perfect for large crowds and family dinners, and most can be frozen without any texture or flavor loss. Add quinoa, and your favorite soups, stews, and chilies become satisfying one-dish meals, as you'll discover in this chapter.

Quinoa can be added at the beginning of the cooking process or near the end. In some recipes, cooked quinoa is added, and in others, uncooked quinoa is mixed in with the liquid near the beginning of the recipe so the quinoa and other ingredients cook together. The main point of adding cooked quinoa is to save time. I suggest reserving leftover quinoa from other meals to use in soups. When adding uncooked quinoa during the cooking process, the flavors are allowed to develop together from beginning to end. Either way, quinoa can be substituted equally for both pasta and rice.

Flavorful Soups, Stews, and Chilies

No matter how long you simmer something, if you don't have the right combination of herbs and spices, your finished dish will fall flat in the flavor department. An easy fix? Herbs! Both dried and fresh herbs are quick and easy to use to flavor dishes.

Here are a few tips on using herbs:

- Add dried herbs near the beginning of the cooking process for the most flavor.

- Use dried herbs in smaller quantities than fresh herbs because their flavor is more concentrated. Use up to three times more fresh herbs than dried.

- Use only dried herbs that are fresh and greenish in color. Brown herbs are stale and should be discarded.

- Because of their delicate nature, add fresh herbs at the very end of the cooking process or as a garnish on the finished product.

- When using fresh herbs in soups, stews, and chilies, use only the leaves, discarding the stems.

Vegetable Soup with Quinoa

Simple vegetable soup gets a taste lift with quinoa and fresh oregano and Italian flat-leaf parsley. Plus the quinoa provides protein, which is usually lacking in traditional vegetable soups.

Yield:	Prep time:	Cook time:	Serving size
about 8 cups	15 minutes	30 minutes	1 cup

Each serving has:			
349.7 calories	74.6 g carbohydrates	2.8 g fat	14.3 g fiber
6.7 g protein			

1 TB. olive oil	1 cup chopped frozen spinach
½ cup chopped yellow onion	4 cups vegetable broth
1 clove garlic, chopped	2 cups water
1 tsp. dried Italian seasoning	¼ cup uncooked quinoa, rinsed and drained
1 (32-oz.) can diced tomatoes, with juice	1 tsp. chopped fresh oregano leaves
1 cup chopped fresh celery	¼ cup chopped fresh Italian flat-leaf parsley leaves
1 (14-oz.) can kernel corn, with liquid	1 tsp. sea salt
2 medium carrots, peeled and sliced into ½-in. rounds	1 tsp. ground black pepper
1 (15-oz.) can lima beans, with liquid	

1. In a large saucepan over medium heat, heat olive oil. Add yellow onion, garlic, and Italian seasoning, and cook, stirring, for about 1 minute.

2. Add diced tomatoes, celery, corn, carrots, lima beans, and spinach, and sauté, stirring, for about 1 minute.

3. Stir in vegetable broth, water, quinoa, oregano leaves, and Italian flat-leaf parsley leaves. Bring to a boil, reduce heat to low, and simmer for about 25 minutes or until carrots are tender.

4. Add sea salt and black pepper, and serve.

Variation: For **Chicken Vegetable Quinoa Soup,** add 1 cup diced cooked chicken breast when you add the quinoa. Add an additional $1\frac{1}{2}$ cups water at the same time. Other vegetables that work well in this soup include diced red bell pepper, diced zucchini, green beans cut into 1-inch pieces, and chopped broccoli florets.

Quinoa Leek Soup

If you're tired of potato *leek* soup, you'll love this twist on the classic with quinoa, lemongrass, ancho chile powder, and smoky bacon.

Yield:	Prep time:	Cook time:	Serving size
4 cups	15 minutes	30 minutes	1 cup

Each serving has:			
221.6 calories	34.0 g carbohydrates	6.5 g fat	3.0 g fiber
6.5 g protein			

2 medium leeks	4 cups vegetable broth
1 slice bacon	1 cup uncooked quinoa, rinsed and drained
¼ cup chopped white onion	1 tsp. sea salt
1 TB. unsalted butter	1 tsp. ground black pepper
2 TB. finely chopped lemongrass, outer husks removed and root chopped	1 tsp. ancho chile powder

1. Slice leeks into ¼ inch slices, from the base up to where the leaves begin to separate. Rinse well, and set aside.

2. In a large saucepan over medium-high heat, cook bacon for 2 or 3 minutes or until slightly crisp. Add white onion and unsalted butter, and cook for about 2 more minutes or until onion is tender.

3. Add leeks and lemongrass, and cook for about 2 minutes or until leeks are lightly browned. Stir in vegetable broth.

4. In a food processor fitted with a chopping blade or a blender, and working in batches, purée leek mixture. Return puréed mixture to the saucepan, set over high heat, and add quinoa. Bring to a boil, cover, reduce heat to low, and simmer for 20 minutes.

5. Add sea salt, black pepper, and ancho chile powder, simmer 5 more minutes, and serve.

DEFINITION

Kin to the onion family, **leeks** are milder in flavor than onions. The edible portion is the white base, and the green stalks are usually discarded because they're often woody and chewy. Naturally low in calories and fat, leeks are high in vitamins such as A, B vitamins, C, and iron. Always wash leeks thoroughly because dirt can embed deep between the leaves.

Cream of Broccoli Soup with Quinoa

Coconut milk is the key ingredient here, giving a sweetness to the nutty flavor of quinoa and blending well with earthy broccoli and mushrooms.

Yield:	Prep time:	Cook time:	Serving size
6 cups	15 minutes	25 minutes	1 cup

Each serving has:			
189.3 calories	16.2 g carbohydrates	13.0 g fat	2.3 g fiber
4.1 g protein			

2 TB. unsalted butter

1 cup chopped yellow onion

$\frac{1}{2}$ TB. chopped garlic

1 cup sliced crimini mushrooms

1$\frac{1}{2}$ cups chopped broccoli florets

$\frac{1}{2}$ cup uncooked quinoa, rinsed and drained

1 (14-oz.) can coconut milk

2 cups vegetable broth

1 tsp. sea salt

1 tsp. ground black pepper

1. In a large saucepan over medium-high heat, melt unsalted butter. Add yellow onions and garlic, and sauté for about 1 or 2 minutes or until onion is tender and garlic is fragrant.

2. Stir in crimini mushrooms and broccoli florets, and mix well to combine.

3. Stir in quinoa, coconut milk, and vegetable broth. Bring to a boil, cover, reduce heat to low, and simmer for about 20 minutes. Stir in sea salt and black pepper.

4. In a food processor fitted with a chopping blade or a blender, and working in batches, purée soup. Serve hot.

Quinoa Minestrone

This Italian-style soup is traditionally made with vegetables and pasta. Here, quinoa is substituted for the pasta, adding extra protein and fiber to the oregano, Italian flat-leaf parsley, cayenne, celery, carrot, green bell pepper, and zucchini. Yum.

Yield:	Prep time:	Cook time:	Serving size
8 cups	15 minutes	30 minutes	1 cup

Each serving has:			
281.2 calories	47.0 g carbohydrates	5.4 g fat	10.0 g fiber
13.9 g protein			

1 TB. olive oil

¾ cup chopped white onion

1 TB. chopped garlic

1 cup chopped fresh celery

1 cup chopped peeled fresh carrot

1 cup chopped fresh green bell pepper

1 cup chopped fresh zucchini

2 cups chopped frozen spinach, thawed

4 cups vegetable broth

1 (28-oz.) can diced tomatoes, with juice

1 (15-oz.) can cannellini beans or Great Northern beans, rinsed and drained

½ cup uncooked quinoa, rinsed and drained

1 cup water

1 tsp. paprika

1 tsp. celery seed

½ tsp. dried oregano

1 tsp. cayenne

1 tsp. sea salt

1 tsp. ground black pepper

½ cup grated Parmesan cheese (optional)

½ cup chopped Italian flat-leaf parsley leaves

1. In a large saucepan over medium heat, heat olive oil. Add white onion and garlic, and sauté for about 1 minute or until fragrant and just tender.

2. Stir in celery, carrot, green bell pepper, zucchini, and spinach. Add vegetable broth, diced tomatoes with juice, and cannellini beans, and stir.

3. Add quinoa, water, paprika, celery seed, oregano, and cayenne. Bring to a boil, cover, reduce heat to low, and simmer for 25 minutes.

4. Remove lid, and stir in sea salt and black pepper. Simmer for 5 more minutes.

5. Ladle soup into bowls, and top each with 1 or 2 tablespoons Parmesan cheese (if using) and 1 or 2 tablespoons Italian flat-leaf parsley leaves.

Tuscan Bean Quinoa Soup

Tuscan bean soup is traditionally made with cannellini beans. These are sometimes hard to find, so I suggest Great Northern beans instead. Here the quinoa adds a nice texture and enhances the already delicious flavors of lemon, rosemary, and garlic.

Yield:	Prep time:	Cook time:	Serving size:
8 cups	10 minutes	30 minutes	1 cup

Each serving has:			
254.7 calories	35.0 g carbohydrates	8.2 g fat	7.0 g fiber
11.7 g protein			

4 TB. olive oil	4 cups chicken broth
3 cloves garlic, chopped	2 (16-oz.) cans Great Northern beans, with liquid
¼ cup uncooked quinoa, rinsed and drained	2 cups water
1 cup chopped green onion, white and green parts	¼ cup diced ham
1 TB. chopped fresh rosemary leaves	2 (½-in.-thick) lemon slices
	1 tsp. sea salt
	1 tsp. ground black pepper

1. In a large stockpot over medium heat, heat olive oil. Add garlic, quinoa, and green onion, and sauté for about 3 minutes.

2. Add rosemary, chicken broth, Great Northern beans with liquid, water, ham, and lemon slices, and stir. Bring to a boil, cover, reduce heat to low, and simmer for 25 minutes.

3. Stir in sea salt and black pepper, and serve.

Lentil Stew with Quinoa

Two protein-packed ingredients come together in this delicious stew—quinoa and lentils—and star alongside cloves, cumin, turmeric, and lemon along with carrots, zucchini, and a hint of Parmesan cheese.

Yield:	Prep time:	Cook time:	Serving size
6 cups	15 minutes	55 minutes	1 cup

Each serving has:			
253.1 calories	37.4 g carbohydrates	5.9 g fat	6.8 g fiber
13.2 g protein			

2 TB. unsalted butter

1 cup diced onion

½ TB. chopped garlic

1 large carrot, peeled and diced

1 cup diced fresh zucchini

1 tsp. cumin

3 whole cloves

1 tsp. turmeric

1 cup uncooked lentils, rinsed and drained

5 cups vegetable broth

1 cup diced fresh tomatoes

1 tsp. sea salt

1 tsp. ground black pepper

1 cup uncooked quinoa, rinsed and drained

½ tsp. ground mustard

½ TB. fresh lemon juice

½ cup chopped fresh cilantro leaves

¾ cup grated Parmesan cheese

1. In a large stockpot over medium heat, melt unsalted butter. Add onion and garlic, and sauté for about 2 minutes or until fragrant.

2. Add carrots, zucchini, cumin, cloves, and turmeric, and stir for about 1 minute.

3. Reduce heat to medium-low, add lentils, vegetable broth, tomatoes, sea salt, and black pepper. Cover, reduce heat to low, and simmer for about 30 minutes.

4. Stir in quinoa and ground mustard, and simmer for about 20 more minutes.

5. Remove from heat, and stir in lemon juice and cilantro.

6. Ladle soup into bowls, top each with 2 tablespoons grated Parmesan cheese, and serve.

♔ Chicken and Quinoa Confetti Soup

Denice Fladeboe, executive producer of *Bikini Lifestyles*, practices what she preaches with healthy meals for her family. Here quinoa is used in place of rice for a delicious soup with avocado, lime, carrots, tomatoes, and spices.

Yield:	Prep time:	Cook time:	Serving size:
6 cups	15 minutes	15 minutes	1 cup

Each serving has:			
444.0 calories	59.4 g carbohydrates	10.2 g fat	8.3 g fiber
29.3 g protein			

4 cups water

2 cups chicken broth

1 medium white onion, diced

3 medium carrots, shredded and chopped

4 (6-oz.) boneless, skinless chicken breast halves, cubed

1 tsp. lemon pepper

2½ cups Quick-and-Easy Quinoa (recipe in Chapter 1)

2 hothouse or vine-ripened tomatoes, seeded and diced

1 small avocado, peeled, seeded, and cubed

3 TB. minced fresh cilantro

3 TB. fresh lime juice

⅛ tsp. crushed red pepper flakes

1. In a large saucepan over medium heat, bring water, chicken broth, white onion, and carrots to a boil. Reduce heat to low and simmer for about 12 minutes or until carrots are tender.

2. Meanwhile, coat chicken with the lemon pepper. Place on a grill pan over medium heat, and grill for about 7 minutes, turning once or twice as needed.

3. Add cooked chicken to chicken broth mixture, and cook for 2 minutes.

4. Add Quick-and-Easy Quinoa, tomatoes, avocado, cilantro, lime juice, and crushed red pepper flakes. Stir, and cook for 5 more minutes. Do not allow to boil. Serve hot.

Quinoa Beef Stew

Chuck roast, fresh vegetables, oregano, basil, and cayenne bring together this delicious comfort food stew, set off by the nutty flavor of quinoa.

Yield:	Prep time:	Cook time:	Serving size
8 cups	15 minutes	45 minutes	1 cup

Each serving has:			
279.4 calories	17.2 g carbohydrates	15.2 g fat	4.2 g fiber
19.3 g protein			

2 TB. olive oil	2 tsp. dried basil
1 cup chopped white onion	1 tsp. cayenne
1 TB. chopped garlic	5 cups chicken broth
1 lb. chuck roast, diced	1 (28-oz.) can diced tomatoes, with juice
1 cup chopped fresh celery	
1½ cups peeled and sliced fresh carrots	¼ cup uncooked quinoa, rinsed and drained
1 cup chopped fresh green bell pepper	1 tsp. sea salt
	1 tsp. ground black pepper
1 cup chopped fresh zucchini	¼ cup chopped fresh Italian flat-leaf parsley leaves
1 tsp. dried oregano	

1. In a large stockpot over medium heat, heat olive oil. Add white onion and garlic, and cook, stirring, for about 1 minute.

2. Add diced chuck roast, and sauté for about 5 minutes or until browned.

3. Add celery, carrots, green bell pepper, and zucchini, and stir. Stir in oregano, basil, and cayenne.

4. Add chicken broth, tomatoes with juice, quinoa, sea salt, and black pepper, and stir to combine. Bring to a boil, reduce heat to low , and simmer for about 25 minutes or until carrots are tender.

5. Serve hot with a sprinkle of Italian flat-leaf parsley leaves.

Quinoa Texas Chili

Texas does everything big and bold, and this chili proves that point. Four varieties of peppers, beef, chili powder, cumin, four types of beans, and quinoa combine for a delicious and healthy chili.

Yield:	Prep time:	Cook time:	Serving size
About 10 cups	20 minutes	65 minutes	1 cup
Each serving has:			
432.2 calories 28.8 g protein	54.6 g carbohydrates	11.5 g fat	16.3 g fiber

1 TB. olive oil

1 large white onion, diced

1 lb. chuck roast, cut into $\frac{1}{2}$-in. cubes

2 cloves garlic, chopped

2 medium fresh jalapeños, seeded and diced

1 medium fresh red bell pepper, ribs and seeds removed, and diced

1 medium fresh yellow bell pepper, ribs and seeds removed, and diced

2 medium fresh serrano peppers, seeded and diced

2 (2.25-oz.) pkg. mild or spicy chili mix

$\frac{1}{4}$ cup chili powder

1 TB. ground cumin

1 (28-oz.) can diced or crushed tomatoes, with juice

1 (46-oz.) can tomato juice blend

1 (16-oz.) can dark kidney beans, with liquid

1 (16-oz.) can light red kidney beans, with liquid

1 (16-oz.) can black beans, with liquid

1 (16-oz.) can Great Northern beans, with liquid

1 tsp. sea salt

1 tsp. ground black pepper

$\frac{1}{4}$ cup uncooked quinoa, rinsed and drained

3 cups water

$\frac{1}{2}$ cup chopped fresh cilantro leaves

1. In a large stockpot over medium heat, heat olive oil. Add white onion, and sauté for about 1 minute.

2. Add diced chuck roast, garlic, jalapeños, red bell pepper, yellow bell pepper, and serrano peppers, and sauté for about 5 minutes.

3. Add chili mix, chili powder, and cumin, and stir well. Add diced tomatoes with juice and $\frac{1}{2}$ of tomato juice blend. Reduce heat to medium-low, and simmer, stirring occasionally, for about 30 minutes, being careful not to allow chili to come to a rapid boil.

4. Add dark kidney beans, light red kidney beans, black beans, Great Northern beans, sea salt, black pepper, and remaining tomato juice blend, and simmer for about 5 minutes.

5. Add quinoa and water, and simmer, stirring occasionally, for 25 more minutes.

6. Ladle soup into bowls, and top each with $\frac{1}{2}$ tablespoon cilantro leaves.

WHOA!

Easy on the spice! Unless you like it really hot, stick with mild chili mix. If you're like most people, the heat of the fresh peppers is all the spice you need.

Turkey Chili with Quinoa

Turkey is leaner and healthier than beef, but sometimes people shy away from turkey because it can lack flavor. Not here, thanks to cayenne, paprika, chili powder, and cumin blended with tomato sauce and quinoa.

Yield:	Prep time:	Cook time:	Serving size
6 cups	12 minutes	30 minutes	1 cup

Each serving has:			
235.8 calories	41.3 g carbohydrates	3.6 g fat	13.2 g fiber
11.4 g protein			

1 TB. olive oil	1 (16-oz.) can dark red kidney beans, with liquid
1 cup chopped white onion	2 cups vegetable broth
1½ TB. chopped garlic	¼ cup uncooked quinoa, rinsed and drained
1 lb. lean ground turkey	2 cups water
2 cups tomato sauce	1 tsp. sea salt
1 tsp. cayenne	1 tsp. ground black pepper
1 tsp. paprika	¼ cup chopped fresh cilantro leaves
1 tsp. chili powder	
½ tsp. cumin	

1. In a large stockpot over medium heat, heat olive oil. Add white onion and garlic, and sauté for about 1 minute.

2. Add ground turkey, and cook for about 5 minutes or until cooked through and very lightly browned.

3. Stir in tomato sauce, cayenne, paprika, chili powder, and cumin. Add dark red kidney beans, vegetable broth, quinoa, and water, and stir to combine. Stir in sea salt and black pepper. Bring to a boil, reduce heat to medium-low, and simmer about 25 minutes.

4. Ladle soup into bowls, and sprinkle each with 1 or 2 teaspoons fresh cilantro leaves.

KEEN ON QUINOA

This dish is packed with protein: lean ground turkey, dark red kidney beans, and quinoa. Plus, both beans and quinoa are high in fiber, making this chili easy to digest!

Quinoa Corn Chowder

There's something comforting about corn chowder. Red bell pepper, cubed potatoes, jalapeño, pepper jack cheese, quinoa, fresh basil, and taco seasoning mix make this spicy chowder a winner.

Yield:	Prep time:	Cook time:	Serving size
8 cups	20 minutes	50 minutes	1 cup

Each serving has:			
332.3 calories	37.5 g carbohydrates	15.2 g fat	4.3 g fiber
13.1 g protein			

2 TB. olive oil

1 cup diced yellow onion

1 (1.25-oz.) pkg. taco seasoning mix

2 small russet baking potatoes, peeled and cut into 1-in. cubes

1 (15- to 16-oz.) can creamed corn

1 cup fresh or frozen kernel corn

1 medium jalapeño, seeded and diced

1 cup diced red bell pepper

½ cup uncooked quinoa, rinsed and drained

5 cups vegetable broth

2 cups water

1 tsp. sea salt (optional)

1 tsp. ground black pepper (optional)

2 cups shredded pepper jack cheese

1 cup chopped fresh basil leaves

1. In a large saucepan over medium heat, heat olive oil. Add yellow onion and taco seasoning mix, and sauté for 1 minute or until onion is just tender, not more than 2 minutes.

2. Add russet baking potatoes, creamed corn, kernel corn, jalapeño, and red bell pepper, and stir. Stir in quinoa, and add vegetable broth and water. Increase heat to medium-high, if necessary, to bring to a boil. Cover, reduce heat to low, and simmer for 15 minutes.

3. Taste for flavor. Add sea salt and black pepper (if needed), and simmer for 10 more minutes.

4. Add pepper jack cheese, and stir until melted.

5. Ladle chowder into bowls, top with 2 tablespoons chopped fresh basil leaves, and serve.

Quinoa Seafood Gumbo

New Orleans–style gumbo is an American favorite. This simple recipe gets its flavor from the shrimp, andouille sausage, Cajun seasoning, tomatoes, peppers, and fresh parsley.

Yield:	Prep time:	Cook time:	Serving size
8 cups	20 minutes	60 minutes	1 cup

Each serving has:			
399.3 calories	31.0 g carbohydrates	25.1 g fat	4.0 g fiber
37.2 g protein			

2 TB. olive oil	3 TB. paprika
3 TB. all-purpose flour	1 tsp. chopped fresh thyme leaves
2 large white onions, chopped	1 lb. andouille sausage, sliced into $\frac{1}{2}$-in. rounds
2 TB. chopped garlic	
1 large green bell pepper, ribs and seeds removed, and diced	10 cups fish stock
	2 cups fresh okra, sliced into $\frac{1}{2}$-in. slices
1 cup chopped fresh celery	
1 bay leaf	1 cup diced tomatoes
3 tsp. cayenne	2 lb. (about 41 to 50) medium shrimp, peeled and deveined
2 TB. ground black pepper	
3 TB. dried basil	3 cups Quick-and-Easy Quinoa (recipe in Chapter 1)
2 TB. dried oregano	
2 TB. garlic powder	$\frac{3}{4}$ cup chopped fresh Italian flat-leaf parsley leaves
3 TB. onion powder	

1. In a large saucepan over medium heat, combine olive oil and all-purpose flour. Cook, stirring, for about 7 or 8 minutes or until mixture begins to brown.

2. Stir in white onions, garlic, green bell pepper, celery, bay leaf, cayenne, black pepper, basil, oregano, garlic powder, onion powder, paprika, thyme leaves, andouille sausage, fish stock, okra, and diced tomatoes. Reduce heat to low, and simmer for about 45 minutes.

3. Add shrimp, and cook for about 5 minutes or until all shrimp have turned pink. Remove bay leaf.

4. Stir in Quick-and-Easy Quinoa.

5. Ladle gumbo into bowls, top each with 1 or 2 tablespoons Italian flat-leaf parsley, and serve.

> **QUICK FIX**
>
> Look for fish stock with the canned seafood items at your grocery store. If you can't find it, you may substitute an equal amount of chicken broth.

Shrimp and Corn Quinoa Bisque

This easy bisque is seasoned with Cajun spices, cayenne, and jalapeño and gets a creamy yet crunchy texture from low-fat milk, nonfat sour cream, and quinoa, all topped off with flavorful fresh cilantro leaves.

Yield:	Prep time:	Cook time:	Serving size
8 cups	20 minutes	30 minutes	1 cup

Each serving has:			
342.8 calories	38.6 g carbohydrates	10.7 g fat	3.7 g fiber
22.2 g protein			

1 TB. olive oil	1 tsp. chili powder
1 cup diced yellow onion	1 tsp. garlic powder
1 small jalapeño, seeded and diced	1 tsp. onion powder
2 small russet baking potatoes, peeled and cut into 1-in. cubes	$\frac{1}{2}$ tsp. ground dry mustard
5 cups low-fat milk	2 (15-oz.) cans creamed corn
$1\frac{1}{2}$ cups nonfat sour cream	1 lb. (20 to 25) medium shrimp, peeled and deveined
1 tsp. cayenne	1 cup Quick-and-Easy Quinoa (recipe in Chapter 1)
1 tsp. sea salt	$\frac{1}{2}$ cup chopped fresh cilantro leaves
1 tsp. black pepper	

1. In a large stockpot over medium heat, heat olive oil. Add yellow onion, and sauté for about 1 minute. Add jalapeño and russet baking potatoes, and sauté 1 more minute.

2. Stir in low-fat milk, nonfat sour cream, cayenne, sea salt, black pepper, chili powder, garlic powder, onion powder, and dry mustard until well blended. Stir in creamed corn, and simmer for about 10 minutes.

3. Add shrimp, and cook for about 5 minutes or until they turn pink.

4. Stir in Quick-and-Easy Quinoa.

5. Ladle bisque into bowls, garnish each with 1 tablespoon chopped fresh cilantro leaves, and serve.

Easy Snacks and Appetizers

Snacks and appetizers are the small-bite supports to help get you through the day or soothe rumbling tummies before a party starts. They're essential edibles! But that doesn't mean they needn't be nutritious.

The chapters in Part 4 give you recipes loaded with quinoa's many health benefits. They cook up quickly in most cases, too, so you can serve them to hungry kids or guests. But be sure to make extra—you're almost guaranteed to get requests for seconds (and thirds!).

Delicious Dips and Spreads

In This Chapter

- Quick and easy quinoa dips
- Healthy quinoa hummus
- Savory quinoa spreads
- Making friends with your food processor

Dips and spreads are a delicious solution for an afternoon snack or the perfect party food, whether the party is at your house or someone else's, and quinoa is a perfect addition to these favorites. It adds bulk and flavor in addition to nutrients, and tastes delicious with roasted red peppers, sun-dried tomatoes, black beans, and many other savory ingredients.

Have fun making these easy, fun dips and spreads, all starring quinoa!

Behold, the Food Processor

Many dips and spreads are puréed to a smooth consistency, and a food processor can be a huge help accomplishing this.

Don't be intimidated by food processors. They're really easy to use and enable you to whip up all kinds of creative combinations with the press of a button. Think food processors are tricky? The only trick is to be aware of the pulse. For chunkier dips and spreads, use the pulse button or quickly press and release the purée button for short, quick pulses to achieve the desired texture. If you're looking for a smooth purée, just press the purée button and let the processor do its thing until your dip is smooth.

KEEN ON QUINOA

Although your food processor might come with many types of blades, my go-to blade is the chopping blade. It has curved, serrated blades on opposite sides of the central shaft.

Quinoa Cannellini Bean Dip

This vegan, gluten-free dip is a flavorful way to get both fiber and protein in your diet. In addition to quinoa, lemon, basil, red pepper flakes, and cannellini beans combine in this party pleaser.

Yield:	Prep time:	Serving size:
2 cups	15 minutes	2 tablespoons

Each serving has:		
44 calories	8.2 g carbohydrates	0.2 g fat
1.7 g fiber	2.6 g protein	

1 clove fresh garlic	$\frac{1}{2}$ tsp. crushed red pepper flakes
1 (15-oz.) can cannellini beans or Great Northern beans, drained, with liquid reserved	$\frac{1}{2}$ cup packed fresh basil leaves
	$\frac{1}{2}$ cup Quick-and-Easy Quinoa (recipe in Chapter 1)
$\frac{1}{2}$ TB. fine lemon zest	1 tsp. sea salt
2 TB. fresh lemon juice	1 tsp. ground white pepper

1. In a food processor fitted with a chopping blade, combine garlic, cannellini beans, lemon zest, lemon juice, crushed red pepper flakes, basil leaves, Quick-and-Easy Quinoa, sea salt, and white pepper.

2. Purée on maximum speed until smooth. Dip will have some texture because of quinoa; for a thinner dip, add water in 1 tablespoon increments until the desired texture is reached.

3. Serve with fresh celery stalks or red bell pepper slices, or crackers.

Spinach Dip with Quinoa

This take on the traditional party classic features spinach, cayenne, water chestnuts, sour cream, cream cheese, lemon, and of course, quinoa.

Yield:	Prep time:	Cook time:	Serving size:
4 cups	15 minutes	55 minutes	¼ cup

Each serving has:			
117.8 calories	7.3 g carbohydrates	8.0 g fat	0.8 g fiber
4.3 g protein			

¾ cup packed fresh basil leaves

¼ cup packed fresh Italian flat-leaf parsley leaves

¾ cup roughly chopped green onion, green and white parts

1 TB. fine lemon zest

2 TB. fresh lemon juice

1 tsp. cayenne

1 tsp. chili powder

¾ cup grated Parmesan cheese

1 (4-oz.) can water chestnuts, drained

½ cup reduced-fat cream cheese

1 (10-oz.) pkg. frozen chopped spinach, thawed and drained

¾ cup Quick-and-Easy Quinoa (recipe in Chapter 1)

¼ tsp. sea salt

½ tsp. ground black pepper

1 cup nonfat mayonnaise

1 cup nonfat sour cream

1. Preheat the oven to 375°F. Lightly coat a 1½-quart round casserole dish with nonstick cooking spray.

2. In a large bowl, stir together basil leaves, Italian flat-leaf parsley leaves, green onion, lemon zest, lemon juice, cayenne, chili powder, Parmesan cheese, water chestnuts, cream cheese, spinach, and Quick-and-Easy Quinoa.

3. In a food processor fitted with a chopping blade, and working in batches, purée dip until well combined and textured, not completely smooth.

4. Return dip to the bowl, and stir in sea salt, black pepper, nonfat mayonnaise, and nonfat sour cream. Spread dip into prepared casserole dish, cover, and bake for about 45 minutes or until heated through.

5. Uncover and bake for 10 more minutes. Serve hot with crackers or fresh vegetables.

> **QUICK FIX**
>
> If you're in a hurry or looking for a chilled dip, skip the baking and refrigerate this dip overnight. Remove from refrigerator about 20 minutes before serving, and stir to recombine the ingredients.

Layered Mexican Quinoa Dip

A blend of traditional Mexican cheeses, cilantro, black olives, tomatoes, avocado, refried beans with taco seasoning, and lemon combine with quinoa for maximum flavor and protein in this hearty dip.

Yield:	Prep time:	Cook time:	Serving size:
1 (8-inch) casserole	15 minutes	15 to 20 minutes	½ cup

Each serving has:			
141.0 calories 7.2 g protein	10.9 g carbohydrates	7.1 g fat	2.9 g fiber

2 (15-oz.) cans refried beans

1 cup Quick-and-Easy Quinoa (recipe in Chapter 1)

2 medium avocados, halved, pitted, and diced

1 TB. fresh lemon juice

½ cup nonfat sour cream

½ cup nonfat mayonnaise

½ (1.5-oz.) pkg. taco seasoning mix

¼ cup sliced black olives

½ cup chopped fresh tomatoes

¼ cup diced white onion

¼ cup chopped fresh cilantro

2 cups shredded Mexican cheese blend

1. Preheat the oven to 400°F. Lightly coat an 8-inch square casserole dish with nonstick cooking spray.

2. Spread refried beans evenly across the bottom of the prepared casserole dish, and evenly sprinkle Quick-and-Easy Quinoa over top.

3. In a small bowl, toss diced avocado with lemon juice. Sprinkle avocado over quinoa.

4. In the small bowl, combine nonfat sour cream, nonfat mayonnaise, and taco seasoning mix. Spread over top of avocado.

5. In a medium bowl, toss black olives, tomatoes, white onion, and cilantro. Spread over top of sour cream mixture, and top evenly with Mexican cheese blend. Bake for about 15 to 20 minutes or until cheese is melted.

6. Serve with tortilla chips; pita bread wedges; melba rounds; or fresh celery, cucumber, or endive leaves.

Eggplant Quinoa Dip

This dip combines eggplant, lemon, tahini, garlic, cumin, chili powder, and quinoa. Fresh cilantro and parsley round out the flavor while jalapeño provides spice.

Yield:	Prep time:	Cook time:	Serving size:
4 cups	20 minutes	30 minutes	$\frac{1}{2}$ cup

Each serving has:			
136.3 calories	11.9 g carbohydrates	9.5 g fat	4.5 g fiber
3.1 g protein			

$2\frac{1}{4}$ tsp. sea salt

2 medium eggplants, each cut into 8 round slices

3 TB. olive oil

2 TB. fresh lemon juice

$\frac{1}{2}$ cup Quick-and-Easy Quinoa (recipe in Chapter 1)

$\frac{1}{4}$ cup tahini

2 cloves fresh garlic

$\frac{1}{2}$ tsp. ground cumin

$\frac{1}{2}$ tsp. chili powder

1 jalapeño, seeded and roughly chopped

$\frac{1}{4}$ cup packed fresh cilantro leaves

$\frac{1}{4}$ cup packed fresh Italian flat-leaf parsley

$\frac{1}{4}$ tsp. ground black pepper

1. Preheat the oven to 400°F. Line a baking sheet with parchment paper.

2. Using 2 teaspoons sea salt, salt each eggplant slice, and place on a plate, stacking if necessary. Top slices with another plate, place a weight on top, and let rest about 15 minutes.

3. Place eggplant on the prepared baking sheet, and bake for 30 minutes or until soft. Allow to cool slightly.

4. In a large bowl, toss eggplant, olive oil, lemon juice, Quick-and-Easy Quinoa, tahini, garlic, cumin, chili powder, jalapeño, cilantro leaves, Italian flat-leaf parsley leaves, sea salt, and black pepper.

5. In a food processor fitted with a chopping blade, and working in batches, purée eggplant mixture until smooth.

6. Serve with pita bread wedges or fresh cut vegetables.

Black Bean Hummus with Quinoa

Cilantro, parsley, cayenne, chili powder, lemon juice, lime juice, black beans, and *hominy*, along with tomato paste and quinoa, are the stars in this gluten-free vegan hummus.

Yield:	Prep time:	Serving size:
4 cups	10 minutes	¼ cup

Each serving has:		
63.0 calories	11.9 g carbohydrates	0.6 g fat
3.0 g fiber	2.8 g protein	

1 (15-oz.) can black beans, with liquid

1 (28-oz.) can whole hominy, drained

¾ cup Quick-and-Easy Quinoa (recipe in Chapter 1)

2 TB. tomato paste

1 clove fresh garlic

2 tsp. cayenne

1 tsp. chili powder

¼ cup plus 1 TB. packed chopped fresh cilantro leaves

¼ cup plus 2 TB. chopped fresh Italian flat-leaf parsley leaves

Juice of ½ lemon

Juice of 1 lime

1 tsp. sea salt

1 tsp. ground black pepper

¼ cup vegetable broth, or as needed

1. In a food processor fitted with a chopping blade or a blender, purée black beans, hominy, Quick-and-Easy Quinoa, tomato paste, garlic, cayenne, chili powder, ¼ cup fresh cilantro leaves, fresh Italian flat-leaf parsley leaves, lemon juice, lime juice, sea salt, and black pepper until smooth, adding vegetable broth, if needed, for a thinner purée.

2. Garnish with remaining 1 tablespoon cilantro, and serve with baked tortilla chips or your favorite crackers.

> **DEFINITION**
>
> Available both whole and ground, **hominy** is hulled corn where the hulls have been removed by soaking in lye. Hominy is sold canned in water or dried. Dried hominy is ground and commonly referred to as *hominy grits*. It's often used in casseroles.

Cucumber Mousse with Quinoa Caviar

Fresh cucumber, dill, and cream cheese combine with quinoa to make a caviar-like dip for fresh vegetables.

Yield:	Prep time:	Serving size:
2 cups	15 minutes, plus 1 hour chill time	¼ cup

Each serving has:			
126.5 calories 4.7 g protein	6.4 g carbohydrates	9.2 g fat	0.5 g fiber

2 cloves fresh garlic

1 tsp. sea salt

1 TB. fine lemon zest

½ TB. fresh lemon juice

1 large cucumber, peeled, seeded, and coarsely chopped

1 cup nonfat sour cream

1 cup nonfat cream cheese

3 TB. fresh dill, stems discarded

½ cup Quick-and-Easy Quinoa (recipe in Chapter 1)

1. In a food processor fitted with a chopping blade or a blender, purée garlic, sea salt, lemon zest, lemon juice, cucumber, nonfat sour cream, nonfat cream cheese, dill, and Quick-and-Easy Quinoa on high until completely blended and almost smooth but not chunky.

2. Transfer mousse to a bowl, cover with plastic wrap, and refrigerate for 1 hour or until ready to use.

3. Serve with fresh cucumber slices, celery stalks, broccoli florets, red bell pepper slices, or your favorite vegetables.

Stuffed and Wrapped Snacks

In This Chapter

- Easy wontons
- Great stuffed grape leaf snacks
- Tips on using puff pastry dough and shells
- Make-ahead time-saving tips

Snacks that taste good and are especially good for you can seem hard to find and make. It doesn't have to be that way! In this chapter, I share many delicious snacks you can make ahead and enjoy all week. These recipes are perfect for party snacks, too!

Tips for Make-Ahead Dishes

Anything stuffed and wrapped can make a fun, delicious snack, but the stuffing and wrapping part can be time-consuming and sometimes tedious. Prepare multistep dishes in stages to save time and split up the tasks so you don't bear the pressure of cooking and assembling everything on the same day.

Got leftovers? They're perfect for quick-and-easy snacks. Dice leftover chicken or beef, and toss it into any of the healthy snacks in this chapter. Leftover corn on the cob? Cut off the kernels, and add them to Braised Cabbage Rolls with Quinoa, Cranberries, and Walnuts or to Quinoa Stuffed Wontons. When in doubt, don't throw it out—that's my motto.

A general rule of cooking is to be sure you have all the ingredients you need before beginning a recipe. For anything that requires some assembly, be sure you have all the parts you need to assemble, including ingredients like grape leaves, puff pastry crust, or phyllo dough, as well as the filling ingredients.

Keep in mind that most fillings can be prepared a day or two ahead of time. As a bonus, this results in better, richer flavor in some recipes. Other recipes can be prepared up to the point of the baking step and kept in the refrigerator or freezer until the day they need to be prepared.

Tips for Stuffing and Wrapping

Whether it's a grape leaf, tortilla, lettuce leaf, or wonton wrapper, a few simple guidelines will help make your life easier when assembling stuffed and wrapped snacks:

- Have plenty of room on a flat working surface.

- When working with pastry dough and wonton wrappers, have a small bowl of water handy for dipping a pastry brush or your finger. Wetting the edges of the dough makes the dough stick together and hold in the filling.

- Be careful not to overstuff the dough, wrapper, or even lettuce leaf. Overstuffing can cause the outer wrap to tear, resulting in a messy and unattractive dish.

- When it comes to using tortillas and lettuce leaves, start at one side and tuck the outer edges in as you roll. This prevents food from spilling out of the wrap.

Crispy Quinoa-Stuffed Wontons

A Thai food lover's favorite, these lightly fried wontons boast flavors of sesame, carrot, mushroom, spinach, garlic, ginger, and soy. Tofu takes on the flavors of the dish and, along with the toasted quinoa, adds protein.

Yield:	Prep time:	Cook time:	Serving size:
50 wontons	25 minutes	30 minutes	4 wontons

Each serving has:			
108.1 calories	16.0 g carbohydrates	3.9 g fat	1.6 g fiber
2.9 g protein			

½ cup uncooked quinoa, rinsed and drained

1 cup vegetable broth

1 TB. sesame oil

1 TB. chopped fresh garlic

1 TB. peeled and chopped fresh ginger

1 large carrot, peeled and finely chopped

½ cup chopped fresh shiitake mushrooms

1 small Thai chile pepper, seeded, and minced

1 cup chopped fresh spinach

1 cup chopped fresh napa cabbage leaves

1 tsp. sea salt

½ tsp. ground black pepper

1 cup diced extra-firm tofu

¼ cup chopped green onion, white and green parts

1 TB. soy sauce

¼ cup chopped fresh cilantro leaves

50 wonton wrappers

4 to 6 cups canola oil

1 cup hoisin sauce

1. Preheat the oven to 300°F. Line a baking sheet with parchment paper.

2. In a small saucepan over medium-high heat, combine quinoa and vegetable broth. Bring to a boil, cover, reduce heat to low, and simmer for 15 minutes or until almost all liquid has been absorbed. Remove from heat and set aside.

3. Spread cooked quinoa evenly across the prepared baking sheet. Roast for about 15 minutes or until slightly crisp and dried. Remove from the oven, and set aside.

4. In a large sauté pan over medium heat, heat sesame oil. Add garlic and ginger, and sauté for about 1 minute.

5. Add carrot, shiitake mushrooms, Thai chile pepper, spinach, napa cabbage, sea salt, and black pepper, and sauté for about 5 minutes or until cabbage is wilted and flavors are starting to blend.

6. Add tofu, green onion, and soy sauce, and sauté for 5 more minutes. Add cilantro, remove from heat, and drain any excess liquid. Transfer mixture to large bowl, add roasted quinoa, and toss to combine.

7. Fill a small bowl with water to use while assembling wontons.

8. Place 6 wonton wrappers on a flat surface. Spoon 1 or 2 teaspoons quinoa mixture in center of each wonton. Dip your index finger into water, and lightly coat outer edges of wonton wrapper. Fold wonton in half, encasing filling, and press edges together to seal. Repeat until all wontons are filled. (If you have any leftover filling, enjoy as a side dish or save for making additional wontons.)

9. Layer 3 paper towels on the countertop for draining cooked wontons.

10. In a heavy iron skillet or saucepan over medium-high heat, heat canola oil until hot but not smoking (between 350°F and 375°F). Using a slotted spatula, carefully place wontons in hot oil and fry for about 1 minute or until crisp and light brown. Using the spatula, remove cooked wontons and transfer to the paper towels to drain. Serve warm with hoisin sauce.

WHOA!

Frying foods is not difficult, but it can be tricky. Avoid getting any water into the pan or oil before frying. Water and oil don't mix, and the water will cause the oil to pop and could burn you.

Herb and Quinoa Stuffed Mushrooms

Stuffed mushrooms are always a hit as a snack or appetizer for mushroom lovers. Prominent flavors in these high-fiber 'shrooms include quinoa, curry, Italian flat-leaf parsley, cilantro, garlic, and Parmesan cheese.

Yield:	Prep time:	Cook time:	Serving size:
12 large crimini mushrooms	15 minutes	25 minutes	2 mushrooms

Each serving has:			
251.6 calories 9.5 g protein	24.1 g carbohydrates	13.7 g fat	2.9 g fiber

3 TB. balsamic vinegar	1 tsp. ground black pepper
4 TB. olive oil	$\frac{1}{4}$ cup chopped fresh Italian flat-leaf parsley leaves
$\frac{1}{2}$ medium yellow onion, chopped	
$\frac{1}{2}$ TB. chopped garlic	$\frac{1}{4}$ cup chopped fresh cilantro leaves
1 cup uncooked quinoa, rinsed and drained	12 large crimini mushrooms, stems removed
2 cups vegetable broth	
$\frac{1}{2}$ TB. curry powder	$\frac{1}{2}$ cup freshly grated Parmesan cheese
1 tsp. sea salt	

1. Preheat the oven to 350°F. Line a baking sheet with parchment paper.

2. In a small bowl, whisk together balsamic vinegar and 2 tablespoons olive oil.

3. In a heavy saucepan over medium-high heat, heat remaining 2 tablespoons olive oil. Add yellow onion, garlic, quinoa, and vegetable broth, and stir. Bring to a boil, cover, reduce heat to low, and simmer for about 15 minutes or until almost all liquid is absorbed.

4. Stir in curry powder, sea salt, black pepper, Italian flat-leaf parsley leaves, and cilantro leaves.

5. Stuff mushrooms with quinoa mixture, top with $\frac{1}{2}$ to 1 tablespoon Parmesan cheese, and place on the prepared baking sheet. Bake for about 15 minutes or until mushrooms are heated and Parmesan cheese is melted.

6. Place on serving plates, drizzle with balsamic vinegar mixture, and serve.

Feta and Quinoa Stuffed Grape Leaves

Feta cheese, fresh mint, and lemon are commonly found in Middle Eastern cuisines. Here, quinoa replaces rice for a more flavorful version of this snack favorite.

Yield:	Prep time:	Cook time:	Serving size:
24 stuffed grape leaves	18 minutes	25 minutes	2 stuffed grape leaves

Each serving has:			
104.1 calories	12.7 g carbohydrates	4.3 g fat	1.5 g fiber
4.1 g protein			

$\frac{1}{2}$ TB. olive oil

$\frac{1}{4}$ cup chopped green onion

1 large tomato, seeded and diced

1 cup uncooked quinoa, rinsed and drained

1$\frac{3}{4}$ cups vegetable broth

1$\frac{1}{2}$ tsp. fine lemon zest

$\frac{1}{2}$ tsp. cayenne

$\frac{1}{8}$ tsp. coriander

$\frac{1}{8}$ tsp. cumin

1 tsp. sea salt

1 tsp. ground black pepper

1 TB. chopped fresh mint leaves

1 cup feta cheese, crumbled

24 jarred grape leaves

1 cup water

1. Preheat the oven to 375°F. Lightly coat an 11×7-inch baking dish with nonstick cooking spray.

2. In medium saucepan over medium heat, heat olive oil. Add green onion, tomato, quinoa, and vegetable broth, and stir. Bring to a boil, cover, reduce heat to low, and simmer for 15 minutes or until almost all liquid is absorbed.

3. Remove from heat, and stir in lemon zest, cayenne, coriander, cumin, sea salt, black pepper, and mint leaves. Stir in feta cheese.

4. Spread 1 grape leaf on a flat work surface. Place 2 teaspoons quinoa mixture down middle of grape leaf. Fold sides of grape leaf into center. Wrap grape leaf into a roll or log, and place seam side down on the prepared baking dish. Repeat until all filling or grape leaves have been used.

6. Pour 1 cup water over stuffed grape leaves. Cover with aluminum foil, and bake for about 25 minutes.

KEEN ON QUINOA

Other delicious ingredients for stuffed grape leaves include fresh dill; fresh Italian flat-leaf parsley; chopped pine nuts, walnuts, or almonds; or cooked ground turkey, chicken, pork, or beef.

Wild Mushroom Goat Cheese Quinoa Puff Pastries

Crimini and porcini mushrooms, fresh thyme, goat cheese, and quinoa wrapped in a puff pastry crust—these are the perfect snack for afternoons, weekends, or any time.

Yield:	Prep time:	Cook time:	Serving size:
24 puff pastries	35 minutes	25 minutes	2 pastries

Each serving has:			
225.0 calories	15.7 g carbohydrates	14.7 g fat	0.6 g fiber
6.9 g protein			

½ cup dried porcini mushrooms	½ TB. fine lemon zest
2 cups warm water	2 tsp. fine lime zest
½ cup plus 1 TB. water	1 tsp. sea salt
1 large egg	1 tsp. ground black pepper
1 TB. olive oil	1 cup goat cheese
½ medium yellow onion, chopped	½ cup Quick-and-Easy Quinoa (recipe in Chapter 1)
½ cup chopped fresh crimini mushrooms	2 puff pastry sheets (1 box)
½ TB. chopped fresh thyme leaves, stems removed	

1. In a medium bowl, soak porcini mushrooms in 2 cups warm water (or enough to cover mushrooms) for about 30 minutes. Strain off liquid, and finely chop mushrooms.

2. Preheat the oven to 400°F. Line a baking sheet with parchment paper.

3. Place ½ cup water into a small bowl.

4. In a separate small bowl, whisk together remaining 1 tablespoon water and egg.

5. In a heavy saucepan over medium heat, heat olive oil. Add yellow onion, and sauté about 1 minute. Add porcini mushrooms, crimini mushrooms, thyme leaves, lemon zest, lime zest, sea salt, and ground black pepper, and sauté for 2 minutes or until any liquid has evaporated and ingredients are tender and well blended.

6. Stir in goat cheese until melted and well blended. Remove from heat, stir in quiona, and set aside.

7. Cover a flat work surface with parchment paper, and place puff pastry sheets on paper. Using a rolling pin, roll out 1 puff pastry sheet to about $\frac{1}{2}$ its thickness. Using a 4- or 5-inch-diameter round cookie cutter, cut out pastry.

8. Place about 1 to $1\frac{1}{2}$ tablespoons mushroom mixture in the center of each pastry. Dip your index finger into water and lightly coat edge of pastry with water. Fold one side over to form a half-moon shape and press edges together to seal. Place on prepared baking sheet. Using a pastry brush or the back of a spoon, lightly coat prepared pastries with egg mixture.

9. Bake for 12 to 15 minutes or until golden brown.

Spinach Parmesan Quinoa Puffs

Spinach and Parmesan cheese are a delicious combination in these puffs, highlighted with a hint of nutmeg, onion, and quinoa.

Yield:	Prep time:	Cook time:	Serving size:
24 puffs	18 minutes	25 minutes	2 puffs

Each serving has:			
352.7 calories	26.5 g carbohydrates	23.2 g fat	2.0 g fiber
10.1 g protein			

1 TB. olive oil

$\frac{3}{4}$ cup chopped yellow onion

$\frac{3}{4}$ cup part-skim ricotta cheese

2 cups frozen spinach, thawed and squeezed dry

$\frac{1}{4}$ tsp. ground nutmeg

$\frac{1}{2}$ tsp. sea salt

1 tsp. ground white pepper

1 cup grated Parmesan cheese

24 puff pastry shells

$\frac{1}{2}$ cup Quick-and-Easy Quinoa (recipe in Chapter 1)

1. Preheat the oven to 400°F. Line a baking sheet with parchment paper.

2. In a heavy saucepan over medium heat, heat olive oil. Add yellow onion, and sauté for about 1 minute. Stir in ricotta cheese, spinach, nutmeg, sea salt, and white pepper, and sauté for 1 or 2 minutes. Stir in Parmesan cheese.

3. Place puff pastry shells on the prepared baking sheet. Carefully remove and discard center of puff pastry shell, leaving bottom intact.

4. Spoon 2 or 3 tablespoons spinach mixture into each puff pastry, and top with $\frac{1}{2}$ to 1 tablespoon Quick-and-Easy Quinoa. Bake for about 25 to 30 minutes or until pastry is lightly browned. Serve warm.

Ricotta Eggplant Quinoa Rolls

These incredibly flavorful baked rolls get their flavor from ricotta, goat, and Parmesan cheeses; fresh basil; eggplant; and fresh tomato sauce.

Yield:	Prep time:	Cook time:	Serving size:
12 rolls	40 minutes	40 minutes	2 rolls
Each serving has:			
352.8 calories	20.4 g carbohydrates	21.3 g fat	4.7 g fiber
22.2 g protein			

5 TB. olive oil	$\frac{3}{4}$ cup ricotta cheese
1 cup chopped yellow onion	$\frac{3}{4}$ cup goat cheese
$\frac{1}{2}$ TB. chopped garlic	$\frac{3}{4}$ cup grated Parmesan cheese
6 medium Roma tomatoes, seeded and diced	$\frac{1}{2}$ cup chopped fresh basil leaves
1 tsp. sugar	$\frac{1}{2}$ cup Quick-and-Easy Quinoa (recipe in Chapter 1)
1 large eggplant	1 tsp. ground black pepper
$1\frac{1}{2}$ tsp. sea salt	

1. In a heavy skillet or sauté pan over medium heat, heat 1 tablespoon olive oil. Add yellow onion, and sauté for about 1 minute. Add garlic, and sauté for about 1 minute or until fragrant.

2. Add Roma tomatoes and sugar, and cook, stirring, for about 15 minutes. Remove from heat, and set aside.

3. Using a mandoline or sharp chef's knife, slice eggplant into 12 ($\frac{1}{4}$-inch) length-wise slices. Place eggplant in a strainer, and sprinkle with 1 teaspoon sea salt. Let drain for about 30 minutes.

4. Preheat the broiler to high. Lightly coat a 9×13-inch casserole dish with nonstick cooking spray.

5. In a large bowl, combine ricotta cheese, goat cheese, and Parmesan cheese. Add $\frac{1}{4}$ cup chopped basil, and mix well.

6. Arrange eggplant slices on a broiler pan or baking sheet, and brush with about 2 tablespoons olive oil. Broil for about 3 minutes, turn over eggplant slices, and brush again lightly with remaining 2 tablespoons olive oil. Broil for 3 more minutes.

7. Place broiled eggplant on a serving platter. Spread $\frac{1}{2}$ tablespoon ricotta cheese mixture down center of each eggplant slice, and top with 1 or 2 teaspoons Quick-and-Easy Quinoa. Beginning at narrow end of eggplant slices, roll into a log. Place rolled eggplant seam side down in the prepared casserole dish. Broil for about 3 minutes or until cheese is melted.

8. Transfer eggplant rolls back to the serving platter. Top with about 2 tablespoons tomato mixture, remaining $\frac{1}{2}$ teaspoon sea salt, black pepper, and remaining $\frac{1}{4}$ cup basil, and serve.

KEEN ON QUINOA

If you're lactose intolerant or have chosen to cut dairy products from your diet, almond, soy, and rice cheeses taste delicious and work well as a substitute for ricotta, goat, and Parmesan cheese. Substitute cheeses one for one.

Quinoa Lettuce Wraps with Sausage, Cranberries, and Pine Nuts

Cumin, coriander, dry mustard, and Worcestershire sauce flavor the pork sausage in this recipe, while sweet dried cranberries, nutty pine nuts, and quinoa balance out these crispy red leaf lettuce wraps.

Yield:	Prep time:	Cook time:	Serving size:
8 wraps	15 minutes	17 minutes	1 wrap

Each serving has:			
201.8 calories	6.9 g carbohydrates	16.4 g fat	0.9 g fiber
7.2 g protein			

½ medium yellow onion, chopped

¾ lb. ground pork sausage

½ tsp. cumin

½ tsp. coriander

½ tsp. dry mustard

2 TB. Worcestershire sauce

1 tsp. sea salt

1 tsp. ground black pepper

¼ cup plus 1 TB. Quick-and-Easy Quinoa (recipe in Chapter 1)

2 tsp. finely chopped fresh dill

½ TB. lemon zest

¼ cup plus 2 TB. dried cranberries

¼ cup pine nuts, lightly toasted

8 large red leaf lettuce leaves

1. In a large saucepan over medium-high heat, combine yellow onion and pork sausage, and sauté for about 1 or 2 minutes.

2. Add cumin, coriander, dry mustard, Worcestershire sauce, sea salt, and black pepper, and cook for 5 minutes or until pork is cooked through. Remove from heat and drain off any grease.

3. Add Quick-and-Easy Quinoa, dill, and lemon zest, and stir to combine. Stir in dried cranberries and pine nuts.

4. Place about ¼ cup sausage mixture into 1 red lettuce leaf. Starting at one end, roll lettuce over sausage mixture to make a wrap or log. Serve.

Fantastic Finger Foods

In This Chapter

- Serving perfect-size finger foods
- Healthy savory quinoa cakes
- Excellent quinoa empanadas
- Quick-and-easy make-ahead appetizers

Finger foods are perfect party pleasers. The key to successful finger foods is size. Be sure to keep each piece no larger than 1 or 2 inches in diameter. If the portions are too large, you might end up with a lot of leftovers.

The recipes in this chapter offer many delicious quinoa finger foods to get your party started!

The Basics of Bruschetta

Bruschetta originated in Italy and consists simply of olive oil, fresh diced tomato, fresh chopped garlic, and fresh chopped basil leaves served on toasted bread rubbed with fresh garlic.

Italian *pane toscano* bread is customarily used but can be difficult to find in the States, so other thick breads, such as French bread, can be thinly sliced and grilled instead of toasted. Sourdough baguettes work perfectly and produce just the right size crostini (thinly sliced toasted bread) for finger foods and snacks. Avoid using ciabatta bread. The bruschetta may fall through its large holes.

DEFINITION

Pane toscano is handmade Italian bread that uses no salt. Due to its low salt content, the bread hardens and becomes stale quicker than other breads, making it great for soups and stews—and bruschetta!

Quinoa Tomato Bruschetta

Tomato, red bell pepper, basil, lemon, garlic, and a hint of green onion are delicious atop Parmesan crisps.

Yield:	Prep time:	Cook time:	Serving size:
24 bruschetta	20 minutes	27 minutes	2 bruschetta
Each serving has:			
61.6 calories 2.6 g protein	4.8 g carbohydrates	3.6 g fat	0.5 g fiber

24 slices sourdough baguette

2 cups seeded and diced tomato

¼ cup diced fresh red bell pepper

¼ cup Quick-and-Easy Quinoa (recipe in Chapter 1)

¼ cup chopped fresh basil leaves

½ TB. fine lemon zest

1 clove garlic, chopped

¼ cup chopped green onion, green and white parts

½ tsp. sea salt

½ tsp. ground black pepper

2 TB. olive oil

¾ cup grated Parmesan cheese

1. Preheat the oven to 275°F. Line a baking sheet with parchment paper.

2. Place baguette slices on the prepared baking sheet, and bake for about 20 minutes.

3. Meanwhile, in a large bowl, toss together tomato, red bell pepper, Quick-and-Easy Quinoa, basil, lemon zest, garlic, green onion, sea salt, and black pepper. Add olive oil, and toss to coat.

4. Remove baguette slices from oven. Increase oven temperature to 400°F. Top each baguette slice with about ½ tablespoon grated Parmesan cheese. Return baguette slices to the oven, and bake for about 3 minutes or just until cheese is melted. Remove from the oven, and transfer baguette slices to a large serving platter.

5. Top each baguette slice with about 1 tablespoon tomato mixture, and serve.

Baked Quinoa Crab Cakes

Lump crabmeat, cilantro, parsley, cayenne, dry mustard, *Old Bay Seasoning*, lemon, and quinoa are the reasons these crab cakes are so delicious. Plus, they're baked for maximum flavor and minimum fat.

Yield:	Prep time:	Cook time:	Serving size
24 crab cakes	15 minutes	12 to 15 minutes	2 crab cakes

Each serving has:			
34.8 calories	1.1 g carbohydrates	1.2 g fat	0.1 g fiber
4.8 g protein			

¼ cup plus 1 TB. nonfat
  mayonnaise

1 TB. minced fresh cilantro leaves

1 TB. minced fresh Italian flat-leaf
  parsley leaves

½ tsp. cayenne

½ tsp. dry mustard

1 TB. Old Bay Seasoning

2 large egg whites

½ TB. fine lemon zest

¼ cup Quick-and-Easy Quinoa
  (recipe in Chapter 1)

1 (1-lb.) can lump crabmeat, well
  drained

1. Preheat the oven to 425°F. Line a baking sheet with parchment paper.

2. In a large bowl, combine nonfat mayonnaise, cilantro, Italian flat-leaf parsley, cayenne, dry mustard, and Old Bay Seasoning. Stir in egg whites, lemon zest, and Quick-and-Easy Quinoa until just blended. Fold in crabmeat until just combined.

3. Form crabmeat mixture into 24 (half-dollar-size) round crab cakes. Place on the prepared baking sheet, and bake for 12 to 15 minutes or until golden. Serve hot.

DEFINITION

A blend of herbs and spices, **Old Bay Seasoning** is for crab cakes and shrimp dishes. It can also be used on many other dishes, including salads, grilled foods such as steaks, mixed vegetables, and corn on the cob.

Wild Mushroom Risotto Quinoa Cakes

Flavorful porcini, shiitake, and morel mushrooms take on the additional tastes of quinoa, shallots, thyme, oregano, white pepper, and Parmesan cheese in this yummy *risotto* cake recipe.

Yield:	Prep time:	Cook time:	Serving size:
36 mushroom quinoa cakes	30 minutes	45 minutes	2 mushroom quinoa cakes

Each serving has:			
84.2 calories	11.3 g carbohydrates	2.7 g fat	0.7 g fiber
3.5 g protein			

½ cup finely chopped dried porcini mushrooms

½ cup finely chopped dried shiitake mushrooms

½ cup finely chopped dried morel mushrooms

3 cups tepid water

1 TB. olive oil

2 shallots, finely chopped

½ TB. chopped fresh thyme leaves

½ TB. chopped fresh oregano leaves

1 cup arborio rice

5¾ cups vegetable broth

1 tsp. ground white pepper

1 tsp. sea salt

¾ cup grated Parmesan cheese

1 TB. chopped fresh Italian flat-leaf parsley leaves

1 cup uncooked quinoa, rinsed and drained

1. In a medium bowl, place porcini mushrooms, shiitake mushrooms, and morel mushrooms, and add water. (Add additional water, if needed, to cover.) Let mushrooms soak for at least 30 minutes, and pour off ½ cup water and set aside. Drain remaining liquid.

2. In medium stockpot over medium heat, heat olive oil until just hot. Stir in shallots, and sauté for about 1 minute. Add thyme, oregano, and arborio rice, and cook, stirring, for about 2 minutes or until rice appears light golden in color.

3. Add mushrooms, and cook, stirring, for about 1 minute or until well combined. Add ½ cup reserved mushroom water, and stir until almost all liquid is absorbed. Add ½ cup vegetable broth, and stir until almost all liquid is absorbed, repeating this process until 4 cups vegetable broth have been absorbed into rice. Rice should be plumped and soft but still *al dente*.

4. Stir in white pepper, sea salt, Parmesan cheese, and Italian flat-leaf parsley leaves. Set aside.

5. Preheat the oven to 450°F. Line a baking sheet with parchment paper.

6. In a large saucepan over medium-high heat, combine quinoa and remaining 1¾ cups vegetable broth. Bring to a boil, cover, reduce heat to low, and simmer for 15 minutes or until almost all liquid is absorbed.

7. Stir quinoa into rice mixture until well combined. Form mixture into 36 (1½- to 2-inch) round cakes. Place cakes on the prepared baking sheet, and bake for about 15 minutes or until hot and slightly crisp. Serve hot.

DEFINITION

Risotto is a creamy rice dish made by using arborio rice, which can absorb higher amounts of water than long-grain rice. **Al dente** literally translates as "to the tooth" and means the food, in this case the rice, has been cooked but is still firm when you bite it.

Sausage Quinoa Croquettes

Turkey sausage, cheese, quinoa, and cayenne make these baked *croquettes* so delicious you won't be able to stop at one!

Yield:	Prep time:	Cook time:	Serving size
24 croquettes	10 minutes	20 minutes	2 croquettes
Each serving has:			
209.8 calories	11.4 g carbohydrates	12.0 g fat	0.5 g fiber
14.2 g protein			

1½ cups baking mix such as Bisquick

½ cup Quick-and-Easy Quinoa (recipe in Chapter 1)

1 lb. turkey sausage

2 cups grated sharp cheddar cheese

1 tsp. cayenne

1. Preheat the oven to 400°F. Line a baking sheet with parchment paper.

2. In a large bowl, combine baking mix, Quick-and-Easy Quinoa, turkey sausage, sharp cheddar cheese, and cayenne. Mix well, and form into 24 (1-inch) balls. Place balls on the prepared baking sheet about 1 inch apart.

2. Bake for 20 minutes or until croquettes are slightly crisp and golden brown. Serve hot.

> **DEFINITION**
>
> A **croquette** is a usually a ball or roll made of vegetables such as mashed potatoes and lentils, meats, spices, herbs. Usually fried to give a nice crunch to foods, croquettes get their name from the French word *croquer,* which means "to crunch."

Rosemary Quinoa Polenta Cakes

The natural corn flavor of cornmeal matches perfectly with fresh rosemary, buttery buttermilk, and freshly grated Parmesan cheese in these tasty *polenta* cakes.

Yield:	Prep time:	Cook time:	Serving size
12 cakes	10 minutes	35 minutes	2 cakes
Each serving has:			
360.3 calories	47.1 g carbohydrates	13.1 g fat	3.8 g fiber
14.8 g protein			

¼ cup uncooked quinoa, rinsed and drained	2 tsp. sea salt
½ cup vegetable broth	1 tsp. ground white pepper
3 cups plus 2 TB. reduced-fat buttermilk	3 TB. unsalted butter
3 cups water	2 TB. chopped fresh rosemary leaves
1¾ cups cornmeal	½ cup grated Parmesan cheese

1. Preheat the oven to 375°F. Lightly coat an 8-inch-square baking dish with non-stick cooking spray.

2. In a small saucepan over medium-high heat, combine quinoa and vegetable broth. Bring to a boil, cover, reduce heat to low, and simmer for about 15 minutes or until almost all liquid is absorbed. Remove from heat and let stand, covered, until ready to use.

3. In a large saucepan over medium-high heat, combine 3 cups buttermilk and water. Bring to a boil. Gradually whisk in cornmeal, and reduce heat to low. Add sea salt and white pepper, and cook, stirring, for about 15 minutes or until mixture thickens. Turn off heat.

4. Add unsalted butter, and stir until melted. Stir in rosemary, Parmesan cheese, remaining 2 tablespoons buttermilk, and quinoa until well combined.

5. Pour cornmeal quinoa mixture into the prepared baking dish, and spread evenly. Bake for about 20 minutes. Remove from the oven, and slice into 12 equal squares. Serve warm.

Variation: If desired, heat a grill or a grill pan to medium-high heat. Carefully place polenta squares on the grill and grill for about 45 seconds. Turn and grill the other side for about 20 to 30 seconds. Place squares on a serving plate, and brush each square with olive oil. Serve warm.

DEFINITION

Polenta is a dish made from ground yellow or white cornmeal. Enjoy it immediately after it's boiled, or bake or grill it.

Baked Quinoa Artichoke Squares with Sun-Dried Tomato Pesto

Artichoke hearts, basil, Parmesan, quinoa, and sun-dried tomatoes will win over your taste buds and your tummy in this simple, delicious recipe. It's easy to make ahead and freeze, too!

Yield:	Prep time:	Cook time:	Serving size
16 squares	20 minutes	45 minutes	2 squares
Each serving has:			
134.1 calories	14.5 g carbohydrates	4.3 g fat	4.2 g fiber
8.5 g protein			

2½ TB. plus ½ cup olive oil	1½ tsp. sea salt
1 medium yellow onion, diced	1½ tsp. ground black pepper
2 cloves garlic, minced	2 cups dry-packed sun-dried tomatoes
2 (14-oz.) cans artichoke hearts, drained, with liquid reserved	¾ cup water
3 large eggs	¾ cup sauvignon blanc
1 TB. chopped fresh basil leaves	3 whole cloves garlic
½ cup grated Parmesan cheese	4 whole fresh basil leaves
1½ cups Quick-and-Easy Quinoa (recipe in Chapter 1)	

1. Preheat the oven to 375°F. Lightly coat an 8-inch-square baking dish with non-stick cooking spray.

2. In a heavy, medium skillet over medium-high heat, heat ½ tablespoon olive oil. Stir in yellow onion and minced garlic, and sauté for about 1 minute. Remove from heat, and set aside.

3. Place artichoke hearts in a large mixing bowl. Using your hands (wear plastic kitchen gloves if you prefer), mash artichokes until they're broken into small, chunky pieces. Mash in reserved artichoke heart liquid, eggs, and 2 tablespoons olive oil, and mix well. Stir in sautéed onion and garlic, and mix well. Add 1 tablespoon chopped basil, Parmesan cheese, Quick-and-Easy Quinoa, 1 teaspoon sea salt, and 1 teaspoon black pepper.

4. Spread artichoke mixture into the prepared baking dish, and bake for 45 minutes or until set.

5. Meanwhile, in a large saucepan over medium heat, cook sun-dried tomatoes, water, sauvignon blanc, and 3 whole cloves garlic for about 15 minutes or until tomatoes are softened. Transfer mixture to a food processor fitted with a chopping blade or blender, add 4 whole basil leaves and remaining $\frac{1}{2}$ cup olive oil, and process on high until smooth, stopping halfway through to add remaining $\frac{1}{2}$ teaspoon sea salt and $\frac{1}{2}$ teaspoon black pepper.

6. Remove artichoke dish from the oven, and let rest for about 5 minutes. Slice into 16 squares, and top with $\frac{1}{2}$ to 1 tablespoon sun-dried tomato pesto.

Vegetarian Empanadas with Quinoa

Corn, broccoli, red bell pepper, onion, cilantro, and quinoa combine for great flavor and color. Cayenne, paprika, and cumin add just the right amount of spice in these *empanadas.*

Yield:	Prep time:	Cook time:	Serving size
24 empanadas	20 minutes	15 minutes	2 empanadas
Each serving has:			
82.9 calories	13.5 g carbohydrates	2.0 g fat	1.1 g fiber
2.9 g protein			

1 TB. olive oil	$\frac{1}{2}$ tsp. paprika
$\frac{3}{4}$ cup chopped yellow onion	$\frac{1}{4}$ tsp. ground cumin
1 clove garlic, chopped	1 tsp. sea salt
$\frac{1}{2}$ cup fresh corn kernels	1 tsp. ground black pepper
$\frac{1}{2}$ cup coarsely chopped broccoli florets	$\frac{1}{2}$ cup Quick-and-Easy Quinoa (recipe in Chapter 1)
1 small to medium red bell pepper, ribs and seeds removed, and chopped	$\frac{1}{2}$ cup plus 1 TB. water
	24 square wonton wrappers
1 TB. chopped fresh cilantro leaves	1 large egg
$\frac{1}{2}$ tsp. cayenne	

1. Preheat the oven to 375°F. Line a baking sheet with parchment paper.

2. In a large sauté pan over medium-high heat, stir together olive oil, yellow onion, and garlic for about 2 minutes.

3. Stir in corn, broccoli, and red bell pepper until just heated through. Add cilantro leaves, cayenne, paprika, cumin, sea salt, black pepper, and Quick-and-Easy Quinoa.

4. Place $\frac{1}{2}$ cup water in a small bowl.

5. Place 1 wonton wrapper on a flat work surface. Spoon $\frac{1}{2}$ tablespoon quinoa mixture into center of wonton. Dip your index finger in water, and lightly coat edges of wonton with water. Fold $\frac{1}{2}$ of wonton over other $\frac{1}{2}$ to cover filling. Press edges with your finger to seal. Transfer filled wontons to the prepared baking sheet.

6. In a small bowl, whisk together egg and 1 tablespoon water. Using a pastry brush or back of a small spoon, brush top of each filled wonton with egg mixture.

7. Bake for about 15 minutes or until golden brown. Serve hot.

DEFINITION

Popular in Latin American and southern European countries, **empanadas** consist of savory fillings encased in pastry and baked or fried. Popular fillings include meats, cheese, and vegetables. With quinoa's light consistency, it makes the perfect high-protein, high-fiber, flavorful addition.

Blackened Chicken Quinoa Empanadas

In these empanadas, chicken is flavored with white onion, lemon, corn, cilantro, and quinoa with a hint of blackened seasoning.

Yield:	Prep time:	Cook time:	Serving size
24 empanadas	25 minutes	40 minutes	2 empanadas

Each serving has:			
114.3 calories	10.8 g carbohydrates	2.2 g fat	0.5 g fiber
12.0 g protein			

2 (6-oz.) boneless, skinless chicken breasts	$\frac{1}{4}$ cup Quick-and-Easy Quinoa (recipe in Chapter 1)
2 TB. blackened seasoning	1 tsp. sea salt (optional)
$\frac{1}{4}$ cup chicken broth	1 tsp. ground black pepper (optional)
$\frac{1}{2}$ TB. olive oil	$\frac{1}{4}$ cup plus 2 TB. water
$\frac{1}{4}$ cup diced white onion	24 (3$\frac{1}{4}$-in.) square wonton wrappers
Juice of $\frac{1}{2}$ lemon	2 large eggs
$\frac{1}{4}$ cup kernel corn, fresh or frozen	
$\frac{1}{4}$ cup chopped fresh cilantro leaves	

1. Preheat the oven to 375°F. Line a baking sheet with parchment paper.

2. In a small bowl, combine chicken with blackened seasoning to coat.

3. In a medium saucepan over medium heat, heat chicken broth. Add chicken, cover, and cook for about 10 minutes. Turn over chicken, cover, and cook for 10 more minutes or until cooked through. Transfer to a plate, and allow to cool.

4. In same saucepan over medium heat, heat olive oil. Add white onion, lemon juice, corn, and cilantro, and sauté for about 2 minutes or until onion is tender. Remove from heat, and stir in Quick-and-Easy Quinoa until well combined.

5. Chop chicken into small $\frac{1}{2}$-inch pieces, and toss into quinoa mixture until well coated. Stir in sea salt (if using) and black pepper (if using).

6. Place $\frac{1}{2}$ cup water in a small bowl.

7. Place wonton wrappers on a flat work surface. Spoon $\frac{1}{2}$ to 1 tablespoon quinoa mixture onto center of each wonton. Dip your index finger into water, and lightly coat outer edges of wonton wrapper. Fold one side of wrapper over quinoa mixture, press edges securely together, and place on the prepared baking sheet.

8. In another small bowl, whisk together remaining 2 tablespoons water and eggs. Using a pastry brush or the back of a spoon, lightly brush tops of wonton wrappers. Bake for 12 to 15 minutes or until lightly golden and crisp.

Quinoa Spinach Balls

These Tuscan-style balls will have you coming back for more, thanks to delicious spinach, Parmesan cheese, nutmeg, and nutty quinoa.

Yield:	Prep time:	Cook time:	Serving size
24 balls	20 minutes	10 minutes	2 balls

Each serving has:			
77.4 calories	6.0 g carbohydrates	3.5 g fat	1.1 g fiber
6.1 g protein			

$\frac{1}{4}$ cup Quick-and-Easy Quinoa (recipe in Chapter 1)	$\frac{1}{2}$ cup grated Parmesan cheese
1 tsp. ground nutmeg	$\frac{1}{2}$ tsp. sea salt
2 cups chopped frozen spinach, squeezed dry	$\frac{1}{2}$ tsp. ground black pepper
1 large egg, lightly beaten	$\frac{1}{4}$ cup all-purpose flour
$1\frac{1}{2}$ cups part-skim milk ricotta cheese	3 qt. water

1. In a small bowl, combine Quick-and-Easy Quinoa and nutmeg. Set aside.

2. In a large bowl, combine spinach, egg, part-skim ricotta cheese, Parmesan cheese, sea salt, and black pepper, and mix well. Add quinoa. Form mixture into about 24 (1-inch) balls, and lightly roll each ball in all-purpose flour.

3. In a large stockpot over medium-high heat, bring water to a boil. Gently drop balls into boiling water, about 5 balls at a time, and boil for about 5 minutes. Using a slotted spoon, lift balls out of water and place in a serving bowl. Repeat until all balls have been cooked. Serve.

Baked Quinoa-Crusted Chicken Tenders

A healthier crust than breadcrumbs, crispy quinoa adds nutty flavor while basil, parsley, and cayenne perfectly accompany tender chicken.

Yield:	Prep time:	Cook time:	Serving size:
24 tenders	18 minutes	20 minutes	4 tenders

Each serving has:			
229.1 calories	19.6 g carbohydrates	4.8 g fat	1.5 g fiber
25.2 g protein			

2 cups nonfat milk

2 large eggs

3 cups Quick-and-Easy Quinoa
   (recipe in Chapter 1)

1 tsp. cayenne

1 tsp. dried basil

1 tsp. dried parsley

$\frac{1}{2}$ tsp. sea salt

$\frac{1}{2}$ tsp. ground black pepper

24 chicken tenders

1. Preheat the oven to 375°F. Line a baking sheet with parchment paper.

2. In a medium bowl, whisk together nonfat milk and eggs. Set aside.

3. In a separate medium bowl, toss together Quick-and-Easy Quinoa, cayenne, basil, parsley, sea salt, and black pepper.

4. Using one hand, dip 1 chicken tender in milk mixture, and place in quinoa mixture. Use your other hand to coat the chicken tender with quinoa. Place coated chicken tender on the prepared baking sheet, and repeat with remaining ingredients.

5. Bake for about 20 minutes or until cooked through. Serve warm with your favorite dipping sauce.

Starter Salads

In This Chapter

- Super simple quinoa salads
- Easy DIY vinaigrettes
- Creative ways to serve salads

Perfect before a large meal or terrific as stand-alone dishes, the flavorful and nutritious starter salads in this chapter are extremely versatile. Enjoy them for midweek lunches, for light dinners, or at brunches and other parties.

Quinoa in Salads and Slaw

As you've discovered by now, quinoa makes a deliciously healthy base for all kinds of recipes, including salads and slaws, and is a healthy fiber-filled substitute for rice.

Rice can be a little heavy and is, in general, a heavier grain that adds bulk to foods—and often your waistline. Quinoa is a smaller, lighter seed that, in effect, is a natural crumble. Its light and puffy nature fluffs up foods rather than weighs them down, and it fluffs up your diet, too, by providing valuable nutrients and fiber. Crumble cooked quinoa on top of finished slaws and salads, or toss it all together. You'll find it light and delicious either way.

The Basics of Vinaigrettes

Vinaigrettes often get overlooked as a good addition to quinoa, but they are a delicious way to add flavor to your favorite quinoa salads. Vinaigrettes are easy to make and much healthier for you when you make them yourself, so throw out those bottled vinaigrettes that are filled with preservatives.

Here are my go-to vinegars and how to use them:

Apple cider vinegar: Made from fermenting apples, this medium-flavored highly acid vinegar has a sharp tangy flavor that's best when diluted with juices such as lemon, lime, and orange. It's delicious as a base to salads with richly flavored fruits and nuts like cranberries, pomegranates, walnuts, and pecans.

Wine vinegar: Wine vinegars are made from red wine, white wine, champagne, and rice wine, as in rice wine vinegar. Milder in flavor and lower in acidity than apple cider vinegar, wine vinegars are best when paired with more subtle-flavored foods like pears, summer squash, and cashews.

Balsamic vinegar: Although dark in color, balsamic vinegar is made from white grapes. Commercially produced balsamic vinegars are typically made with concentrated grape juice and vinegar and have slightly sweet, bold, rich flavors that pair well with most foods. Genuine balsamic vinegars are aged for 12 years or longer—and some are aged for 40 to 100 years. Aging the vinegar makes it sweeter and gives it a thicker consistency. Balsamic vinegar tastes delicious with most foods and can be used as a base for vinaigrettes or drizzled over foods by itself.

🍳 Quinoa Carbonara with Fresh Spring Peas, Topped with Quail Eggs

Spring peas, bacon, pancetta, and Parmigiano Reggiano cheese are tossed with quinoa fettuccine in this recipe by Hailey Kehoe, owner, Culinartist Catering (San Francisco, CA).

Yield:	Prep time:	Cook time:	Serving size:
8 cups	15 minutes	25 minutes	2 cups
Each serving has:			
933 calories	33.2 g carbohydrates	63.0 g fat	3.0 g fiber
56.2 g protein			

$\frac{1}{2}$ cup fresh or frozen spring peas	1 tsp. ground black pepper
1 (16-oz.) box quinoa fettuccini	1 cup grated Parmigiano Reggiano
1 TB. extra-virgin olive oil	2 large eggs
3 strips bacon, diced small	Pinch of nutmeg
2 cloves fresh garlic, minced	4 ($\frac{1}{2}$-in.) slices round pancetta
1 tsp. sea salt	4 quail eggs

1. Bring a medium stockpot full of salted water to a boil over medium-high heat. Place spring peas in a small strainer, and blanch in salt water for 2 or 3 minutes. Quickly remove from hot water and run under cool water.

2. Add quinoa fettuccine to salted water, and cook according to package directions or until *al dente*. Drain.

3. Meanwhile, in a medium or large skillet over medium heat, heat extra-virgin olive oil. Add bacon, and cook for 3 minutes or until crispy. Remove bacon from the skillet, drain on paper towels, and reduce heat to low.

4. Add garlic to the skillet, and cook for 30 to 45 seconds or until just starting to become golden. Return bacon to the skillet. Add blanched spring peas. Do not let garlic overcook, or you'll have to start the whole process from scratch.

5. Add cooked fettuccini to the skillet, and remove from heat.

6. In a medium bowl, combine Parmigiano Reggiano, eggs, and nutmeg.

7. In a medium, dry skillet over medium heat, fry pancetta rounds for 1 minutes or until crispy. Remove pancetta from the skillet, and drain on paper towels, reserving fat in the skillet.

8. Return fettuccine mixture to medium heat, and after it's heated a bit, add egg mixture and stir very well. Be sure heat isn't too high or eggs will scramble. If skillet becomes too hot, remove it from heat for a minute before resuming.

9. Meanwhile, in the medium, dry skillet over medium heat, fry quail eggs in pancetta fat.

10. To serve, use tongs to grab some fettuccini, and twirl to create a nest. Top fettuccini nest with pancetta round, followed by quail egg.

Variation: If you can't find a quail egg, enjoy the dish without!

KEEN ON QUINOA

My catering business was founded on creating gluten-free menus for gourmet dinners. Naturally gluten-free quinoa is the perfect unexpected ingredient that allows me to wow guests with healthy, delicious menus.

—Hailey Kehoe

♨ Wild Arugula Quinoa Salad with Lemon Vinaigrette

Chef Chris Barnett of Sherbourne (Los Angeles, CA) combines honey, mustard, and lemon in a simple vinaigrette tossed with quinoa and arugula.

Yield:	Prep time:	Cook time:	Serving size:
4 cups	15 minutes	15 minutes	1 cup

Each serving has:			
1,047.5 calories	59.1 g carbohydrates	86.4 g fat	6.6 g fiber
12.0 g protein			

½ cup Dijon mustard

¼ cup honey

½ cup fresh lemon juice

1½ tsp. sea salt

½ tsp. ground black pepper

1½ cups olive oil

1 cup uncooked quinoa, rinsed and drained

2 cups water

2 medium celery stalks, finely diced

2 ears corn, kernels cut off cob

1 cup cherry tomatoes, halved

¼ cup pomegranate seeds

1 cup edamame beans

3 cups arugula greens

1. In a medium bowl, whisk together Dijon mustard, honey, lemon juice, ½ teaspoon sea salt, black pepper, and olive oil until well combined and thickened.

2. In a medium saucepan over medium heat, bring quinoa, remaining 1 teaspoon sea salt, and water to a boil. Cook for about 15 minutes or until tender. Drain and set aside to cool.

3. In a large bowl, combine celery, corn kernels, cherry tomatoes, pomegranate seeds, edamame beans, arugula greens, and quinoa. Toss with Dijon-lemon vinaigrette, and serve.

♟ M Café's Scarlet Quinoa Salad

Red beets, lemon, cucumber, chives, dill, and quinoa are tossed with a umeboshi vinegar, a light citrusy vinegar common to Asian dishes in this recipe by Chef Lee Gross, Executive Chef, M Café (Los Angeles, CA).

Yield:	**Prep time:**	**Cook time:**	**Serving size:**
4 cups	15 minutes	30 minutes	1 cup
Each serving has:			
198.4 calories	34.5 g carbohydrates	4.0 g fat	3.6 g fiber
6.4 g protein			

½ cup diced red beet

2 cups vegetable stock

¼ tsp. sea salt

1 tsp. olive oil

2 tsp. fresh lemon juice

1 cup uncooked quinoa, rinsed and drained

2 tsp. umeboshi vinegar

2 TB. dill pickle juice

1 TB. extra-virgin olive oil

¼ cup diced Japanese or Persian cucumber

2 tsp. minced fresh chives

1 TB. minced fresh dill

1 tsp. fine lemon zest

1. In a heavy-bottomed 2-quart saucepan over medium heat, bring beet, vegetable stock, sea salt, olive oil, and 1 teaspoon lemon juice to a boil.

2. Add quinoa, cover, reduce heat to low, and simmer for 20 minutes or until almost all liquid has been absorbed. Let stand 10 minutes before uncovering. Fluff quinoa with a fork and transfer to a plate or baking sheet to cool.

3. In a small bowl, whisk together umeboshi vinegar, remaining 1 teaspoon lemon juice, dill pickle juice, and extra-virgin olive oil.

4. In a large bowl, combine scarlet quinoa mixture, Japanese cucumber, chives, dill, and lemon zest. Moisten salad with a few tablespoons umeboshi vinegar mixture. Serve immediately, or refrigerate and serve later. Taste salad after refrigerating and add additional dressing, if desired.

KEEN ON QUINOA

Whole grains are the basis of the macrobiotic way of eating. Quinoa is the only whole grain that is also a complete protein. Light, nourishing, and satisfying, it is the perfect whole grain for southern California, the home of M Café. Scarlet Quinoa Salad highlights this supergrain's nutty flavor and pleasing texture.

—Chef Lee Gross

Smoked Turkey Quinoa Salad on Endive

Smoked turkey, nutty quinoa, crisp celery, refreshing mint, and sweet cranberries, all mixed with a little creamy mayo, are the perfect topping for bitter endive.

Yield:	Prep time:	Serving size:
4 cups	15 minutes	1 cup

Each serving has:		
369.3 calories	31.6 g carbohydrates	17.6 g fat
9.6 g fiber	23.2 g protein	

2 cups diced smoked turkey breast

$\frac{1}{2}$ cup nonfat mayonnaise

$\frac{1}{4}$ cup diced celery

$\frac{1}{4}$ cup Quick-and-Easy Quinoa (recipe in Chapter 1)

1 TB. fine lemon zest

$\frac{1}{2}$ cup dried cranberries

2 TB. chopped fresh mint leaves

1 tsp. sea salt

1 tsp. ground black pepper

2 heads fresh endive, root trimmed

1. In a large bowl, combine turkey, nonfat mayonnaise, celery, Quick-and-Easy Quinoa, lemon zest, dried cranberries, mint leaves, sea salt, and black pepper.

2. Arrange about 6 endive leaves on a serving plate. Top with $\frac{1}{2}$ cup quinoa mixture, and serve.

Five-Spice Chicken Quinoa in Radicchio Cups

Chinese five-spice powder adds the perfect balance of flavors with chicken breast, shallots, fresh orange, honey, rice wine vinegar, cilantro, and quinoa. Sesame oil gives this salad its final Asian flair.

Yield:	Prep time:	Cook time:	Serving size:
4 radicchio cups with $\frac{1}{2}$ cup quinoa mixture	15 minutes	20 minutes	1 radicchio cup

Each serving has:			
355.6 calories 31.4 g protein	36.1 g carbohydrates	9.8 g fat	3.7 g fiber

2 tsp. Chinese five-spice powder	2 TB. sesame oil
$1\frac{1}{2}$ tsp. sea salt	1 batch Quick-and-Easy Quinoa (recipe in Chapter 1)
2 (6-oz.) boneless, skinless chicken breasts	$\frac{3}{4}$ cup chopped fresh cilantro leaves
2 medium navel oranges	4 medium to large fresh radicchio leaves
2 small shallots, minced	
2 TB. rice wine vinegar	
2 TB. honey	

1. Preheat the oven to 350°F. Line a baking sheet with parchment paper.

2. In a small mixing bowl, combine Chinese five-spice powder and sea salt.

3. Lightly coat each chicken breast with Chinese five-spice powder mixture. Place chicken on the prepared baking sheet, and bake for about 20 minutes or until chicken is cooked through. Allow to cool, and cut chicken into $\frac{1}{2}$-inch pieces.

4. Using a *Microplane* or other fine grate zester, zest navel orange into a small bowl.

5. Slice off ends of oranges, and slice off rind and pith. Working over a small bowl to catch the juice, using a small paring knife, slice between orange membranes to remove the fruit. Place fruit in a small bowl.

6. Squeeze empty membranes, and capture juice in the bowl.

7. In a large bowl, toss together orange slices, shallots, $\frac{1}{2}$ of reserved orange juice, $\frac{1}{2}$ of reserved orange zest, rice wine vinegar, honey, and sesame oil. Gently stir in chopped chicken, Quick-and-Easy Quinoa, and cilantro.

8. Place 1 radicchio leaf on each of 4 serving plates. Spoon about $\frac{1}{2}$ cup quinoa mixture onto each radicchio leaf, and serve.

> **DEFINITION**
>
> **Chinese five-spice powder** is a combination of cinnamon, cloves, fennel seed, star anise, and Szechuan pepper. Make your own with ground star anise, ground fennel seed, ground cinnamon, lemon pepper (or Szechwan pepper), and ground cloves. A **Microplane** is a specific type of zester or grater. It has a rubber handle attached to a long metal shaft with small, sharp metal teeth, perfect for zesting citrus fruits and also for grating hard cheeses like Parmesan.

Chicken Quinoa Lettuce Cups

Quinoa, chicken, Asian pear, blue cheese, and walnuts are tossed with delicious cranberry vinaigrette and served in delicious Bibb lettuce leaf cups.

Yield:	Prep time:	Cook time:	Serving size
6 chicken quinoa lettuce cups	20 minutes	20 minutes	1 chicken quinoa lettuce cup
Each serving has:			
435.9 calories 27.4 g protein	36.4 g carbohydrates	21.2 g fat	6.3 g fiber

2 (6-oz.) boneless, skinless chicken breasts

3 TB. olive oil

$1\frac{1}{4}$ tsp. sea salt

1 tsp. ground black pepper

$\frac{1}{2}$ cup canned whole-berry cranberry sauce

$\frac{1}{4}$ cup plus 2 TB. fresh orange juice (about 1 medium orange)

2 TB. balsamic vinegar

1 tsp. sugar

1 tsp. minced and peeled fresh ginger

1 batch Quick-and-Easy Quinoa (recipe in Chapter 1)

2 cups diced Asian pear

1 cup chopped red onion

2 heads Bibb lettuce

$\frac{1}{2}$ cup crumbled blue cheese

$\frac{1}{2}$ cup roughly chopped walnuts, toasted

1. Preheat the oven to 350°F. Line a baking sheet with parchment paper.

2. Coat chicken breasts with 2 tablespoons olive oil, and season with 1 teaspoon sea salt and black pepper. Place on the prepared baking sheet, and bake for 20 minutes or until chicken is cooked through. Set aside to cool, and cut into $1/2$-inch pieces.

3. In a large bowl, whisk together whole-berry cranberry sauce, $1/4$ cup orange juice, remaining 1 tablespoon olive oil, balsamic vinegar, sugar, and ginger. Add Quick-and-Easy Quinoa, Asian pear, red onion, chicken, and remaining 2 tablespoons orange juice, and toss well to combine.

4. Arrange 3 lettuce leaves on each of 6 serving plates, overlapping them to form a cup in the center. Spoon equal amounts of chicken quinoa mixture (about $3/4$ cup) into center of each lettuce cup. Top with $11/2$ tablespoons blue cheese and $11/2$ tablespoons chopped toasted walnuts, and serve.

Radicchio Cups with Quinoa and Citrus Salsa

Radicchio has a bitter flavor that provides balance to the nutty flavor of quinoa and a sweet citrus salsa of mango, lemon, lime, cilantro, and pepper.

Yield:	Prep time:	Cook time:	Serving size
8 radicchio cups with ½ cup quinoa each	40 minutes	15 minutes	1 radicchio cup with ½ cup quinoa

Each serving has:			
170.9 calories 4.0 g protein	23.9 g carbohydrates	7.2 g fat	3.6 g fiber

1 cup uncooked quinoa, rinsed and drained

2 cups vegetable broth or water

½ TB. fine lemon zest

1 TB. fresh lemon juice

¼ TB. fine lime zest

1 TB. fresh lime juice

2 TB. white wine vinegar

2 TB. olive oil

1 tsp. sea salt

1 tsp. ground black pepper

1 medium mango

1 medium red bell pepper, ribs and seeds removed, and diced

½ medium red onion, diced

1 large cucumber, peeled, seeded, and diced

½ cup diced avocado

¼ cup plus 2 TB. chopped fresh cilantro leaves

8 medium radicchio leaves

1. In a medium saucepan over medium-high heat, combine quinoa and vegetable broth. Bring to a boil, reduce heat to low, cover, and simmer for 15 minutes or until almost all liquid is absorbed. Transfer quinoa to a mixing bowl, and refrigerate for at least 20 minutes or overnight.

2. In a large bowl, whisk together lemon zest, lemon juice, lime zest, lime juice, white wine vinegar, olive oil, sea salt, and black pepper.

3. Dice mango by taking a sharp knife and slicing lengthwise through mango on each side of seed. Make 4 or 5 lengthwise slices on each mango half. Make 4 or 5 crosswise slices on each mango half. Carefully slice along skin of mango and underneath mango "cubes" to release diced mango. Place diced mango on a cutting board, and chop into small chunks, as you would for a fresh salsa.

4. Toss diced mango into the mixing bowl with lemon zest mixture. Add red bell pepper, red onion, cucumber, avocado, cilantro leaves, and quinoa, and toss well to coat.

5. To serve, place 1 radicchio leaf on each of 8 medium serving plates or bowls. Spoon $\frac{1}{2}$ cup quinoa mixture into each radicchio cup, and serve.

Summer Quinoa Slaw with Cider Vinaigrette

I adapted this recipe from my Aunt Carolyn's Southern Coleslaw recipe. The addition of quinoa ensures you get protein and minerals, and adds a nice nutty flavor. Other key flavors include tangy cider vinegar, creamy mayonnaise, and sweet sugar.

Yield:	Prep time:	Serving size:
8 cups	15 minutes plus overnight chill time	1 cup

Each serving has:		
217.8 calories	28.5 g carbohydrates	10.9 g fat
3.4 g fiber	3.3 g protein	

1 medium head green cabbage	1$\frac{1}{2}$ tsp. prepared mustard
1$\frac{1}{2}$ TB. olive oil	$\frac{1}{2}$ tsp. sea salt
$\frac{3}{4}$ cup nonfat mayonnaise	2 TB. apple cider vinegar
$\frac{1}{2}$ cup sugar	1 batch Quick-and-Easy Quinoa (recipe in Chapter 1)
$\frac{1}{2}$ tsp. celery seed	

1. Quarter cabbage, and shred in food processor fitted with a chopping blade or a blender until just grated. Be careful not to overprocess, or cabbage will turn to cabbage purée. Transfer shredded cabbage to a large bowl.

2. In a small bowl, whisk together olive oil, nonfat mayonnaise, sugar, celery seed, prepared mustard, sea salt, and apple cider vinegar.

3. Pour vinegar mixture over cabbage, but *do not stir*. Cover, and refrigerate overnight to allow flavors to meld.

4. Before serving, add Quick-and-Easy Quinoa, and toss to combine.

Delicious Dinners

Whether you're cooking for one, two, four, or more people, having a plan for your dinner ahead of time saves you tons of time and frustration later. Plus, planning and serving a family dinner keeps you from eating in front of the TV, when you'd likely be distracted, not eat mindfully, and risk overeating.

The chapters in Part 5 give you tons of ideas to answer the question, "What's for dinner?" These recipes help you make quinoa an even more delicious meal option and highlight quinoa's real versatility in vegetarian and meat-based dishes alike.

Vegetarian Dinners

In This Chapter

- Deliciously healthy vegetarian main dishes
- Versatile veggie-and-quinoa dinners
- Quinoa burgers, salads, and more

Quinoa can add some real pizzazz—and protein!—to vegetarian dishes, as you'll see by the mouthwatering recipes in this chapter.

Fresh, Frozen, or Canned Vegetables?

Fresh vegetables are always the best tasting and healthiest for you. When it comes to purchasing fresh vegetables, the best, best choice is right off the farm. Farmers' markets are prevalent in cities big and small, and in most cases, the prices are cheaper than if you purchase them at the grocery store because they don't have to pay the store's overhead.

When fresh isn't available, the next best thing is fresh frozen. Fresh frozen vegetables are exactly that—fresh vegetables that have been cleaned, trimmed, and frozen in a convenient package so you can have fresh vegetables year-round.

Canned vegetables are my least favorite option. They're still good for you, but the packing liquid makes the vegetable softer and less crisp. And they've been lightly processed, so they have fewer nutrients than the fresh versions.

🍳 Quinoa "Pasta" and Lentils

Fresh vegetables are tossed with quinoa and lentils and touched off with a hint of harissa paste in this recipe by Chef Serena Palumbo, finalist, *The Next Food Network Star* (Season 6).

Yield:	Prep time:	Cook time:	Serving size:
4 cups	15 minutes, plus 8 hours soak time	25 minutes	1 cup

Each serving has:			
212.8 calories 12.1 g protein	38.0 g carbohydrates	1.8 g fat	9.7 g fiber

2 cups dry green lentils

1 TB. light extra-virgin olive oil

2 cloves garlic, minced

$\frac{1}{4}$ cup chopped white onion

$\frac{1}{4}$ cup chopped celery

$\frac{1}{4}$ cup chopped carrots

1 TB. sea salt

4 cups water

2 cups reduced-sodium vegetable stock

1 bay leaf (optional)

$\frac{1}{2}$ TB. harissa paste

1 batch Quick-and-Easy Quinoa (recipe in Chapter 1)

$\frac{1}{2}$ cup roughly chopped Italian flat-leaf parsley leaves

2 TB. extra-virgin olive oil

1. In a large bowl, soak dry green lentils in warm water to cover for 8 hours or overnight. Drain and rinse lentils.

2. Meanwhile, in a Dutch oven over medium heat, heat light extra-virgin olive oil. Add garlic, white onion, celery, carrots, and sea salt. Sauté for about 2 minutes or until onions are translucent.

3. Drain lentils, add to the Dutch oven, and stir. Add water, vegetable stock, bay leaf (if using), and harissa paste. Cover, bring to a boil, reduce heat to low, and simmer for 20 minutes or until lentils are cooked. Remove bay leaf.

4. Add Quick-and-Easy Quinoa, garnish with Italian flat-leaf parsley, and drizzle with $\frac{1}{2}$ tablespoon extra-virgin olive oil.

KEEN ON QUINOA

I love cooking with quinoa because it is a nonperishable protein! It cooks quickly and you don't need fancy appliances to prepare it. Since quinoa is not used in Italy, I am trying to introduce it to friends and family who live there. This recipe is my way of turning *pasta e lenticchie* (pasta and lentils) into a quinoa-based recipe. Enjoy!

—Chef Serena Palumbo

Quinoa with Roasted Pine Nuts and Cilantro

Pine nuts have a nutty yet almost sweet flavor that's delicious with tangy, fresh cilantro, quinoa, and the other key flavors in this dish: lemon, cayenne, and coriander.

Yield: 4 cups	Prep time: 10 minutes	Cook time: 18 minutes	Serving size: 1 cup
Each serving has:			
142.6 calories 3.4 g protein	11.1 g carbohydrates	10.2 g fat	1.4 g fiber

¼ cup pine nuts	1½ tsp. fine lemon zest
1 TB. olive oil	½ tsp. cayenne
½ medium yellow onion, chopped	¼ tsp. coriander
½ TB. chopped garlic	1 tsp. sea salt
1 cup uncooked quinoa, rinsed and drained	1 tsp. ground black pepper
2 cups vegetable broth	½ cup chopped fresh cilantro leaves

1. In a medium sauté pan over medium heat, heat pine nuts, stirring occasionally, for about 3 minutes or until lightly browned. Be careful not to burn pine nuts. Transfer toasted pine nuts to a bowl, and set aside.

2. In a medium saucepan over medium heat, heat olive oil. Add yellow onion and garlic, and sauté for about 1 or 2 minutes.

3. Stir in quinoa and vegetable broth. Bring to a boil, cover, reduce heat to low, and simmer for 15 minutes or until almost all liquid is absorbed.

4. Remove quinoa from heat, and stir in lemon zest, cayenne, coriander, sea salt, and black pepper. Top each serving with about 2 tablespoons cilantro leaves, and serve.

> **DEFINITION**
>
> **Pine nuts** are the edible seeds from the pine tree. Rich in flavor and nutrients, pine nuts are high in vitamin E and monounsaturated fats (the good fats), and they're naturally gluten free.

🍳 Red Beet Quinoa and Zucchini Noodle

Cooked red beets, lemon, chives, and golden raisins mix with zucchini and avocado basil pesto in this recipe by Chef Manfred Lassahn, senior executive chef of Hyatt Regency Century Plaza (Los Angeles, CA).

Yield:	Prep time:	Cook time:	Serving size:
4 cups	20 minutes	30 minutes	1 cup
Each serving has:			
734.6 calories	46.2 g carbohydrates	59.7 g fat	7.2 g fiber
8.8 g protein			

¾ TB. olive oil	2 TB. toasted almonds
½ small Spanish or yellow onion	2 cups fresh basil leaves
½ TB. minced garlic	2 TB. minced garlic
1 cup uncooked quinoa, rinsed and drained	¼ cup pine nuts
2½ TB. diced roasted baby red beets	¾ cup extra-virgin olive oil
	¼ tsp. kosher salt
2 cups water	¼ tsp. ground black pepper
4 TB. fresh lemon juice	1 medium ripe avocado, pitted and diced
1 TB. chopped fresh chives	¼ cup ¼-inch-thick sliced zucchini, chopped
2 TB. golden raisins	

1. In a medium saucepan over medium heat, heat ½ tablespoon olive oil. Add onion and ½ tablespoon minced garlic, and sauté for 1½ minutes.

2. Add quinoa, red beets, water, 2 tablespoons lemon juice, chives, golden raisins, and almonds. Bring to a boil, cover, reduce heat to low, and cook for 15 to 20 minutes or until liquid is absorbed and quinoa is tender.

3. In a food processor fitted with a chopping blade or a blender, purée basil, remaining minced garlic, pine nuts, extra-virgin olive oil, kosher salt, black pepper, avocado, and remaining 2 tablespoons lemon juice until smooth. Set aside.

4. In a small saucepan over medium heat, heat remaining $\frac{1}{4}$ tablespoon olive oil. Add zucchini, and sauté for 20 seconds or until tender.

5. Add zucchini and 1 teaspoon avocado pesto to quinoa mixture, mix well, and serve. Freeze remaining avocado mixture for later use.

KEEN ON QUINOA

I first stumbled upon quinoa in the 1990s while looking for alternatives to rice and beans for the "progressive" eater. I was surprised to discover that [it] was not only part of the spinach family but highly appreciated for its nutritional value. In today's vegan and gluten-free societies, it's a natural choice for this dish because of its texture and nutrient composition.

—Senior Executive Chef Manfred Lassahn

Egg Fried Quinoa with Green Peas

A healthier spin on traditional Chinese egg fried rice, this quinoa version is packed full of flavor from green peas, corn, carrots, ground fennel, Chinese five-spice powder, and a little soy sauce.

Yield:	Prep time:	Cook time:	Serving size:
4 cups	12 minutes	25 minutes	1 cup

Each serving has:			
378.8 calories	43.2 g carbohydrates	17.5 g fat	6.1 g fiber
14.1 g protein			

3 TB. canola oil	1 tsp. sea salt
1 cup green peas	$\frac{1}{2}$ tsp. ground fennel
$\frac{1}{2}$ cup peeled and diced carrots	$\frac{1}{4}$ tsp. Chinese five-spice powder
$\frac{1}{2}$ cup fresh corn kernels or canned corn kernels, drained	3 large eggs
$\frac{1}{2}$ cup diced celery	2 TB. reduced-sodium soy sauce
4 cups Quick-and-Easy Quinoa (recipe in Chapter 1)	$\frac{1}{2}$ cup chopped scallions, white and green parts

1. In a large sauté pan over medium heat, heat canola oil. Add green peas, carrots, corn, and celery, and sauté, stirring, for about 2 minutes.

2. Add Quick-and-Easy Quinoa, sea salt, fennel, and Chinese five-spice powder, and sauté for another 1 or 2 minutes.

3. Crack eggs into a medium bowl, and whisk together until well combined. Add eggs to quinoa mixture, and using the edge of a metal spatula, *fold* eggs into quinoa mixture. Add soy sauce and scallions, and cook, stirring occasionally, for about 2 minutes. Serve.

DEFINITION

Usually called for when combining a lighter ingredient such as egg whites with a heavier ingredient such as melted chocolate, **folding** is the process of lifting the heavier ingredient and turning it into the lighter one repeatedly until well combined. Here, the heavier quinoa mixture is folded over the egg, and the process is repeated until the egg is cooked and mixed into the quinoa.

♔ Quinoa Veggie Burgers by Chef Chris Barnett

Ground chickpeas, pecans, and red quinoa get a spicy kick from sriracha hot sauce, citrusy lemon, and spices in this recipe by Chef Chris Barnett, executive chef, Sherbourne Restaurant (Los Angeles, CA).

Yield:	Prep time:	Cook time:	Serving size:
6 burgers	15 minutes	25 minutes	1 burger with bun

Each serving has:			
330.5 calories 9.2 g protein	40.9 g carbohydrates	15.7 g fat	5.6 g fiber

$\frac{1}{2}$ cup uncooked red quinoa, rinsed and drained

1 cup water

$1\frac{1}{2}$ tsp. sea salt

1 (16-oz.) can chickpeas, drained and rinsed

$\frac{1}{2}$ cup ground pecans

1 tsp. ground coriander

$\frac{1}{2}$ tsp. ground cumin

2 TB. sriracha hot sauce

1 TB. fresh lemon juice

2 TB. chopped fresh parsley leaves

2 TB. minced scallions

$\frac{1}{2}$ tsp. ground black pepper

2 TB. olive oil

6 whole-wheat hamburger buns, toasted

6 tomato slices

6 butter lettuce leaves

6 red onion slices

1. In a medium saucepan over medium-high heat, bring red quinoa, water, and 1 teaspoon sea salt to a boil. Cover and cook for about 15 minutes or until tender. Drain and set aside to cool.

2. Meanwhile, in a food processor fitted with a chopping blade or a blender, purée chickpeas until almost smooth.

3. In a large bowl, combine chickpea purée, pecans, coriander, cumin, sriracha hot sauce, lemon juice, parsley leaves, scallions, remaining $\frac{1}{2}$ teaspoon sea salt, and black pepper.

4. Form mixture into 6 burgers.

5. In a large sauté pan over medium-high heat, heat olive oil. Add burgers, and sauté for about $2\frac{1}{2}$ minutes per side or until brown.

6. Serve burgers on toasted whole-wheat buns with tomato slices, butter lettuce leaves, and red onion slices.

🍳 Quinoa Lentil Burgers

Chickpeas, lentils, and quinoa combine with carrots, celery, and cilantro for a delicious, high-protein, high-fiber burger by Chef Mark Ellman, executive chef of Honu (Maui, HI) and executive chef and owner of Mala (Wailea, HI).

Yield:	Prep time:	Cook time:	Serving size:
6 burgers	20 minutes	30 minutes	1 burger

Each serving has:			
1,027.4 calories	145.1 g carbohydrates	30.9 g fat	29.4 g fiber
46.6 g protein			

¼ cup ground cumin

⅛ cup ground coriander

1½ (14-oz.) cans chickpeas, rinsed and drained, chopped

7 cups cooked lentils

7 cups Quick-and-Easy Quinoa (recipe in Chapter 1)

2 cups chopped cooked carrots

1 cup chopped celery

8 large eggs

1 cup chopped fresh cilantro leaves

1 cup chopped fresh mint leaves

1 medium yellow onion, chopped

Fine lemon zest from 2 lemons

5 cups panko breadcrumbs

½ cup plus 2 TB. extra-virgin olive oil

⅛ cup sweet paprika

¼ cup fennel pollen

1. In a large heavy skillet over medium-low heat, combine cumin and coriander. Cook, shaking occasionally, for about 3 minutes or until lightly fragrant. Set aside.

2. In a large bowl, combine chickpeas, lentils, Quick-and-Easy Quinoa, carrots, celery, eggs, cilantro, mint, yellow onion, lemon zest, panko breadcrumbs, ½ cup extra-virgin olive oil, toasted cumin, toasted coriander, sweet paprika, and fennel pollen. Form mixture into 6 burgers.

3. In the skillet over medium heat, heat remaining 2 tablespoons extra-virgin olive oil. Add burgers, and sear for 1 or 2 minutes on each side or until crispy on both sides. Remove from the skillet and transfer to a platter.

4. Serve 1 patty per person on lettuce or over pasta.

KEEN ON QUINOA

I wanted to make something special for the health-conscious market. My daughter, Michelle, does not eat meat, so she was my inspiration. We also use quinoa with our Dore Fish at Honu, which has pomegranate and cumin in the recipe.

—Chef Mark Ellman

Lemon Herb Quinoa with Asparagus

Asparagus can have a slightly bitter flavor, but not in this recipe—tangy, crisp lemon brings a nice balance of flavor that's heightened by fresh thyme leaves.

Yield:	Prep time:	Cook time:	Serving size:
4 cups	10 minutes	25 minutes	1 cup

Each serving has:			
179.7 calories 6.8 g protein	32.5 g carbohydrates	2.9 g fat	3.7 g fiber

4 cups water	2 TB. chopped white onion
1¼ tsp. sea salt	1 tsp. fine lemon zest
3 medium spears asparagus, trimmed and cut into 1-in. pieces	1 tsp. fresh lemon juice
	2 tsp. chopped fresh thyme leaves
1 cup uncooked quinoa, rinsed and drained	1 tsp. ground black pepper

1. Fill a small bowl with ice, and add about 2 cups water or enough to cover ice. Set aside.

2. Fill a medium stockpot or saucepan ½ full of water. Set over high heat, add ¼ teaspoon sea salt, and bring to a boil. Add asparagus pieces, and when all asparagus is in, drain and quickly pour asparagus into ice bath. Set aside.

3. In a medium saucepan over high heat, combine quinoa, white onion, and remaining 2 cups water. Bring to a boil, cover, reduce heat to low, and simmer for 15 minutes or until almost all liquid has been absorbed.

4. Drain asparagus from ice bath, and pat dry with a paper towel or clean kitchen towel. Add asparagus, lemon zest, lemon juice, thyme leaves, remaining 1 teaspoon sea salt, and black pepper to quinoa mixture, stir well, and serve.

Eggplant Quinoa Parmesan

Richly flavored eggplant; tomato sauce; and Parmesan, ricotta, and mozzarella cheeses are the perfect match for quinoa. Dried oregano gives this recipe an Italian-style finish.

Yield:	Prep time:	Cook time:	Serving size:
1 (2-quart) casserole	20 minutes	45 minutes	1½cups

Each serving has:			
507.1 calories	44.8 g carbohydrates	27.4 g fat	6.3 g fiber
22.3 g protein			

2 TB. sea salt	½ cup olive oil
2 medium eggplants, cut into 16 round slices	2 cups tomato sauce
1 cup uncooked quinoa, rinsed and drained	2 cups part skim milk ricotta cheese
2 cups vegetable broth or water	1 cup shredded Parmesan cheese
1 cup corn flour	2 large eggs
1 tsp. ground black pepper	1 TB. dried oregano
	1 cup grated mozzarella cheese

1. Using sea salt, salt each eggplant slice, and place on a plate, stacking if necessary. Top slices with another plate, and place a weight on top. Let rest for about 15 minutes.

2. In a medium saucepan over high heat, combine quinoa and vegetable broth. Bring to a boil, cover, reduce heat to low, and simmer for 15 minutes or until almost all liquid has been absorbed. Remove from heat, and set aside, covered.

3. In a medium bowl, combine corn flour and black pepper. Dredge eggplant slices in flour mixture, and set aside.

4. In a large saucepan over medium-high heat, heat olive oil. When hot but not smoking, add eggplant, and fry for about 5 minutes total or until browned and lightly crisp. Transfer to a paper towel to drain.

5. Preheat the oven to 325°F. Lightly coat a 2-quart casserole dish with nonstick cooking spray.

6. Spread a thin layer of tomato sauce in the prepared casserole dish.

7. In a large bowl, combine ricotta cheese, $\frac{1}{2}$ cup Parmesan cheese, eggs, and oregano. Place 1 tablespoon egg-cheese mixture onto 1 slice eggplant, and roll eggplant slice into a log. Place seam side down in the prepared casserole dish. Repeat with remaining egg-cheese mixture and eggplant.

8. Spread remaining tomato sauce over top of eggplant logs. Sprinkle quinoa over eggplant. Top with remaining $\frac{1}{2}$ cup Parmesan cheese and mozzarella cheese. Bake for about 40 minutes. Let rest for about 5 minutes before serving.

Grilled Vegetables on Quinoa Muffins with Basil Aioli

Get that grilled flavor you love with red peppers, zucchini, and red onion over nutty quinoa, golden raisins, and brown sugar. Basil aioli tops off the wonderful flavors in this recipe.

Yield:	Prep time:	Cook time:	Serving size:
12 muffins plus 2 cups roasted vegetables	20 minutes	35 minutes	1 muffin plus 2 tablespoons roasted vegetables and 1 or 2 tablespoons aioli

Each serving has:			
377.7 calories 5.9 g protein	55.1 g carbohydrates	17.5 g fat	2.5 g fiber

2 cloves garlic

2 tsp. sea salt

2 tsp. ground black pepper

$\frac{1}{2}$ TB. fine lemon zest

$\frac{1}{2}$ TB. fresh lemon juice

$1\frac{1}{2}$ cups nonfat mayonnaise

2 cups fresh basil leaves, lightly packed

$\frac{1}{2}$ tsp. cayenne

2 cups all-purpose flour

$1\frac{1}{2}$ tsp. baking powder

$\frac{3}{4}$ cup brown sugar, firmly packed

$\frac{1}{4}$ cup canola oil

$\frac{3}{4}$ cup 2 percent milk

1 large egg

1 tsp. pure vanilla extract

4 cups Quick-and-Easy Quinoa (recipe in Chapter 1)

$\frac{1}{2}$ cup golden raisins

1 TB. olive oil

1 large red bell pepper, ribs and seeds removed, sliced lengthwise

1 medium zucchini, sliced into strips

1 medium red onion, thinly sliced

1. In a food processor fitted with a chopping blade or a blender, purée garlic, 1 teaspoon sea salt, black pepper, lemon zest, lemon juice, nonfat mayonnaise, basil, and cayenne on high until completely blended. Transfer to a bowl, cover with plastic wrap, and refrigerate until ready to use.

2. Preheat the oven to 350°F. Lightly coat a 12-cup muffin pan with nonstick cooking spray, or line with cupcake liners.

3. In a medium bowl, stir together all-purpose flour, baking powder, and remaining 1 teaspoon sea salt.

4. In a separate medium bowl, whisk together brown sugar, canola oil, 2 percent milk, egg, and vanilla extract. Stir brown sugar mixture into flour mixture until combined.

5. Add Quick-and-Easy Quinoa and golden raisins, and stir until just coming together. Using a large tablespoon, spoon equal amounts of quinoa mixture into muffin cups. Bake for about 25 minutes or until a toothpick inserted comes out clean. Remove from the oven, and cool for about 5 minutes.

6. Meanwhile, in a heavy skillet or grill pan over medium heat, heat olive oil. Add red bell pepper, zucchini, and red onion, and cook for 5 to 7 minutes or until vegetables are tender and have a lightly grilled color.

7. To serve, slice muffins in $\frac{1}{2}$ crosswise and top with 1 or 2 tablespoons grilled vegetables followed by 1 or 2 tablespoons basil aioli.

Quinoa Tamale Casserole with Golden Raisins

Garlic, lime, oregano, golden raisins, and quinoa—along with a green chile tomato sauce with fresh cilantro topping—make this a tamale to remember.

Yield:	Prep time:	Cook time:	Serving size:
1 (9×5-inch) loaf	20 minutes	60 minutes	$\frac{1}{10}$ loaf

Each serving has:			
237.8 calories	28.3 g carbohydrates	9.7 g fat	3.1 g fiber
10.2 g protein			

1 TB. olive oil	1 tsp. ground black pepper
1 large white onion, chopped	2 cups uncooked quinoa, rinsed and drained
1 garlic clove, chopped	4 cups plus 3 TB. water
3 (3.5-oz.) cans diced green chiles, with liquid	$\frac{1}{2}$ tsp. baking powder
1 cup tomato juice	$1\frac{1}{2}$ cups grated Monterey Jack cheese
2 TB. tomato paste	$\frac{1}{2}$ cup golden raisins
3 tsp. sea salt	1 TB. chili powder
1 TB. chopped fresh oregano leaves	$\frac{3}{4}$ cup chopped fresh cilantro leaves
2 TB. fresh lime juice	

1. In a sauté pan over medium heat, heat olive oil. Add white onion and garlic, and sauté for about 1 or 2 minutes or until fragrant and tender.

2. Add onion and garlic to a food processor fitted with a chopping blade, followed by green chiles, tomato juice, tomato paste, 2 teaspoons sea salt, oregano leaves, lime juice, and ground black pepper. Purée until nearly smooth.

3. Meanwhile, in a large saucepan over medium-high heat, combine quinoa and 4 cups water. Bring to a boil, cover, reduce heat to low, and simmer for 15 minutes or until almost all liquid is absorbed. Remove from heat, and set aside.

4. Preheat the oven to 400°F. Lightly coat a 9×5-inch loaf pan with nonstick cooking spray.

5. In a large bowl, combine quinoa and baking powder, adding remaining 3 table-spoons water if mixture is overly dry.

6. Spread $\frac{1}{2}$ of quinoa mixture into the prepared loaf pan. Top evenly with 1 cup Monterey Jack cheese, golden raisins, and chili powder. Add remaining quinoa, and press evenly to seal loaf. Cover the pan with aluminum foil, and bake for about 30 minutes. Uncover and bake an additional 30 minutes.

7. Remove loaf from the oven, and let rest about for 10 minutes. Turn tamale out onto a platter, top with remaining $\frac{1}{2}$ cup Monterey Jack cheese and cilantro, cut into slices, and serve with green chile tomato sauce.

KEEN ON QUINOA

To make this dish vegan, opt for soy, rice, or almond cheese instead, substituting equal parts nondairy cheese for the real thing. These cheeses and other delicious options are available in the organic specialty section of your grocery store or online (see Appendix B).

Perfect Poultry Entrées

In This Chapter

- Quinoa and poultry dishes everyone will love
- Easy baked quinoa casseroles
- Quinoa curries, stir-fries, risottos, and more

Chicken has a delicious flavor that goes with practically everything. Barbecued chicken, chicken with lemon and herbs, baked chicken, broiled chicken—you get the idea.

Chicken and other poultry pair well with quinoa. Plus, the two taste great with pretty much anything else you pair them with, as you'll see by the recipes in this chapter.

Chicken Cooking Tips

Because of its dense texture, chicken can take a while to cook and must be cooked all the way through to be safe to eat. When stovetop grilling or pan frying, it's best to sear the chicken until golden on the outside and finish cooking the chicken in the oven. For a 4- to 6-ounce chicken breast, sear the outside for about 4 minutes per side, transfer chicken to a baking sheet or an ovenproof skillet, and bake for about 20 minutes or until cooked through.

For stuffed poultry, stuff first and then bake until cooked through.

For fried chicken, fry until the skin is crisp, and transfer to the oven to finish cooking. The chicken will still be moist, tender, and flavorful and have the grilled look you love, but it won't burn from excess time on the stovetop or grill.

Herb-Baked Chicken Quinoa Casserole

Crimini mushrooms, fresh thyme, and fresh dill enhance the flavors of traditional chicken and mushroom soup in this delicious chicken quinoa casserole.

Yield:	Prep time:	Cook time:	Serving size:
1 (9×13-inch) casserole	20 minutes	90 minutes	1 cup

Each serving has:			
336.1 calories 31.8 g protein	25.5 g carbohydrates	11.3 g fat	1.8 g fiber

2 cups low-fat milk

1 cup uncooked quinoa, rinsed and drained

1 (10.75-oz.) can cream of chicken soup

1 (10.75-oz.) can cream of mushroom soup

2 tsp. chicken bouillon powder

1 tsp. ground black pepper

1 tsp. ground mustard

$\frac{1}{2}$ TB. fine lemon zest

$\frac{1}{2}$ TB. chopped fresh thyme leaves

2 tsp. chopped fresh dill

$\frac{1}{2}$ cup chopped white onion

1 cup sliced fresh crimini mushrooms

4 (6-oz.) boneless, skinless chicken breasts, cut into 1-in.-thick slices

1 cup grated Parmesan cheese

1. Preheat the oven to 350°F. Lightly coat a 9×13-inch casserole dish with nonstick cooking spray.

2. In a large bowl, whisk together low-fat milk, quinoa, cream of chicken soup, cream of mushroom soup, chicken bouillon powder, black pepper, ground mustard, lemon zest, thyme, and dill. Pour quinoa mixture into the prepared casserole dish.

3. Evenly distribute white onion, crimini mushrooms, and chicken slices atop quinoa mixture, stirring with a wooden spoon if necessary to incorporate. Cover with aluminum foil, and bake for 90 minutes, stirring every 30 minutes.

4. Remove aluminum foil, top with Parmesan cheese, and bake for 10 more minutes.

Variation: For **Herb-Baked Chicken Quinoa Casserole with Broccoli and Pine Nuts,** add 1 cup chopped fresh broccoli florets and $\frac{1}{2}$ cup toasted pine nuts with the onion and chicken.

Barbeque Chicken Quinoa Casserole

Homemade barbecue sauce, chicken, quinoa, fresh green bell pepper, corn, onion, fresh cilantro, and white cheddar cheese—that's all it takes.

Yield:	Prep time:	Cook time:	Serving size:
1 chicken plus 4 cups quinoa mixture	25 minutes	65 minutes	1 piece chicken with $\frac{1}{2}$ cup quinoa mixture

Each serving has:			
336.5 calories 15.1 g protein	52.5 g carbohydrates	7.8 g fat	3.5 g fiber

1 cup ketchup	2 TB. canola oil
$\frac{1}{2}$ cup water	1 cup chopped fresh white onion
4 tsp. curry powder	1 cup chopped fresh green bell pepper
3 TB. brown sugar, firmly packed	2 cups kernel corn, fresh or frozen
3 TB. Worcestershire sauce	4 cups Quick-and-Easy Quinoa (recipe in Chapter 1)
$\frac{1}{2}$ tsp. cayenne	
1 cup all-purpose flour	1 cup grated white cheddar cheese
$\frac{1}{2}$ tsp. sea salt	$\frac{1}{2}$ cup chopped fresh cilantro leaves
$\frac{1}{2}$ tsp. ground black pepper	
1 (4-lb.) whole chicken, cut into pieces	

1. Preheat the oven to 350°F. Lightly coat a 9×13-inch casserole dish with nonstick cooking spray.

2. In a small bowl, whisk together ketchup, water, curry powder, brown sugar, Worcestershire sauce, and cayenne. Set aside.

3. In a large zipper-lock plastic bag, shake together all-purpose flour, sea salt, and black pepper. Working in batches, add chicken pieces to bag, seal the bag, and toss chicken to coat.

4. In a large cast-iron skillet over medium-high heat, heat canola oil. Add chicken, and brown on both sides. Transfer chicken to the prepared baking dish, and top with ketchup mixture, cheddar cheese, and cilantro.

5. Return the skillet, with drippings, to medium heat. Add white onion, green bell pepper, and corn, and sauté for about 3 minutes or until just tender.

6. Stir in Quick-and-Easy Quinoa. Spoon mixture over chicken, gently pushing quinoa mixture all around chicken and lightly mixing quinoa mixture into sauce. Cover with aluminum foil, and bake for about 50 minutes or until chicken is cooked through.

7. Remove aluminum foil, and bake for 5 more minutes. Remove from the oven, and let rest for about 5 minutes before serving.

Grilled Chicken with Sweet Quinoa Relish

The sweetness in this recipe doesn't come from sugar but from fresh mango, red bell pepper, and tomato. Balancing out the chicken and quinoa flavors are tangy cider vinegar and citrus zest and juices.

Yield:	Prep time:	Cook time:	Serving size:
4 chicken breasts with quinoa relish	15 minutes	25 minutes with	1 chicken breast 1 cup quinoa relish
Each serving has:			
534.8 calories 34.7 g protein	43.6 g carbohydrates	25.1 g fat	5.0 g fiber

1 cup uncooked quinoa, rinsed and drained

2 cups vegetable broth

2 medium Roma tomatoes, seeded and diced

1 medium mango, diced

1 medium red bell pepper, ribs and seeds removed, and diced

3 green onions, white and green parts, chopped

1 clove garlic, chopped

$\frac{1}{2}$ TB. fine lemon zest

$\frac{1}{4}$ cup chopped fresh cilantro leaves

1 TB. apple cider vinegar

1 TB. fresh lime juice

1 TB. fresh lemon juice

$\frac{1}{4}$ cup plus 2 TB. olive oil

4 (4- or 5-oz.) boneless, skinless chicken breasts

$\frac{1}{2}$ tsp. sea salt

$\frac{1}{2}$ tsp. ground black pepper

1. In a medium saucepan over medium-high heat, combine quinoa and vegetable broth. Bring to a boil, cover, reduce heat to low, and simmer for 15 minutes or until almost all liquid has been absorbed.

2. Meanwhile, in a large bowl, toss together Roma tomatoes, mango, red bell pepper, green onions, garlic, lemon zest, and cilantro leaves.

3. In a small bowl, whisk together apple cider vinegar, lime juice, and lemon juice. Whisk in $\frac{1}{4}$ cup olive oil, and set aside.

4. Coat chicken with sea salt and black pepper.

5. In a heavy skillet or sauté pan over medium heat, heat remaining 2 tablespoons olive oil. Add chicken, cook for about 6 minutes, turn, and cook for 6 more minutes. Continue cooking for about 8 more minutes or until chicken is cooked through (about 20 minutes total).

6. Add cooked quinoa to tomato mixture, and toss well to combine. Drizzle olive oil mixture over tomato-quinoa mixture, and toss to coat.

7. To serve, place 1 chicken breast on a serving plate and top with 1 cup quinoa relish.

KEEN ON QUINOA

Acidic ingredients like lime juice, lemon juice, and apple cider vinegar help break down proteins and fat in the body, giving your metabolism a boost.

Quinoa Cornish Hens with Lemon

Cornish hens are essentially little chickens and make the perfect individual dinner. In this recipe, the hens are stuffed with a mixture of quinoa, onion, red bell pepper, rosemary, and lemon.

Yield:	Prep time:	Cook time:	Serving size:
2 stuffed Cornish hens	20 minutes	35 minutes	1 stuffed Cornish hen

Each serving has:			
659.6 calories 59.4 g protein	60.1 g carbohydrates	19.8 g fat	7.9 g fiber

¾ cup uncooked quinoa, rinsed and drained

1½ cups chicken broth

1 medium lemon

1 TB. olive oil

1 medium white onion, chopped

1 clove garlic, minced

1 medium red bell pepper, ribs and seeds removed, and chopped

¼ cup chopped fresh rosemary leaves

2 Cornish hens

1 tsp. sea salt

1 tsp. ground black pepper

½ cup water

1. Preheat the oven to 425°F.

2. In a medium saucepan over medium-high heat, combine quinoa and chicken broth. Bring to a boil, cover, reduce heat to low, and simmer for about 15 minutes or until almost all liquid has been absorbed.

3. Finely zest lemon, and place zest in a small bowl. Slice lemon into 4 or 5 slices.

4. In a separate medium saucepan over medium heat, heat olive oil. Add white onion and garlic, and sauté for about 1 minute. Remove from heat.

6. Add red bell pepper, lemon zest, and rosemary, and stir onion mixture into cooked quinoa.

7. Place Cornish hens on a flat work surface. Divide quinoa mixture in half and stuff each hen as much as possible, allowing stuffing to come out the front of the hen if overflowing. Place stuffed hens in a small roasting pan, and sprinkle with sea salt and black pepper. Arrange lemon slices around hens, and pour in water. Bake for 25 minutes or until juices run clear and temperature of hens reaches 165°F.

8. Let hens rest for about 5 minutes before serving 1 hen per person or sliced in half down the middle for 4 smaller servings.

≈⌒

Quinoa Indian Chicken Curry

Curry powder, fennel, cumin, green peas, cauliflower, and cashews taste wonderful with chicken and quinoa in this delicious and fiber-filled recipe sure to please.

Yield:	Prep time:	Cook time:	Serving size:
5 cups	20 minutes	35 minutes	1¼ cups

Each serving has:			
588.9 calories	57.6 g carbohydrates	28.7 g fat	9.5 g fiber
29.9 g protein			

1 cup uncooked quinoa, rinsed and drained	½ tsp. ground cumin
4 cups vegetable or chicken broth	1 tsp. celery seed
5 or 6 chicken tenders, chopped into 1-in. pieces	½ tsp. fennel seed
4 TB. olive oil	½ tsp. turmeric
6 tsp. curry powder	⅓ cup plain low-fat yogurt
1 cup chopped yellow onion	⅓ cup nonfat sour cream
2 TB. minced garlic	½ cup cashew halves
1 cup frozen peas	¼ cup chopped fresh cilantro leaves
1 medium head cauliflower, chopped into 1-in. pieces	½ tsp. sea salt
	½ tsp. ground black pepper

1. In a medium saucepan over medium heat, combine quinoa and 2 cups vegetable broth. Bring to a boil, cover, reduce heat to low, and simmer for 15 minutes or until almost all liquid has been absorbed.

2. Meanwhile, in a medium bowl, coat chicken tenders with 1 tablespoon olive oil and 2 teaspoons curry powder.

3. In a large saucepan over medium heat, heat 1 tablespoon olive oil. Add chicken tenders, and cook for about 7 minutes or until just done. Transfer chicken to a bowl, and set aside.

4. In the same large saucepan over medium heat, heat remaining 2 tablespoons olive oil. Add yellow onion and garlic, and sauté, stirring, for about 1 minute.

5. Add peas, cauliflower, cumin, celery seed, fennel seed, turmeric, remaining 4 teaspoons curry powder, and remaining 2 cups vegetable broth. Cover and cook, stirring occasionally, for about 5 minutes.

6. Stir in low-fat yogurt and nonfat sour cream until well combined. Remove from heat, and stir in quinoa, cashew halves, cilantro, sea salt, and black pepper. Serve warm.

KEEN ON QUINOA

Curry powder, the essence of Indian cuisine, is a blend of ground spices. A little goes a long way, both in flavor and health benefits. Curry may help reduce inflammation and can help protect against some cancers.

Turkey Quinoa Picadillo

In this Latin American–inspired dish usually served with rice, you get double the protein and flavor with quinoa. Ginger, serrano pepper, chili powder, lime, red bell pepper, and golden currants lend flavor to lean ground turkey.

Yield:	Prep time:	Cook time:	Serving size:
6 cups	15 minutes	28 minutes	1 cup

Each serving has:			
286.7 calories	31.4 g carbohydrates	9.8 g fat	3.4 g fiber
20.0 g protein			

1 cup uncooked quinoa, rinsed and drained

2 cups vegetable or chicken broth

1 TB. olive oil

1 cup chopped white onion

1 TB. minced garlic

1 TB. peeled and minced fresh ginger

2 small serrano peppers, minced

1 lb. lean ground turkey

2 tsp. chili powder

1 medium red bell pepper, ribs and seeds removed, and diced

1 (15-oz.) can diced tomatoes, with juice

$\frac{1}{2}$ cup water

$\frac{1}{4}$ cup firmly packed golden currants

$\frac{1}{4}$ cup chopped fresh cilantro leaves

1. In a medium stockpot over medium heat, combine quinoa and vegetable broth. Bring to a boil, cover, reduce heat to low, and simmer for 15 minutes or until almost all liquid has been absorbed. Remove from heat, and set aside.

2. In a large saucepan over medium heat, heat olive oil. Add white onion, garlic, ginger, and serrano peppers, and sauté for about 1 minute.

3. Add ground turkey, and cook, using a wooden spoon to break up chunks, for 7 to 10 minutes or until turkey is lightly browned and cooked through.

4. Reduce heat to low, and stir in chili powder, red bell pepper, diced tomatoes, water, and lime juice. Sauté for about 10 minutes.

5. Stir in golden currants, and simmer for 1 more minute.

6. Stir in quinoa and fresh cilantro, and serve.

Turkey with Quinoa Wild Mushroom Risotto

This quinoa risotto gets its creamy texture and rich flavor from milk and sour cream, earthy mushrooms, shallots, and fresh parsley, all served over turkey.

Yield:	Prep time:	Cook time:	Serving size:
8 turkey cutlets plus 8 cups risotto	15 minutes	35 minutes	1 turkey cutlet plus 1 cup risotto

Each serving has:			
496.3 calories 33.4 g protein	49.4 g carbohydrates	18.1 g fat	4.6 g fiber

8 (5-oz.) turkey cutlets

5 TB. olive oil

2 tsp. sea salt

2 tsp. ground black pepper

3 medium shallots, peeled and diced

1 TB. chopped garlic

$\frac{1}{4}$ cup sauvignon blanc

2$\frac{1}{2}$ cups uncooked quinoa, rinsed and drained

4 cups vegetable broth

$\frac{1}{2}$ cup chopped shiitake mushrooms

$\frac{1}{2}$ cup chopped porcini mushrooms

$\frac{1}{2}$ cup chopped crimini mushrooms

$\frac{1}{4}$ cup nonfat milk

1 cup nonfat sour cream

1 TB. fine lemon zest

$\frac{1}{4}$ cup plus 2 TB. chopped fresh Italian flat-leaf parsley leaves

$\frac{1}{2}$ cup grated Parmesan cheese

1. Coat turkey cutlets with 2 tablespoons olive oil, and season with 1 teaspoon sea salt and 1 teaspoon black pepper.

2. In a large stockpot over medium heat, stir together 2 tablespoons olive oil, shallots, and garlic for about 3 minutes.

3. Stir in sauvignon blanc and quinoa. Add vegetable broth, shiitake mushrooms, porcini mushrooms, and crimini mushrooms. Cover, reduce heat to low, and simmer for about 15 minutes.

4. Meanwhile, in a grill pan over medium heat, heat remaining 1 tablespoon olive oil. Add turkey cutlets, and cook for about 5 minutes per side or until cooked through.

5. Uncover, and stir in nonfat milk, nonfat sour cream, lemon zest, remaining 1 teaspoon sea salt, and remaining 1 teaspoon black pepper until combined and mixture has thickened slightly, about 1 minute.

6. Stir in Italian flat-leaf parsley and Parmesan cheese until combined and cheese has melted.

7. To serve, place 1 grilled turkey cutlet on each serving plate and top with 1 cup quinoa risotto.

Meaty Main Dishes

In This Chapter

- Can red meat be healthy for you?
- A lot of fiber goes a long way
- Hearty, quinoa-based dinners

If meat's your thing, this chapter is for you! You'll love these hearty recipes with a healthy quinoa twist.

Pros and Cons of Eating Beef, Pork, and Lamb

Often the only news we hear about eating beef, pork, and lamb is negative. Yet despite all the bad press, these red meats do have their benefits.

Red meats are naturally higher in iron and zinc, both of which are needed for a healthy immune system and energy. Lean red meats like filet mignon, boneless trimmed pork chops, and lamb chops are filled with vitamins and minerals, including B vitamins, potassium, selenium, magnesium, and other vital nutrients. And consuming proper portions of leaner red meats (about a 4- or 5-ounce serving) is proven to aid in weight loss.

That said, high consumption of red meat (on average 2 or more servings per week) can lead to higher risk of osteoporosis, heart disease, cancer, high cholesterol, and an increased chance of diseases like Alzheimer's. Most of the increased risks from eating red meat are likely due to overconsumption. Remember, everything in moderation.

Why Quinoa Is an Important Part of Meat Dishes

It's true that meats like beef and pork have tons of protein, and quinoa is a great source of protein as well. Adding quinoa to already protein-rich dishes might not seem relevant, but in the recipes in this chapter, it's not about the protein quinoa adds. It's about fiber.

Your body doesn't absorb fiber, so fiber essentially acts like a sweeper, flushing out fat and toxins from your body, and helps break down proteins in foods, making it easier for your body to digest them. Fiber also helps reduce your risk of heart disease, cancers, diabetes, and ulcers and has a host of other positive effects on the body.

Beef and Quinoa Stuffed Artichokes

Here, quinoa and beef are mixed with garlic, cilantro, spices, and tomatoes and spooned into fresh artichoke bottoms.

Yield:	Prep time:	Cook time:	Serving size:
8 stuffed artichoke bottoms	20 minutes	65 minutes	2 stuffed artichoke bottoms
Each serving has:			
319.8 calories 16.1 g protein	20.6 g carbohydrates	20.2 g fat	4.0 g fiber

8 large fresh artichoke bottoms

8 slices lemon

2 TB. olive oil

½ cup chopped white onion

1 TB. minced garlic

¾ cup lean ground beef

¼ tsp. paprika

¼ tsp. ground cumin

¼ tsp. ground ginger

¼ tsp. sea salt

¼ tsp. ground black pepper

⅛ tsp. ground turmeric

1½ cups diced tomatoes, canned or fresh

¼ cup golden raisins

½ cup Quick-and-Easy Quinoa (recipe in Chapter 1)

¼ cup chopped fresh cilantro leaves

½ cup water

½ cup grated Parmesan cheese

1. Preheat the oven to 350°F.

2. Using a melon baller, remove chokes and small leaves from center of artichoke bottoms. Rub each artichoke bottom with a slice of lemon, and place in a bowl of water.

3. In a large saucepan over medium heat, heat olive oil. Add white onion and garlic, and sauté for 1 minute.

4. Add ground beef, and cook for about 5 minutes or until browned. Drain beef without removing from the pan. Return to heat. Add paprika, cumin, ginger, sea salt, black pepper, turmeric, tomatoes, and golden raisins, and simmer for about 5 minutes to allow flavors to blend. Remove from heat and stir in Quick-and-Easy Quinoa and cilantro.

5. Drain artichoke bottoms and pat dry. Spoon equal amounts of quinoa mixture into artichoke bottoms, and place in a Dutch oven or casserole dish with a lid. Pour in water, and bake for 45 minutes.

6. Remove from the oven, top artichokes with Parmesan cheese, and bake for 10 more minutes or until cheese is melted. Serve 2 hot artichokes per person.

QUICK FIX

Artichoke bottoms are the fleshy base of the artichoke. They're as tasty as the artichoke hearts and are the perfect base for dishes like this one, which can be served as an entrée or single-serving appetizer.

Beef with Smothered Peppers, Onions, and Quinoa

Top round steak, green and red bell peppers, onions, pepper, cayenne, parsley, green onion, oregano, and thyme are served over cooked quinoa in this protein lover's dream.

Yield:	Prep time:	Cook time:	Serving size:
6 cups steak, peppers, and onions	15 minutes	60 minutes	1 cups steak, peppers, and onions

Each serving has:			
558.5 calories 59.3 g protein	35.8 g carbohydrates	19.0 g fat	3.4 g fiber

2 TB. paprika

1 small red chile pepper, minced

1 tsp. sea salt

2 TB. garlic powder

1 tsp. ground black pepper

1 TB. onion powder

½ TB. cayenne

½ TB. dried oregano

½ TB. dried thyme

2 TB. all-purpose flour

1 (2-lb.) top round steak, sliced into ¼-in.-thick strips

2 TB. olive oil

4 cups chicken broth

2 medium yellow onions, thinly sliced

2 medium red bell peppers, ribs and seeds removed, sliced

2 medium green bell peppers, ribs and seeds removed, sliced

¼ cup chopped fresh Italian flat-leaf parsley leaves

4 cups Quick-and-Easy Quinoa (recipe in Chapter 1)

1. In a medium bowl, combine paprika, red chile pepper, sea salt, garlic powder, black pepper, onion powder, cayenne, oregano, thyme, and all-purpose flour. Add beef strips, and toss to coat.

2. In a large skillet or saucepan over medium heat, heat olive oil. Add coated beef strips, and cook, turning as needed to brown all sides, for about 5 minutes.

3. Stir in 2 cups chicken broth, onions, red bell peppers, and green bell peppers. Reduce heat to medium-low, cover, and cook for about 15 minutes.

4. Add remaining 2 cups chicken broth, cover, and cook for 15 more minutes.

5. Uncover, reduce heat to low, and simmer for 25 to 30 more minutes.

6. Remove from heat and stir in parsley. Serve over Quick-and-Easy Quinoa.

Beef Quinoa Tamales

Tamales are easier to make than it seems. (Don't get discouraged by the long cooking time and use of corn husks.) Their great flavor comes from beef spiced with cumin, oregano, and crushed red pepper wrapped in a *masa harina* and quinoa flour tamale.

Yield:	Prep time:	Cook time:	Serving size:
36 tamales	1 hour	6 hours	2 tamales
Each serving has:			
548.0 calories	43.9 g carbohydrates	26.2 g fat	4.3 g fiber
34.9 g protein			

4 lb. boneless chuck roast	2 TB. ancho chile powder
4 cloves garlic, roughly chopped	2 tsp. chopped fresh oregano leaves
1 large yellow onion, sliced into 8 pieces	1 tsp. crushed red pepper flakes
7 cups water, plus more if needed	1 tsp. apple cider vinegar
3 (8-oz.) pkg. dried corn husks	1 tsp. plus 1 TB. sea salt
2 TB. canola oil	¼ cup coconut oil
2 TB. all-purpose flour	2 tsp. baking powder
1 cup beef broth	3 cups quinoa flour
1 tsp. ground cumin	6 cups masa harina

1. In a large stockpot over medium-high heat, combine chuck roast, garlic, and yellow onion. Cover with water. Bring to a boil, cover, reduce heat to low, and simmer for about 3½ hours or until beef is tender. (Test tenderness by shredding a small portion with a fork.) Remove beef from pot, reserve cooking liquid, and shred beef with a fork.

2. Meanwhile, in a large bowl, soak corn husks in water, weighting down husks with a plate or other heavy item if necessary, for 3 hours or until husks are soft and pliable.

3. In a large sauté pan over medium heat, heat canola oil. Stir in all-purpose flour until lightly browned. Stir in beef broth until smooth. Stir in cumin, ancho chile powder, oregano, crushed red pepper flakes, apple cider vinegar, and 1 teaspoon sea salt. Add shredded beef, reduce heat to low, cover, and simmer for about 45 minutes.

4. In a large bowl, and using a hand mixer on low speed, beat coconut oil, baking powder, quinoa flour, and masa harina until well combined. Slowly add reserved cooking liquid, ¼ cup at a time, until mixture forms a soft dough (about 5 cups total).

5. Drain corn husks, and flatten out each husk on a flat work surface. Spread about 2 tablespoons quinoa flour mixture onto ⅔ of each husk. Spread about 1 tablespoon beef mixture down middle of quinoa flour mixture. Starting at one end of long side of husk, roll husk and secure with butcher's twine.

6. Place tamales in a steamer basket, add about 1½ inches water to the bottom of the steamer, and season with remaining 1 tablespoon sea salt. Steam over boiling water for about 1 hour, adding liquid as needed during the cooking process. Serve immediately, alone or with green chile sauce or your favorite sauce.

DEFINITION

Masa harina is a coarse flour made from ground corn. It is used in many recipes traditional to Mexico, Central America, and South America. It is easy to form a dough using masa harina and water, as in this recipe, which also uses quinoa flour.

Skillet-Baked Quinoa-Crusted Pork Chops

Flavorful Italian breadcrumbs and quinoa provide a crisp, delicious flavor to these pork chops that get a flavor boost from cayenne and lemon pepper.

Yield:	Prep time:	Cook time:	Serving size:
4 pork chops	10 minutes	15 minutes	1 pork chop

Each serving has:			
658.8 calories	25.6 g carbohydrates	35.3 g fat	2.4 g fiber
56.4 g protein			

1 batch Quick-and-Easy Quinoa (recipe in Chapter 1)	$\frac{1}{2}$ tsp. sea salt
	2 large eggs
$\frac{1}{4}$ cup Italian seasoned breadcrumbs	$\frac{1}{4}$ cup low-fat milk
$\frac{1}{2}$ tsp. cayenne	2 TB. olive oil
1 tsp. lemon pepper	4 (6-oz.) bone-in pork chops

1. Preheat the oven to 375°F.

2. In a medium bowl, combine Quick-and-Easy Quinoa, Italian breadcrumbs, cayenne, lemon pepper, and sea salt.

3. In a small bowl, whisk together eggs and low-fat milk.

4. In a heavy cast-iron or other ovenproof skillet over medium heat, heat olive oil.

5. Working quickly, dredge each pork chop in egg mixture and then in quinoa mixture, and place in the skillet. Sear for about 2 or 3 minutes per side.

6. Transfer the skillet to the oven and bake for about 3 minutes, depending on thickness of pork chop, or until done. Serve hot.

Variation: For a leaner and lighter recipe, substitute lean chicken breasts for the pork chops. This saves more than 200 calories per serving and more than 50 percent of the fat.

Beef and Pork Quinoa Meatballs

These protein-packed meatballs get their flavor from fresh basil and cilantro, onion, Worcestershire sauce, a hint of lemon zest, and quinoa, combined with lean beef and pork sausage.

Yield:	Prep time:	Cook time:	Serving size:
24 meatballs	25 minutes	18 minutes	3 meatballs

Each serving has:			
362.3 calories	14.9 g carbohydrates	25.6 g fat	2.5 g fiber
16.9 g protein			

¾ lb. lean ground beef

¾ lb. ground pork sausage, mild or medium-hot

1 cup Quick-and-Easy Quinoa (recipe in Chapter 1)

¼ cup finely chopped white onion

1 TB. minced fresh garlic

1 TB. Worcestershire sauce

½ TB. ground mustard

1 tsp. fine lemon zest

2 TB. finely chopped basil leaves

2 TB. finely chopped cilantro leaves

1 tsp. sea salt

1 tsp. ground black pepper

1 large egg

1 (32-oz.) jar marinara sauce

1. Preheat the oven to 450°F. Line a baking sheet with parchment paper.

2. In a large bowl, combine ground beef, ground pork sausage, Quick-and-Easy Quinoa, white onion, garlic, Worcestershire sauce, mustard, lemon zest, basil, cilantro, sea salt, black pepper, and egg.

3. Shape mixture into 24 (1½- to 2-inch) balls and place on the prepared baking sheet. Bake for 15 to 18 minutes or until meatballs are cooked through.

4. Meanwhile, in a medium saucepan over medium heat, heat marinara sauce. Add cooked meatballs, and stir to coat. Transfer to serving plates and enjoy alone or over cooked pasta.

Variation: For a healthier, high-fiber and high-protein option, serve the cooked meatballs over cooked quinoa in place of pasta.

🍳 Pork Chops with a Twist

Breaded pork chops are dipped in lime juice, seasoned, and baked with quinoa until tender in this recipe by Denice Fladeboe, executive producer of *Bikini Lifestyles*.

Yield:	Prep time:	Cook time:	Serving size:
6 pork chops with quinoa	15 minutes	1 hour	1 pork chop with ½ cup quinoa

Each serving has:			
638.1 calories 68.4 g protein	25.8 g carbohydrates	27.3 g fat	2.4 g fiber

1 TB. fresh lime juice	½ cup chopped green bell pepper
2 TB. olive oil	1 clove garlic, minced
3 TB. all-purpose flour	1 cup uncooked quinoa, rinsed and drained
2½ tsp. sea salt	
¼ tsp. ground black pepper	1 (2.5-oz.) jar chopped pimentos, with liquid
¼ tsp. ground allspice	
6 (¾-in.-thick) boneless pork chops	2 cups chicken broth
1 medium white onion, chopped	1 medium lime

1. Preheat the oven to 350°F.

2. Place lime juice in a wide, shallow bowl.

3. In a heavy skillet over medium-high heat, heat olive oil.

4. In a medium bowl, combine all-purpose flour, 1½ teaspoons salt, black pepper, and allspice.

5. Dip pork chops in lime juice, and dredge in flour mixture. Add pork chops to the skillet, and brown for about 2 minutes per side. Remove pork chops from the skillet, and set aside.

6. Add white onion, green bell pepper, and garlic to the skillet, reduce heat to medium, and sauté for about 3 minutes.

7. Add quinoa, pimentos, and remaining 1 teaspoon salt, and stir in chicken broth.

8. Pour quinoa mixture with broth into a 9×13-inch baking dish. Place browned pork chops on top of quinoa mixture, cover tightly with aluminum foil, and bake for 1 hour or until pork chops are tender.

9. Meanwhile, slice lime crosswise into 6 slices, and cut a slit to the center of each slice. Twist slices, and place 1 on top of each pork chop before serving hot.

KEEN ON QUINOA

Cooking easy, flavorful meals for my family has always been at the top of my list, and incorporating quinoa with traditional Italian breadcrumbs is a great way to sneak in extra nutrients. My family loves the flavor without realizing how healthy these pork chops really are.

—Denice Fladeboe

Herb-Crusted Pork Tenderloin with Lemon Quinoa

Fresh rosemary, thyme, and parsley coat tender pork served over quinoa cooked with vermicelli noodles and lemon.

Yield:	Prep time:	Cook time:	Serving size:
About 2 pounds pork tenderloin	20 minutes	65 minutes	1 slice pork tenderloin (about 4 ounces) plus 1 cup quinoa

Each serving has:			
546.5 calories 46.9 g protein	23.1 g carbohydrates	25.1 g fat	5.6 g fiber

1 TB. ground black pepper

½ TB. sea salt

1 TB. chopped fresh Italian flat-leaf parsley leaves

1 TB. chopped fresh rosemary leaves

1 TB. chopped fresh thyme leaves

1 tsp. minced garlic

2½ lb. pork tenderloin

1 stick unsalted butter (8 TB.)

1 cup uncooked red quinoa, rinsed and drained

1 cup vermicelli noodles, crushed

2 cups chicken broth

1 cup vermouth

1. Preheat the oven to 350°F.

2. In a medium bowl, combine ground black pepper, sea salt, Italian flat-leaf parsley, rosemary, thyme, and garlic.

3. Rub mixture over pork tenderloin, and place tenderloin on a rack in a roasting pan. Bake for about 40 minutes or until internal temperature of pork reaches 142°F. (Pork will be slightly pink inside. If too pink, roast for 8 more minutes or until desired level of doneness. Be careful not to over-roast pork or it'll become dry.) Remove from the oven, and let rest for about 10 minutes before slicing.

3. Meanwhile, in a large saucepan over medium heat, melt unsalted butter. Add quinoa and vermicelli noodles, and sauté for about 2 minutes or until mixture is golden brown.

4. Pour in chicken broth and vermouth, and stir to combine. Bring to a boil, reduce heat to low, cover, and simmer for about 20 minutes or until almost all liquid is absorbed.

5. Slice pork into 8 ($^1\!/_2$-inch-thick) slices, and serve each over 1 cup quinoa mixture.

Seafood Suppers

In This Chapter

- Baked, grilled, and stir-fried seafood dishes
- Versatile quinoa crust for fish
- Sushi and quinoa from top chefs

Don't be intimidated at the thought of cooking seafood. In the quinoa seafood dishes in this chapter, you learn how quickly seafood cooks and how simple it is to use.

Seafood Suggestions

The most common types of fish and seafood are mild in flavor and include shrimp, tilapia, scallops, and tuna. They're delicious paired with a variety of different ingredients such as tomato-based sauces, fruit salsas, and spices like blackened or peppery seasonings. Spice, citrus, and sweet bring out the flavors of the fish.

Quality is the most important aspect to look for when making your selections. Whether fresh or fresh frozen, be sure you purchase from reputable sources, and don't be afraid to ask questions.

No matter the type of fish, it should smell fresh and mild. The eyes should be clear, and whole fish and fillets should have a firm, shiny flesh that springs back when lightly pressed. The fish should not appear mushy or be drying out around the edges.

When purchasing shellfish, avoid those with shells that are open or cracked. When buying frozen fish, avoid packages that are torn or ripped. Avoid buying frozen seafood in which you can visibly see ice crystals.

At home, store fresh fish in the refrigerator and use within 2 days.

WHOA!

When it comes to sushi-grade or sashimi-grade fish, inspection guidelines recommend fish be frozen at −4°F for at least 7 days to kill any parasites as one way to guarantee quality. For further details and recommendations on purchasing fish, visit fda.gov.

For the best flavor and texture, cook fish to an internal temperature of about 145°F. (Undercooking runs the risk of foodborne illness and overcooking makes the fish dry, tough, and unsavory.)

Quinoa Jambalaya

Cajun spices, andouille sausage, shrimp, celery, bell pepper, and onion are all you expect from jambalaya but with a quinoa twist.

Yield:	Prep time:	Cook time:	Serving size:
5 cups	15 minutes	35 minutes	1½ cups
Each serving has:			
433.0 calories	27.6 g carbohydrates	22.3 g fat	3.4 g fiber
30.6 g protein			

½ lb. (15 to 20) medium shrimp, peeled, deveined, and chopped

3 or 4 chicken tenders, diced

¼ cup pine nuts

½ TB. paprika

1 tsp. sea salt

½ tsp. ground black pepper

1 tsp. onion powder

1 tsp. cayenne

¼ tsp. dried oregano

¼ tsp. dried thyme

2 TB. olive oil

½ chopped yellow onion

½ cup chopped green bell pepper

½ cup chopped celery

1 TB. chopped fresh garlic

½ cup chopped tomatoes

1 bay leaf

1 tsp. Worcestershire sauce

1 medium jalapeño, minced

6 oz. andouille sausage, sliced

4½ cups chicken broth

¾ cup uncooked quinoa, rinsed and drained

¼ cup chopped fresh cilantro leaves

1. In a large bowl, combine shrimp, chicken tenders, pine nuts, paprika, sea salt, black pepper, onion powder, cayenne, oregano, and thyme. Toss to coat shrimp and chicken.

2. In a large saucepan over medium heat, heat olive oil. Add yellow onion, green bell pepper, celery, and garlic, and sauté for about 3 minutes or until slightly tender and fragrant.

3. Add tomatoes, bay leaf, Worcestershire sauce, and jalapeño, and sauté, stirring, for about 2 minutes.

4. Add shrimp and chicken mixture, andouille sausage, and chicken broth. Bring to a boil, and cook, stirring occasionally, for 5 minutes.

5. Stir in quinoa, cover, reduce heat to low, and simmer for about 15 minutes or until quinoa is cooked.

6. Uncover and simmer for 10 more minutes. When ready to serve, ladle into bowls and top with a sprinkle of fresh cilantro leaves.

Quinoa Shrimp Creole

Shrimp creole is a shrimp and rice dish made with tomatoes, onion, celery, bell pepper, and spices. Here, quinoa is used instead of rice for a more healthy and flavorful dish.

Yield:	Prep time:	Cook time:	Serving size:
8 cups	20 minutes	3 hours	1 cup quinoa with 1 cup creole

Each serving has:			
193.6 calories 21.0 g protein	15.5 g carbohydrates	5.5 g fat	2.4 g fiber

2 TB. olive oil

1 medium white onion, chopped

1 medium green bell pepper, ribs and seeds removed, and chopped

3 medium celery stalks, chopped

1 tsp. chili powder

1 (14-oz.) can diced tomatoes, with juice

1 (8-oz.) can tomato sauce

1 TB. hot sauce

1 TB. Worcestershire sauce

1 tsp. sugar

1 tsp. sea salt

1 tsp. ground black pepper

¼ tsp. cayenne

2 cups uncooked quinoa, rinsed and drained

4 cups chicken broth

1½ lb. (50 to 55) medium shrimp, peeled and deveined

1 TB. fine grate lemon zest

¼ cup chopped fresh cilantro leaves

1. In a large sauté pan over medium heat, heat olive oil. Add white onion, green bell pepper, celery, and chili powder, and sauté, stirring, for about 3 minutes or until fragrant and just tender. Transfer to a slow cooker.

2. Add diced tomatoes, tomato sauce, hot sauce, Worcestershire sauce, sugar, sea salt, black pepper, and cayenne to the slow cooker. Cover and cook on low for 3 hours.

3. Meanwhile, in a large stockpot over medium-high heat, combine quinoa and chicken broth. Bring to a boil, cover, reduce heat to low, and simmer for about 15 minutes or until almost all liquid has been absorbed. Remove from heat and set aside.

4. Add shrimp to the slow cooker, and cook for about 3 minutes or just until shrimp turn pink.

5. Serve about 1 cup creole over 1 cup quinoa. Garnish with lemon zest and chopped fresh cilantro leaves.

Variation: If you don't have a slow cooker, use a large saucepan instead. Stir occasionally while the mixture cooks, adding 1½ cups water in ½ cup increments during the cooking process.

KEEN ON QUINOA

Creole is common in Louisiana and combines French, African, and Spanish cuisines. Creole is antioxidant rich with high fiber, lycopene-rich tomatoes and bell pepper. Although the traditional version with rice is tasty, give your metabolism an extra boost by adding fiber-, protein-, and flavor-packed quinoa.

⌒ Achiote Roasted Red Snapper with Quinoa

Chef Ashley James of the Four Seasons Los Angeles at Beverly Hills uses achiote spice with chipotle powder, jalapeño, charred corn, fresh tomatillos, grapefruit, orange, cucumber, and tomato with this red snapper, and finishes with an avocado cilantro crema.

Yield:	Prep time:	Cook time:	Serving size:
4 red snapper filets with quinoa	20 minutes, plus 2 hours marinate time	35 minutes	1 red snapper filet with 1 cup quinoa

Each serving has:			
761 calories 56.1 g protein	61.1 g carbohydrates	34.4 g fat	11.7 g fiber

$\frac{1}{2}$ cup fresh orange juice

$\frac{1}{2}$ cup fresh grapefruit juice

$\frac{1}{2}$ cup achiote seasoning

1 tsp. chipotle chili powder

4 (6-oz.) Pacific red snapper fillets

1 cup uncooked quinoa, rinsed and drained

2 cups chicken broth

$1\frac{1}{2}$ cups charred kernel corn (preferably fresh off the cob)

$\frac{1}{2}$ cup chopped heirloom tomatoes

$\frac{1}{2}$ cup chopped English cucumber

$\frac{1}{2}$ cup chopped red onion

$\frac{1}{2}$ cup plus 1 TB. chopped fresh cilantro leaves

Juice of 4 limes

4 TB. extra-virgin olive oil

1 medium jalapeño, seeded and finely chopped

2 tsp. sea salt

2 tsp. ground black pepper

4 large banana leaves

2 medium avocados, peeled, pitted, and chopped

1 TB. sour cream

2 large ripe tomatillos, husks removed, and chopped

$\frac{1}{2}$ cup water

1. In a blender or a food processor fitted with a chopping blade, blend orange juice, grapefruit juice, achiote seasoning, and chipotle chile powder until smooth.

2. Place Pacific red snapper in a baking dish, and pour orange juice mixture over top. Refrigerate for 2 hours.

3. In a medium stockpot over medium-high heat, combine quinoa and chicken broth. Bring to a boil, cover, reduce heat to low, and simmer for 20 minutes or until almost all liquid has been absorbed. Spread out cooked quinoa on a baking sheet to cool.

4. Preheat the oven to 450°F.

5. In a medium bowl, combine cooled quinoa, charred corn, heirloom tomatoes, English cucumber, red onion, $\frac{1}{2}$ cup cilantro, juice of 2 limes, extra-virgin olive oil, jalapeño, 1 teaspoon sea salt, and 1 teaspoon black pepper.

6. Place banana leaves on a parchment paper–lined baking sheet. Add marinated fish on top of banana leaves, and bake for 6 minutes or until fish is lightly charred and just cooked through.

7. In a food processor fitted with a chopping blade or a blender, combine avocados, sour cream, tomatillos, water, remaining 1 tablespoon cilantro, juice of remaining 2 limes, remaining 1 teaspoon sea salt, and remaining 1 teaspoon black pepper, and purée until smooth.

8. Place 1 cup quinoa mixture onto a serving plate. Top with 1 red snapper fillet and a couple tablespoons avocado mixture.

KEEN ON QUINOA

Quinoa has been a staple of international cuisine for thousands of years. Its sustainable nature brings an earthy quality to seafood such as red snapper.

—Chef Ashley James

♟ Tilapia over Quinoa

Light tilapia filets are dipped in egg whites and sautéed with celery, carrots, and onion and served over cooked quinoa with a touch of grapeseed oil in this recipe by Chef Bruno Serato, executive chef and owner, Anaheim White House (Anaheim, CA).

Yield:	Prep time:	Cook time:	Serving size:
6 tilapia fillets	15 minutes	25 minutes	1 tilapia fillet with 1 cup quinoa

Each serving has:			
367.7 calories 29.6 g protein	35.6 g carbohydrates	12.6 g fat	3.9 g fiber

4¼ cups water

3 TB. grapeseed oil

1½ cups uncooked quinoa, rinsed and drained

6 large egg whites

6 (4-oz.) tilapia fillets

¼ cup plus 1 TB. whole-wheat flour

1½ tsp. sea salt

1½ tsp. ground black pepper

2 tsp. jarred vegetable base

1 medium carrot, diced

½ medium white onion, diced

1 medium stalk celery

6 lemon wedges

1. In a large pot over high heat, bring 3 cups water to a boil. Mix in 1 tablespoon grapeseed oil, and add quinoa. Bring to a boil, cover, reduce heat to low, and simmer for 15 minutes or until almost all liquid has been absorbed. Remove from heat and set aside for at least 6 to 8 minutes.

2. Preheat the oven to 300°F.

3. Place a large ovenproof sauté pan over medium-high heat, and add remaining 2 tablespoons grapeseed oil.

4. Place egg whites in a medium bowl.

5. Lightly dust tilapia fillets with ¼ cup whole-wheat flour, and sprinkle with 1 teaspoon sea salt and 1 teaspoon black pepper. Dip fillets into egg whites, and place in the hot sauté pan. Sear both sides of fillets for 45 seconds on each side or until light golden brown. Remove from heat, and bake for 8 to 10 minutes.

6. Meanwhile, in a separate stockpot over medium high heat, combine remaining 1¼ cups water and vegetable base. Whisk in remaining 1 tablespoon whole-wheat flour. Bring to a boil.

7. In a separate medium sauté pan over medium heat, heat remaining 2 tablespoons grapeseed oil. Add carrot, white onion, and celery, and cook for 5 minutes or until tender.

8. Add vegetable broth and quinoa, reduce heat to low, and cook for 3 to 5 minutes.

9. Place a bed of quinoa on each of 6 serving plates, along with a touch of vegetable broth. Place 1 fillet on top, and garnish with lemon wedges.

KEEN ON QUINOA

Quinoa adds a unique texture that gives depth to the light tilapia fillet and is wonderful as an ingredient because of its high nutrient value.

—Chef Bruno Serato

♙ Grilled Halibut with Quinoa, Asparagus, Spinach, and Fortun's Lemon Dill Caper Wine Sauces

Fortun's Finishing Touch Lemon Dill Caper with White Wine Sauce rounds out this delicious grilled halibut served with sautéed asparagus, spinach, and pine nuts by Chef Keith Otter, executive chef of Desert Sage Restaurant (La Quinta, CA).

Yield:	Prep time:	Cook time:	Serving size:
4 fillets	15 minutes	25 minutes	1 fillet with $\frac{1}{2}$ cup vegetables and 3 tablespoons sauce

Each serving has:			
647 calories	37.2 g carbohydrates	35.7 g fat	5.1 g fiber
47.5 g protein			

1 cup uncooked quinoa, rinsed and drained

2 cups chicken broth

$\frac{1}{4}$ cup plus 1 TB. unsalted butter

1 tsp. chopped shallots

4 cups fresh spinach leaves

$1\frac{1}{2}$ tsp. sea salt

$1\frac{1}{2}$ tsp. ground white pepper

4 (5-oz.) halibut fillets

1 (4-oz.) bag Fortun's Finishing Touch Lemon Dill Caper with White Wine Sauce

6 fresh asparagus spears, cut into 3-in. pieces

$\frac{1}{2}$ cup toasted pine nuts

1. In a medium saucepan over medium-high heat, combine quinoa and chicken broth. Cook, uncovered, for 15 minutes or until almost all liquid has been absorbed.

2. Meanwhile, in a large sauté pan over medium heat, melt $\frac{1}{4}$ cup unsalted butter. Add shallots, spinach, 1 teaspoon sea salt, and 1 teaspoon white pepper, and sauté for about 5 minutes or until spinach is tender. Set aside.

3. Season halibut fillets with remaining $\frac{1}{2}$ teaspoon sea salt and remaining $\frac{1}{2}$ teaspoon white pepper.

4. In a grill pan or heavy skillet over medium heat, cook halibut for about 3 or 4 minutes per side.

5. To prepare Fortun's Finishing Touch Lemon Dill Caper with White Wine Sauce, either place in simmering water for 4 or 5 minutes or microwave on high for 1½ minutes.

6. In a medium sauté pan over medium heat, melt remaining 1 tablespoon unsalted butter. Add asparagus, and sauté for about 2 minutes or until tender. Stir in quinoa and pine nuts.

7. Arrange asparagus on serving plates, add sautéed spinach, top with cooked halibut, and spoon Fortun's Finishing Touch Lemon Dill Caper with White Wine Sauce over top of halibut.

KEEN ON QUINOA

It's important to provide fine dining for guests with special dietary needs and guests who are seeking healthier meals. Quinoa is a nutrient- and flavor-rich food that complements a variety of dishes.

—Chef Keith Otter

♟ Roasted Salmon, Quinoa, Fennel, Radish, and Blood Orange Salad

The title says it all in this nutrient-filled salad by Chef Chris Barnett, executive chef, Sherbourne (Los Angeles, CA), featuring omega-3–rich salmon, protein-packed quinoa, antioxidant-rich fennel, crisp radish, and vitamin C–packed blood orange.

Yield:	Prep time:	Cook time:	Serving size:
6 cups quinoa plus 4 salmon fillets	15 minutes	25 minutes	1½ cups quinoa plus 1 salmon fillet

Each serving has:			
394.0 calories 29.4 g protein	32.3 g carbohydrates	16.5 g fat	5.2 g fiber

1 cup uncooked red quinoa, rinsed and drained	3 TB. extra-virgin olive oil
2 cups water	4 (5-oz.) salmon fillets, skin on
2 tsp. sea salt	1 tsp. ground black pepper
1 medium red bell pepper, ribs and seeds removed, and diced	1 large bulb fennel, shaved
1 medium yellow bell pepper, ribs and seeds removed, and diced	1 large blood orange, peeled and segmented
2 medium celery stalks, diced	1 large navel orange, peeled and segmented
Juice of 1 lemon	2 TB. chopped fresh dill
Juice of 1 lime	4 small red radishes, peeled

1. In a medium saucepan over medium heat, bring red quinoa, water, and 1 teaspoon sea salt to a boil. Cook for about 15 minutes or until quinoa is tender. Drain and set aside to cool.

2. In a large bowl, combine red bell pepper, yellow bell pepper, celery, lemon juice, lime juice, and extra-virgin olive oil.

3. Sprinkle salmon with remaining 1 teaspoon sea salt and black pepper, and sauté, skin side down, in a heavy skillet over medium heat for about 5 minutes or until crispy.

4. Add fennel, blood orange, navel orange, dill, and radishes to bell pepper mixture, and toss to coat.

5. To serve, place quinoa in the center of each serving plate, top with salmon, skin side up, and garnish with fennel salad.

🍳 Poached Salmon with Cucumber and Tomato Quinoa Salad

Cucumbers, olives, tomatoes, and lemon are the primary flavor accents for delicious quinoa and salmon in this recipe by Executive Chef Giselle Wellman, of the Petrossian Boutique and Restaurant (West Hollywood, CA).

Yield:	Prep time:	Cook time:	Serving size:
4 salmon fillets with 4 cups quinoa	20 minutes	30 minutes	1 (8-ounce) salmon fillet with 1 cup quinoa salad

Each serving has:			
822 calories 72.6 g protein	72.0 g carbohydrates	26.7 g fat	8.6 g fiber

4 cups chicken broth	1 TB. fresh lemon juice
2 cups uncooked quinoa, rinsed and drained	½ cup pitted olives
2 medium English cucumbers, diced	1½ tsp. sea salt
1 pt. cherry tomatoes, cut in ½	1½ tsp. ground white pepper
2 TB. chopped red onion	2 cloves garlic
1 TB. chopped Italian flat-leaf parsley leaves	3 cups olive oil
	4 (8-oz.) salmon fillets

1. In a large saucepan over medium-high heat, combine chicken broth and quinoa. Bring to a boil, reduce heat to low, cover, and simmer for about 20 minutes or until liquid has been absorbed and quinoa is tender. Remove from heat, and set aside for 5 minutes. Using a fork, fluff quinoa and place in a separate bowl. Allow to cool to room temperature.

2. In a large bowl, combine English cucumbers, cherry tomatoes, red onion, Italian flat-leaf parsley, lemon juice, and olives. Add quinoa, and toss with $\frac{1}{2}$ teaspoon sea salt and $\frac{1}{2}$ teaspoon white pepper.

3. In a large saucepan over medium heat, combine garlic and olive oil. Add salmon fillets, season with remaining 1 teaspoon sea salt and remaining 1 teaspoon white pepper, and cook for about 8 to 15 minutes. For more rare salmon, cook 8 to 10 minutes. For firmer salmon, cook 12 to 15 minutes.

4. Divide quinoa mixture evenly among 4 plates. Top each with 1 piece salmon.

KEEN ON QUINOA

Quinoa is a great choice to have for a meal, because it's a filling protein that will not slow you down.

—Chef Giselle Wellman

🍳 Quinoa and Lobster Thermidor

Beaufort cheese, fresh herbs, tomato paste, and mouthwatering lobster are served with quinoa and toasted pine nuts in this recipe by Chef Brendan Collins, executive chef and owner of Waterloo and City (Culver City, CA) and Larry's Venice Beach (Venice Beach, CA).

Yield:	Prep time:	Cook time:	Serving size:
8 cups	15 minutes	25 minutes	2 cups
Each serving has:			
1,191.5 calories	32.8 g carbohydrates	57.8 g fat	2.6 g fiber
130.2 g protein			

2¼ cups low-sodium chicken broth	⅛ cup chopped fresh tarragon leaves
1 tsp. tomato paste	2 tsp. sea salt
1 tsp. red wine vinegar	3 tsp. ground black pepper
¾ cup uncooked quinoa, rinsed and drained	1 TB. fresh lemon juice
¼ cup pine nuts	4 large egg yolks
4 TB. olive oil	1 TB. sauvignon blanc
½ cup chopped white onion	1 tsp. white wine vinegar
1 TB. chopped fresh thyme leaves	1 TB. water
4 (1¼-lb.) lobsters, cooked, shelled, and meat diced	½ cup melted unsalted butter
⅛ cup chopped fresh parsley leaves	½ cup grated Beaufort or Gruyère cheese

1. In a medium saucepan over medium heat, combine chicken broth, tomato paste, red wine vinegar, and quinoa. Bring to a boil, reduce heat to low, cover, and cook for 15 to 20 minutes or until almost all liquid is absorbed and quinoa is tender.

2. Meanwhile, in a large, dry skillet over medium-high heat, toast pine nuts for about 2 minutes, stirring frequently, or until golden brown and fragrant. Remove pine nuts from the skillet, and set aside.

3. In the skillet over medium-high heat, heat olive oil. Add white onion and thyme leaves, and cook, stirring occasionally, for about 6 minutes or until onions soften and begin to brown.

4. When quinoa is done, fluff with a fork and transfer to a large ovenproof serving tray. Stir in toasted pine nuts, onions, lobster, parsley, and tarragon. Season with 1 teaspoon sea salt, 1 teaspoon black pepper, and lemon juice.

5. In a round-bottomed bowl, combine egg yolks, sauvignon blanc, white wine vinegar, and water. Place bowl over a pan of simmering water, and whisk briskly until mixture becomes as thick as whipped cream. Remove from heat.

6. Slowly whisk in melted unsalted butter, pouring it in in a slow, steady trickle. If sauce thickens too much, adjust it by whisking in 1 spoonful hot water. Do not allow sauce to boil, or it will separate. Season with remaining 1 teaspoon sea salt and remaining 2 tablespoons black pepper.

7. Spoon hollandaise sauce over quinoa and lobster. Sprinkle Beaufort cheese over top, and broil for 2 or 3 minutes or until topping is golden brown. Serve immediately.

KEEN ON QUINOA

[Quinoa's] earthy essence is key to balancing out the rich cream flavors of this dish, which is a simple twist on the classic lobster favorite.

—Chef Brendan Collins

🍽 Ceviche Nikkei

Chef Katsu Hanamure, Executive Chef, Osaka (Hollywood, CA), shares this Japanese ceviche made with sushi-grade tuna, cucumber, green onion, Key lime juice, and Japanese yuzu sauce (a citrusy sauce).

Yield:	Prep time:	Cook time:	Serving size
8 servings	15 minutes	15 minutes	½ cup
Each serving has:			
243.5 calories	15.5 g carbohydrates	2.8 g fat	1.5 g fiber
37.0 g protein			

2 lb. fresh ahi tuna, sliced into 15 (2.4-oz.) pieces

4 cups julienned cucumber

2 cups julienned green onion, white and green parts

1 tsp. sea salt

1 tsp. ground black pepper

½ cup Key lime juice

2½ cups yuzu sauce

1 cup uncooked quinoa, rinsed and drained

2 cups water

8 cups vegetable oil

1. In a large bowl, toss together ahi tuna, cucumber, and green onion. Add sea salt, black pepper, Key lime juice, and yuzu sauce, and toss to coat.

2. In a medium saucepan over medium-high heat, bring quinoa and water to a boil, cook for 10 minutes. Drain quinoa, and put it on a paper towel–lined tray to dry for about 15 minutes.

3. In a medium saucepan over medium-high heat, heat vegetable oil. Add quinoa, and fry for about 1 minute. Drain quinoa, place ½ cup on each serving plate, and top with about ½ cup tuna mixture.

KEEN ON QUINOA

Osaka restaurant is a concept that is rooted in Peru and Peruvian food and culture. For that reason, we use a lot of quinoa in our dishes. Quinoa is a traditional, classic Peruvian ingredient found in the mountains. It is also very healthy and lends a crunchy texture to the ceviche.

—Chef Katsu Hanamure

Scrumptious Side Dishes

A side dish is all about the flavor, texture, and color, and quinoa satisfies all three. My mom, a nutrition major, taught me a colorful plate is a healthy plate, which is where side dishes truly shine. From vibrant green broccoli to richly red tomatoes, side dishes tie meals together colorfully and deliciously.

In Part 6, you see how quinoa wakes up your side dishes with its naturally nutty flavor and crunchy texture. Veggie-rich sides, hearty nut- and bean-based recipes, and even more sensational sides really round out your evening meal. Dig in!

Versatile Veggie Sides

In This Chapter

- Superstar side dishes
- Show-stealing vegetable and quinoa combos
- Getting spicy with sides
- Transforming sides to one-pot meals

Side dishes are often primarily composed of vegetables, but in all the fuss over the main dish, the flavors of side dishes sometimes get overlooked. Not anymore! As you'll see by the recipes in this chapter, it's easy to integrate spices into your side dishes for memorable meals that will also boost your metabolism.

Spicing up your sides can also be as simple as switching your cooking technique. Grilling, broiling, and roasting add more flavor than sautéing and steaming vegetables. Yet even sautéed and steamed veggies can easily be flavored with a drizzle of aged balsamic vinegar, a small sprinkling of grated Parmesan or feta cheese, or a little goat cheese melted on top.

Quinoa works its nutty-flavored magic with side dishes and tastes delicious with practically every flavor imaginable. Adding quinoa to your side dishes also ensures they contain fiber and powerful nutrients and protein for a healthy lifestyle.

Easy One-Pot Meals

Preparing healthy, delicious meals fast is the name of the game when you're working late, have a hungry family to feed, or just don't feel like spending hours in the kitchen. Transform side dishes into one-dish meals simply by adding chopped grilled chicken, fajita-style steak strips, shredded pork, or grilled shrimp. If you have leftover roasted chicken, save time and money by chopping the leftover chicken and incorporating it into a side dish. Those midweek meals you used to dread will become fast, easy, and delicious!

Red Pepper Broccoli Rabe with Quinoa

Broccoli rabe tastes delicious with red pepper flakes, a little olive oil, garlic, and colorful red quinoa.

Yield:	Prep time:	Cook time:	Serving size:
8 cups broccoli rabe with 2 cups quinoa	15 minutes	5 minutes	½ cup broccoli rabe with ½ cup quinoa

Each serving has:			
212.4 calories 6.1 g protein	20.9 g carbohydrates	14.4 g fat	4.7 g fiber

½ cup red uncooked quinoa, rinsed and drained	1 TB. minced fresh garlic
1 cup vegetable broth	½ cup diced white onion
3 tsp. sea salt	½ tsp. crushed red pepper flakes
8 cups broccoli rabe (rapini), stems trimmed	½ TB. fine lemon zest
3 TB. olive oil	½ cup chopped fresh cilantro leaves

1. In a medium saucepan over medium-high heat, bring red quinoa and vegetable broth to a boil. Cover, reduce heat to low, and simmer for 15 minutes or until almost all liquid has been absorbed.

2. Meanwhile, fill a large stockpot ¾ full of water and bring to a boil over medium-high heat. Add 2 teaspoons sea salt, and add rapini. Boil for about 30 seconds, and, using a slotted spoon, remove rapini and transfer to a bowl or plate.

3. In a large skillet over medium heat, heat olive oil. Add garlic and white onion, and sauté for about 2 minutes or until fragrant and tender.

4. Add rapini, and sauté for about 2 minutes. Stir in quinoa, crushed red pepper flakes, lemon zest, and cilantro leaves, and serve hot.

Variation: Fresh kernel corn; sliced red bell peppers; and pine nuts, almonds, or walnuts also make great additions to this dish.

DEFINITION

Broccoli rabe, also called *Italian broccoli* or *rapini,* is a leafy vegetable that looks like a cross between spinach and broccoli. It has a bit more pungent flavor than broccoli, but don't let that scare you off!

Garlic Kale Quinoa Sauté

Quinoa, carrots, onion, garlic, lemon, and a hint of nutmeg and fennel are sautéed with kale and topped with fresh tomatoes and a sprinkle of feta cheese.

Yield:	Prep time:	Cook time:	Serving size:
4 cups	12 minutes	25 minutes	1 cup

Each serving has:			
377.0 calories	51.9 g carbohydrates	14.5 g fat	8.8 g fiber
13.4 g protein			

1 cup uncooked quinoa, rinsed and drained

2 cups vegetable broth

2 TB. olive oil

1 cup chopped yellow onion

1 TB. minced garlic

1 tsp. crushed red pepper flakes

6 cups roughly chopped kale, stems removed

1 cup chopped fresh carrots

1 TB. fresh lemon juice

$\frac{1}{3}$ cup sauvignon blanc

2 TB. water

$\frac{1}{2}$ TB. fine lemon zest

$\frac{1}{8}$ tsp. ground nutmeg

$\frac{1}{4}$ tsp. ground fennel

$\frac{1}{2}$ tsp. sea salt

$\frac{1}{2}$ tsp. ground black pepper

2 TB. chopped fresh Italian flat-leaf parsley leaves

$\frac{1}{2}$ cup chopped and seeded medium ripe tomatoes

$\frac{1}{2}$ cup crumbled feta cheese

1. In a medium saucepan over medium-high heat, combine quinoa and vegetable broth. Bring to a boil, cover, reduce heat to low, and simmer for 15 minutes or until almost all liquid has been absorbed.

2. In a large saucepan over medium heat, heat olive oil. Add yellow onion, garlic, and crushed red pepper flakes, and sauté for about 2 minutes.

3. Stir in kale, carrots, lemon juice, sauvignon blanc, water, lemon zest, nutmeg, fennel, sea salt, and black pepper. Sauté, stirring occasionally, for about 5 minutes.

4. Remove from heat and stir in quinoa, Italian flat-leaf parsley, and tomatoes. Sprinkle with crumbled feta cheese, and serve.

Quinoa with Tomatoes, Mint, and Lemon

Tomatoes, onion, fresh mint, and tart lemon are tossed with quinoa and black olives and accented with a hint of cayenne.

Yield:	Prep time:	Cook time:	Serving size:
About 6 cups	12 minutes	15 minutes	1½ cups
Each serving has:			
255.9 calories	41.4 g carbohydrates	7.4 g fat	5.2 g fiber
7.5 g protein			

1 cup uncooked quinoa, rinsed and drained

2 cups vegetable broth

1 TB. olive oil

1 cup chopped white onion

2 cups seeded and diced tomatoes

2 TB. fresh lemon juice

¼ cup chopped fresh mint leaves

¼ cup sliced black olives

½ tsp. cayenne

1 tsp. sea salt

1 tsp. ground black pepper

1. In a medium saucepan over medium-high heat, combine quinoa and vegetable broth. Bring to a boil, cover, reduce heat to low, and simmer for 15 minutes or until almost all liquid has been absorbed.

2. In a large saucepan over medium heat, heat olive oil. Add white onion, and sauté for about 1 minute.

3. Stir in tomatoes and lemon juice, and turn off heat. Stir in mint leaves, black olives, cayenne, sea salt, and black pepper. Stir in quinoa until well combined, and serve.

Parmesan Quinoa with Asparagus Tips

Quinoa and Parmesan are the perfect pairing. Rich asparagus and tangy lemon give both balance and flavor to this nutty and cheesy dish, and smoky crisp bacon crumbles add the finishing touch.

Yield:	Prep time:	Cook time:	Serving size:
5 cups	15 minutes	20 minutes	1¼ cups

Each serving has:			
328.1 calories	36.8 g carbohydrates	12.0 g fat	4.4 g fiber
18.9 g protein			

1 cup uncooked quinoa, rinsed and drained	¼ cup water
2 cups vegetable broth	2 TB. fresh lemon juice
2 slices bacon	1½ tsp. sea salt
1 clove garlic, minced	2 cups chopped asparagus tips
¼ cup chopped white onion	½ tsp. ground black pepper
	1 cup grated Parmesan cheese

1. In a medium saucepan over high heat, combine quinoa and vegetable broth. Bring to a boil, cover, reduce heat to low, and simmer for 15 minutes or until almost all liquid has been absorbed.

2. In a large saucepan over medium heat, cook bacon for about 7 minutes or until crisp. Transfer bacon to a paper towel to drain. When cool to the touch, crumble.

3. In the large saucepan over medium heat, heat bacon grease. Add garlic and white onion, and sauté for about 2 minutes.

4. Add water, lemon juice, and 1 teaspoon sea salt, and cook for about 30 seconds. Add asparagus tips, and sauté for about 3 minutes or until just tender but still al dente.

5. Stir in quinoa, remaining $\frac{1}{2}$ teaspoon sea salt, black pepper, and Parmesan cheese, and serve.

> **QUICK FIX**
>
> If you don't care for asparagus, you can use 2 cups broccoli florets in this recipe instead. Both provide vital nutrients, including vitamins A and K, which help prevent certain cancers.

Quinoa au Gratin

Red potatoes replace heavier baking potatoes in this recipe, where a baked quinoa crust adds both flavor and fiber. Rich Gruyère cheese, fresh sage, and a hint of Parmesan seal the deal.

Yield:	Prep time:	Cook time:	Serving size:
1 (9×13-inch) square casserole	15 minutes	45 minutes	1 (3¼-inch) square

Each serving has:			
390.0 calories	57.8 g carbohydrates	10.9 g fat	5.3 g fiber
15.4 g protein			

½ cup uncooked quinoa, rinsed and drained

1 cup vegetable broth

5 large red potatoes

1 TB. olive oil

1 large shallot, peeled and minced

2 TB. all-purpose flour

2 cups nonfat milk

½ cup nonfat sour cream

1 tsp. ground black pepper

½ tsp. dry mustard

⅛ tsp. ground nutmeg

½ cup grated Gruyère cheese

2 TB. chopped fresh sage leaves

¼ cup grated Parmesan cheese

1. Preheat the oven to 375°F. Lightly coat a 9×13-inch baking dish with nonstick cooking spray.

2. In a small saucepan over medium-high heat, combine quinoa and vegetable broth. Bring to a boil, cover, reduce heat to low, and simmer for 15 minutes or until almost all liquid has been absorbed. Remove from heat and set aside.

3. Peel and slice red potatoes into ¼-inch-thick slices, and place in the prepared baking dish.

4. In a heavy saucepan over medium heat, heat olive oil. Add shallot, and sauté for about 2 minutes or until tender.

5. Stir in all-purpose flour, and cook for about 1 or 2 minutes or until lightly browned.

6. Stir in nonfat milk, nonfat sour cream, black pepper, dry mustard, and nutmeg until well combined. Stir in Gruyère cheese until cheese is melted and well combined. Remove from heat, and stir in sage. Pour mixture over potatoes, gently stirring to coat potatoes with milk mixture evenly.

7. Stir Parmesan cheese into cooked quinoa, and sprinkle quinoa evenly on top of potatoes. Cover with aluminum foil, and bake for about 45 minutes.

8. Uncover and bake for 15 more minutes or until quinoa crust is crisp and browned and potatoes are tender. Slice into 6 equal squares, and serve.

Baked Zucchini Quinoa with Gruyère and Parmesan

Zucchini and quinoa bring the perfect blend of protein, fiber, and antioxidants and combine nicely with tomatoes, herbs, and cheese in this healthy side dish.

Yield:	Prep time:	Cook time:	Serving size:
1 (9×13-inch) casserole	20 minutes	35 minutes	1 square, about 1 cup

Each serving has:			
111.6 calories 6.1 g protein	10.5 g carbohydrates	5.4 g fat	2.0 g fiber

$\frac{1}{2}$ cup shredded Gruyère cheese

$\frac{3}{4}$ cup grated Parmesan cheese

3 medium zucchini, sliced into $\frac{1}{4}$-in.-thick slices

1 tsp. sea salt

1 tsp. ground black pepper

1 TB. olive oil

$\frac{1}{2}$ cup chopped white onion

1 TB. minced garlic

3 cups canned diced tomatoes (seasoned okay), with juice

3 TB. finely chopped fresh basil leaves

1 TB. finely chopped fresh thyme leaves

1 tsp. dried oregano or $\frac{1}{2}$ TB. finely chopped fresh oregano leaves

1 batch Quick-and-Easy Quinoa (recipe in Chapter 1)

1. Preheat the oven to 400°F. Lightly coat a 9×13-inch baking dish with nonstick cooking spray.

2. In a small bowl, toss together Gruyère cheese and Parmesan cheese.

3. In a large bowl, toss together zucchini, sea salt, and black pepper, and toss to coat. Distribute $\frac{1}{4}$ of zucchini slices evenly in the bottom of the prepared baking dish.

4. In a large sauté pan over medium heat, heat olive oil. Add white onion, and sauté for about 2 minutes or until fragrant and slightly tender.

5. Stir in garlic, tomatoes, basil, thyme, and oregano, and sauté for about 5 minutes or until almost all liquid has cooked out.

6. Spread ¼ of tomato mixture over zucchini. Sprinkle ¼ of Quick-and-Easy Quinoa over tomatoes, and top with ¼ of cheese mixture. Begin another layer with ⅓ each zucchini, tomato mixture, quinoa, and cheese mixture. Repeat using ½ of remaining zucchini, tomato mixture, quinoa, and cheese mixture, and finish with final layers of zucchini, tomato mixture, quinoa, and cheese mixture. Cover with aluminum foil, and bake for 35 minutes.

7. Uncover, and bake for 15 more minutes. Slice into 12 slices, and serve.

Variation: Diced carrots, corn kernels, and yellow squash are also delicious additions to this dish. For a one-dish meal, add diced chicken or ground turkey.

KEEN ON QUINOA

Filled with antioxidants such as vitamin A, lycopene, and fiber, this dish gets a protein boost from the quinoa. The cheeses add protein, too!

Tri-Color Pepper and Pistachio Quinoa

A gorgeous dish is a healthy one, because lots of color means more nutrients and more flavor. Flavor permeates this dish, thanks to red, yellow, and green bell peppers; quinoa; citrusy orange and lime; and pistachios.

Yield:	Prep time:	Cook time:	Serving size:
About 6 cups	15 minutes	30 minutes	1½ cups

Each serving has:			
391.6 calories	46.1 g carbohydrates	19.7 g fat	6.6 g fiber
10.3 g protein			

1 cup vegetable broth

1 cup uncooked quinoa, rinsed and drained

3 TB. olive oil

3 TB. red wine vinegar

Zest of 1 medium lime

Juice of 1 medium lime

½ tsp. sea salt

½ tsp. ground black pepper

1 medium red bell pepper, ribs and seeds removed, and chopped

1 medium yellow bell pepper, ribs and seeds removed, and chopped

1 medium green bell pepper, ribs and seeds removed, and chopped

1 medium jalapeño, ribs and seeds removed, and chopped

1 medium orange, peeled and cut into 1-in. pieces

½ cup shelled pistachios

¼ cup chopped fresh cilantro leaves

1. In a medium saucepan over medium-high heat, combine vegetable broth and quinoa. Bring to a boil, cover, reduce heat to low, and simmer for 15 minutes or until almost all liquid has been absorbed.

2. In a small bowl, whisk together olive oil, red wine vinegar, lime zest, lime juice, sea salt, and black pepper.

3. In a large bowl, toss together red bell pepper, yellow bell pepper, green bell pepper, jalapeño, orange, pistachios, and quinoa. Drizzle olive oil mixture over the top, and toss well to coat. Add cilantro, and serve.

Caramelized Onion Quinoa

Caramelized onions add a richer flavor to many dishes. Here, they're a key part of this delicious quinoa side dish.

Yield:	Prep time:	Cook time:	Serving size:
4 cups	15 minutes	35 minutes	1 cup

Each serving has:			
266.2 calories	45.9 g carbohydrates	6.2 g fat	5.9 g fiber
8.9 g protein			

3 cups sliced yellow onions	2 cups chicken broth
1 TB. olive oil	½ TB. lemon pepper
1 TB. unsalted butter	½ cup frozen peas
1 tsp. brown sugar	
1 cup uncooked quinoa, rinsed and drained	

1. In a large saucepan over medium-low heat, combine yellow onions, olive oil, and unsalted butter. When butter has melted and all are combined, stir in brown sugar. Cover, reduce heat to low, and simmer, stirring occasionally, for about 20 minutes.

2. Uncover, and cook for 15 more minutes or until onions are lightly browned.

3. Meanwhile, in a large saucepan over medium-high heat, combine quinoa and chicken broth. Bring to a boil, cover, reduce heat to low, and simmer for 15 minutes or until almost all liquid has been absorbed.

4. Remove all from heat. Stir onions into cooked quinoa, add lemon pepper and peas, and serve.

KEEN ON QUINOA

This caramelized onion dish is wonderful as a side, used as the base for stuffed peppers, or served alongside grilled chicken, pork chops, or filet mignon or flank steak strips.

Quinoa with Hearts of Palm and Avocado

Quinoa and hearts of palm combine in this delicious side dish that pairs well with lighter chicken and fish entrées. Lemon, coriander, paprika, fresh avocado, a drizzle of balsamic vinegar, and chopped red onion provide maximum flavor.

Yield:	Prep time:	Serving size:
4 cups	20 minutes	1 cup

Each serving has:		
463.6 calories	43.4 g carbohydrates	30.1 g fat
10.1 g fiber	9.3 g protein	

1 cup uncooked quinoa, rinsed and drained	$\frac{1}{2}$ tsp. paprika
2 cups vegetable broth	$\frac{1}{4}$ cup olive oil
2 tsp. minced fresh garlic	1 (14-oz.) can hearts of palm, drained and chopped
1 TB. ground coriander	2 medium ripe avocados, peeled and diced
3 TB. fresh lemon juice	
1 tsp. sugar	$\frac{1}{2}$ cup chopped red onion
$\frac{1}{2}$ tsp. sea salt	2 TB. aged balsamic vinegar
$\frac{1}{2}$ tsp. ground black pepper	

1. In a medium saucepan over medium-high heat, combine quinoa and vegetable broth. Bring to a boil, cover, reduce heat to low, and simmer for 15 minutes or until almost all liquid has been absorbed.

2. In a large bowl, whisk together garlic, coriander, lemon juice, sugar, sea salt, black pepper, paprika, and olive oil until well blended.

3. In a separate large bowl, toss together hearts of palm, avocados, red onion, and quinoa. Drizzle with garlic mixture, and toss well to coat. Serve 1 cup servings with $\frac{1}{2}$ tablespoon balsamic vinegar drizzled over top.

Nut- and Bean-Based Dishes

In This Chapter

- Piling on the protein with beans
- Sensational sides with quinoa, nuts, and beans
- Metabolism-boosting sides for maximum energy
- Toasting and roasting nuts

Nuts and beans are popular ingredients in vegetarian diets because of their intense earthy flavors and high nutritional value and protein content. Add quinoa, and you double the nutrients, double the protein, and double the flavor, as you'll see by the recipes in this chapter.

Any diet, vegetarian and nonvegetarian alike, can reap the health benefits and metabolism-boosting qualities of the delicious nut, bean, and quinoa combination.

Nutritional Powerhouses

Even though nuts are high in fat, they contain good fats—the kind of fats your body can process efficiently, which translates to an efficient metabolism. Portion control is still necessary when it comes to nuts, but a little goes a long way both in flavor and nutrients.

Beans are known for their high protein content, fiber, and other nutrients. Black beans, for example, have almost 4 grams protein, virtually no fat (less than 1 gram), and only 56.8 calories in a $\frac{1}{4}$ cup serving, plus substantial amounts of vitamins and minerals.

I recommend keeping canned black beans, dark kidney beans, and lentils on hand in your pantry to add to dishes, salads, casseroles, and soups.

Toasting and Roasting Nuts

When cooking with nuts, I recommend you toast them first. Toasting or roasting brings out the natural nut oils, along with the true flavor of the nut. There are times you may choose to use the raw nut, but for the most part, toasting or roasting is best.

Toast nuts easily on the stovetop by adding salted or unsalted nuts directly to a skillet or saucepan over low heat. No butter or oils are needed; just the nuts. Don't leave the nuts unattended. It may seem like it takes a while to toast them, but once the pan and the nuts heat up, they turn brown quickly and will burn if you let them rest too long. Shuffle them around in the skillet while toasting. Transfer slightly browned and fragrant nuts to a bowl or plate immediately to prevent overcooking.

Roast nuts in the oven. Preheat the oven to 300°F. Place nuts on a parchment paper–lined baking sheet, and bake for about 10 minutes, shuffling them about halfway through the cooking process for even cooking.

Toast or roast nuts before chopping for a more evenly roasted quality. Also, chopping the nuts before roasting means the nuts will cook faster and therefore may burn more easily.

Toasted Almond Quinoa Pilaf

Toasted almonds bring the perfect roasted flavor to this simple quinoa dish with garlic, green onions, lemon, and cilantro that's perfect alongside roasted pork, chicken, or turkey entrées.

Yield:	Prep time:	Cook time:	Serving size:
4 cups	10 minutes	18 minutes	1 cup
Each serving has:			
247.5 calories	34.5 g carbohydrates	9.2 g fat	3.9 g fiber
7.4 g protein			

1 cup uncooked quinoa, rinsed and drained	2 medium green onions, white and green parts, chopped
2 cups vegetable broth	1/2 TB. fine grate lemon zest
1 TB. olive oil	1 TB. chopped fresh cilantro leaves
1 clove garlic, minced	1/2 tsp. sea salt
1/4 cup whole almonds	1/2 tsp. ground black pepper

1. In a medium saucepan over medium-high heat, combine quinoa and vegetable broth. Bring to a boil, cover, reduce heat to low, and simmer for 15 minutes or until almost all liquid has been absorbed.

2. In a large sauté pan over medium heat, heat olive oil. Add garlic and almonds, and sauté for about 1 minute.

3. Add green onions and lemon zest, and stir to combine. Remove from heat. Stir in cooked quinoa, cilantro, sea salt, and black pepper, and serve.

QUICK FIX

Although nuts are dry toasted most of the time, adding the almonds with the olive oil and garlic here gives this recipe extra dimension by fusing the garlic and almond flavors.

Roasted Sweet Potatoes with Quinoa and Pecans

Crushed cornflakes and cooked quinoa make a tasty crust for sweet potatoes with cinnamon and nutmeg, dusted with crushed pecans.

Yield:	Prep time:	Cook time:	Serving size:
1 (9×13-inch) casserole	20 minutes	1 hour, 20 minutes	1 cup

Each serving has:			
377.4 calories 7.3 g protein	38.9 g carbohydrates	21.5 g fat	4.4 g fiber

¾ cup unsweetened crushed cornflakes

¾ cup Quick-and-Easy Quinoa (recipe in Chapter 1)

1½ TB. brown sugar

4 large sweet potatoes, peeled and cut into 2-in. pieces

2 TB. unsalted butter, softened

¼ cup sugar

2 TB. honey

1 tsp. ground cinnamon

¼ tsp. ground nutmeg

1 (5-oz.) can nonfat evaporated milk

1 tsp. pure vanilla extract

1 large egg, beaten

3 large egg whites, lightly whipped

1½ cups finely chopped pecans

1. Preheat the oven to 350°F. Lightly coat a 9×13-inch baking dish with nonstick cooking spray.

2. In a small bowl, combine cornflakes, Quick-and-Easy Quinoa, and brown sugar. Press mixture into the bottom of the prepared baking dish.

3. Add sweet potatoes to a large stockpot, and fill with enough water to liberally cover potatoes. Bring to a boil over high heat, and boil for about 20 minutes or until potatoes are tender. Drain thoroughly, and return cooked potatoes to the stockpot.

4. Add unsalted butter, sugar, honey, cinnamon, nutmeg, evaporated milk, and vanilla extract, and mix well. Stir in egg and egg whites.

5. Using a spatula, spoon mixture into the prepared baking dish, and smooth top into an even layer. Sprinkle chopped pecans over top, and bake for 45 minutes to 1 hour. Remove from the oven, and let rest for about 5 to 10 minutes before serving.

Steamed Broccoli with Quinoa and Cashews

Superfood broccoli contains vitamin A, fiber, and cancer-fighting properties. This recipe adds even more flavor and nutrients with cooked quinoa, lemon, and toasted cashews.

Yield:	Prep time:	Cook time:	Serving size:
6 cups	15 minutes	25 minutes	1 cup

Each serving has:			
241.9 calories	36.0 g carbohydrates	7.9 g fat	8.4 g fiber
11.8 g protein			

1 cup uncooked quinoa, rinsed and drained

2 cups vegetable broth

2 medium bunches fresh broccoli, broken into large, bite-size florets and top part of stems

½ TB. fine grate lemon zest

1 TB. fresh lemon juice

½ cup toasted cashews

1. In a large saucepan over medium-high heat, combine quinoa and vegetable broth. Bring to a boil, cover, reduce heat to low, and simmer for 15 minutes or until almost all liquid has been absorbed.

2. Bring 1 inch of water to a boil in a medium to large saucepan with a steamer basket. Place broccoli in the steamer basket, cover, and steam for about 4 or 5 minutes or until broccoli is just fork-tender but still firm.

3. Stir lemon zest and lemon juice into cooked quinoa. Add steamed broccoli and toasted cashews, toss well to combine, and serve immediately.

Quinoa with Fava Beans, Red Onion, and Fresh Mint

Fava beans are large, earthy, hearty beans that pair perfectly with chopped red onion, fresh mint leaves, quinoa, and a lemon vinaigrette.

Yield:	Prep time:	Serving size:
5 cups	20 minutes	1¼ cups

Each serving has:		
460.0 calories	55.8 g carbohydrates	21.3 g fat
3.5 g fiber	18.9 g protein	

2 TB. fresh lemon juice

2 TB. white wine vinegar

1 tsp. ground black pepper

1 tsp. sea salt

4 TB. olive oil

1 (15-oz.) can fava beans, drained and rinsed

½ cup diced red onion

4 cups Quick-and-Easy Quinoa (recipe in Chapter 1)

¼ cup chopped fresh mint leaves

½ cup crumbled feta cheese (optional)

1. In a large bowl, whisk together lemon juice, white wine vinegar, black pepper, and sea salt. Drizzle in olive oil while continuing to whisk.

2. Add fava beans, red onion, Quick-and-Easy Quinoa, mint, and feta cheese (if using). Toss well, tossing from the bottom up to incorporate vinaigrette, and serve.

Fava beans are large beans native to parts of Africa and Asia and are popular in Mediterranean cooking. Also known as *broad beans,* fava beans are often immersed in boiling water (blanched) to remove their outer skins. In addition to their robust flavor, fava beans provide many nutrients, are low in fat, and are a good source of protein. If you can't find fava beans at your local market (most commonly found in cans), substitute black beans or green peas.

Three-Bean Quinoa Salad

Your favorite three-bean salad gets a tasty quinoa twist! Green beans, yellow beans, and dark kidney beans are tossed with red onion, quinoa, apple cider vinaigrette, and Italian parsley in this delicious side salad.

Yield:	Prep time:	Serving size:
8 cups	15 minutes	1 cup

Each serving has:		
273.6 calories	40.0 g carbohydrates	8.6 g fat
10.9 g fiber	10.4 g protein	

1 tsp. minced garlic	1 (16-oz.) can yellow beans, drained
2 TB. apple cider vinegar	1 (16-oz.) can dark red kidney beans, drained
1 TB. fresh lime juice	
$\frac{1}{2}$ TB. sugar	$\frac{1}{2}$ cup chopped red onion
$\frac{1}{2}$ tsp. sea salt	4 cups Quick-and-Easy Quinoa (recipe in Chapter 1)
1 tsp. ground black pepper	
4 TB. olive oil	$\frac{1}{4}$ cup chopped fresh Italian flat-leaf parsley leaves
1 (16-oz.) can green beans, drained	

1. In a large bowl, whisk together garlic, apple cider vinegar, lime juice, sugar, sea salt, and black pepper. Drizzle in olive oil while continuing to whisk.

2. Add green beans, yellow beans, red kidney beans, and red onion, and toss well. Add Quick-and-Easy Quinoa and Italian parsley, toss all to combine, and serve.

Variation: For **Three-Bean Quinoa Salad with Herbs and Feta,** add 1 teaspoon chopped fresh oregano leaves and 1 teaspoon chopped fresh thyme leaves with the Italian flat-leaf parsley. Toss all the ingredients with $\frac{1}{4}$ cup crumbled feta cheese or goat cheese.

Red Beans with Quinoa "Rice"

Quinoa replaces rice in this New Orleans–style bean dish. Dark red kidney beans, cumin, garlic, bay leaves, oregano, lemon, and lime are tossed with quinoa, a little andouille sausage, and a dollop of sour cream.

Yield:	Prep time:	Cook time:	Serving size:
8 cups	15 minutes	30 minutes	1 cup

Each serving has:			
176.8 calories	27.2 g carbohydrates	3.9 g fat	5.8 g fiber
8.6 g protein			

1 cup uncooked quinoa, rinsed and drained

2 cups chicken broth

1 bay leaf

½ tsp. minced garlic

½ cup sliced andouille sausage

½ cup chopped white onion

½ tsp. chili powder

1 tsp. ground cumin

2 tsp. chopped fresh oregano leaves

1 TB. fresh lemon juice

1 TB. fresh lime juice

2 (16-oz.) cans dark red kidney beans, drained and rinsed

½ tsp. sea salt

4 TB. nonfat sour cream

1. In a medium saucepan over medium-high heat, combine quinoa, chicken broth, bay leaf, and garlic. Bring to a boil, cover, reduce heat to low, and simmer for 15 minutes or until almost all liquid has been absorbed.

2. In a medium sauté pan over medium heat, cook andouille sausage and white onion for about 5 minutes or until sausage is cooked and onion is translucent.

3. Stir in chili powder, ground cumin, fresh oregano leaves, lemon juice, and lime juice. Stir in dark red kidney beans, cooked sausage, onions, and sea salt.

4. Remove bay leaf, and serve in 1 cup servings topped with ½ tablespoon sour cream.

Even More Super Sides

In This Chapter

- Baked and stuffed quinoa sides
- Cheesy quinoa dishes
- Flavoring with herbs

We're not through with the side dishes yet! In this chapter, I give you even more mouthwatering sides that go crazy with cheese, take advantage of fresh herbs, feature baked dishes like casseroles and stuffed peppers, or keep things light with quinoa pilaf. You'll forget the main dish when you dive into these taste treasures!

Flavor Fun with Herbs

Fresh herbs bring more flavor to dishes than they often get credit for—and they add vital nutrients, such as vitamin A, vitamin C, and fiber. Popular fresh herbs for cooking are cilantro, dill, rosemary, thyme, oregano, and Italian flat-leaf parsley, the latter of which has a milder flavor than its curly counterpart and is distinguished by pointed flat leaves.

When chopping fresh herbs, gently pull off the leaves and discard the stems. A few leafy stems from herbs like parsley, cilantro, and dill are okay, but steer clear of most of the long, bitter stem and stick to the leaves. For herbs with a woody stem, use only the leaves, and discard the stems. Always chop the leaves of fresh herbs, no matter how small, to unleash the natural oils, juices, and flavor.

Generally, add fresh herbs later in the cooking process for maximum flavor benefit, or stir them in just before serving.

🍳 Quinoa Lentil Paillard

This quinoa and lentil "paillard" by Chef Brock Kleweno, executive chef of Yamashiro Restaurant (Hollywood, CA), is a simple loaf of garlic, caramelized onions, Parmesan cheese, lentils, and quinoa. (For a refresher on carmelizing onions, see Chapter 19's Caramelized Onion Quinoa.)

Yield:	Prep time:	Cook time:	Serving size:
1 (8-inch) loaf	15 minutes	25 minutes	8 slices

Each serving has:			
123.9 calories 7.1 g protein	13.0 g carbohydrates	5.0 g fat	2.7 g fiber

1 batch Quick-and-Easy Quinoa (recipe in Chapter 1)	1 large egg
	2 TB. roasted garlic
1 cup cooked lentils	¼ cup caramelized onions
½ cup grated Parmesan cheese	1 TB. olive oil

1. Preheat the oven to 350°F. Lightly coat an 8-inch nonstick loaf pan with cooking spray.

2. In a large bowl, combine Quick-and-Easy Quinoa, lentils, Parmesan cheese, egg, roasted garlic, and caramelized onions. Transfer to the prepared loaf pan, and bake for about 30 minutes or until a toothpick inserted in the center comes out clean.

3. Cool and slice into 8 (¼-inch-thick) slices.

4. In a medium sauté pan over high heat, heat olive oil. Add "paillard" slices, and sear for 30 seconds per side or until warmed through. Serve.

Variation: These paillard slices are amazing topped with sautéed or grilled tomatoes and mushrooms (or vegetables of choice) or accompanied with a simple arugula/shallot salad on top of the paillard with a light vinaigrette.

KEEN ON QUINOA

I love using quinoa any chance I get, whether in hot or chilled dishes. It brings a whole different complexity to any dish it is used in, is completely delicious, and has the mysterious distinction of being known as the Super Grain.

—Chef Brock Kleweno

Quinoa Polenta with Parmesan and Sage

Here, quinoa is combined with buttermilk, Parmesan cheese, garlic, and sage for a delicious side dish that can also be used as a base for appetizers.

Yield:	Prep time:	Cook time:	Serving size:
1 (9×13-inch) casserole	15 minutes	30 minutes	1 (3¼-inch) square

Each serving has:			
170.1 calories	21.1 g carbohydrates	6.1 g fat	1.4 g fiber
6.9 g protein			

½ TB. olive oil	½ cup Quick-and-Easy Quinoa (recipe in Chapter 1)
¼ cup chopped yellow onion	1 tsp. ground black pepper
½ TB. minced fresh garlic	1 TB. chopped fresh sage leaves
2¼ cups vegetable broth	2 TB. unsalted butter
2 cups reduced-fat buttermilk	¾ cup grated Parmesan cheese
½ tsp. sea salt	
1½ cups quick-cooking polenta, medium or coarse grain	

1. Preheat the oven to 350°F. Lightly coat a 9×13-inch baking dish with nonstick cooking spray.

2. In a medium saucepan over medium-high heat, heat olive oil. Add yellow onion and garlic, and cook for about 1 minute.

3. Add 1 cup vegetable broth, reduced-fat buttermilk, and sea salt, and bring just to a boil. Slowly whisk in polenta, and continue to whisk until mixture begins to thicken.

4. Stir in Quick-and-Easy Quinoa, black pepper, sage leaves, unsalted butter, and Parmesan cheese, and cook, stirring, until very thick. Spread mixture into the prepared baking dish, and bake for 20 minutes.

5. Remove from the oven and let rest for 10 minutes. Slice into 9 squares, and serve.

Herb Quinoa with Lemon and Chives

Quinoa pilaf gets great flavor from a simple combination of lemon, chives, fresh parsley, and fresh cilantro.

Yield:	Prep time:	Cook time:	Serving size:
4 cups	10 minutes	15 minutes	1 cup

Each serving has:			
181.1 calories	32.8 g carbohydrates	2.8 g fat	3.1 g fiber
6.2 g protein			

1 cup uncooked quinoa, rinsed and drained	½ tsp. sea salt
2 cups vegetable broth	1 tsp. lemon pepper
½ TB. fine grate lemon zest	1 TB. chopped fresh Italian flat-leaf parsley leaves
¼ cup chopped fresh chives	1 TB. chopped fresh cilantro leaves

1. In a medium saucepan over medium heat, combine quinoa and vegetable broth. Bring to a boil, cover, reduce heat to low, and simmer for 15 minutes or until almost all liquid has been absorbed.

2. Remove from heat, and stir in lemon zest, chives, sea salt, lemon pepper, Italian flat-leaf parsley, and cilantro. Serve.

Quinoa-Stuffed Chili Peppers

Here, poblano peppers are halved, grilled, and stuffed with a mixture of quinoa, spinach, tomato, and pepper jack cheese.

Yield:	Prep time:	Cook time:	Serving size:
8 stuffed pepper halves	20 minutes	30 minutes	1 stuffed pepper half

Each serving has:			
260.7 calories	24.4 g carbohydrates	13.8 g fat	3.0 g fiber
11.7 g protein			

1 cup uncooked quinoa, rinsed and drained	2 cups packed washed spinach leaves
2¼ cups chicken broth	1 tsp. sea salt
4 large poblano peppers, sliced in ½ lengthwise and seeded	1 tsp. ground black pepper
2 TB. olive oil	1 cup tomato sauce
1 tsp. minced fresh garlic	2 cups shredded pepper jack cheese

1. In a medium saucepan over medium-high heat, combine quinoa and 2 cups chicken broth. Bring to a boil, cover, reduce heat to low, and simmer for 15 minutes or until almost all liquid has been absorbed.

2. Preheat the broiler to high.

3. Heat a griddle or grill pan over medium-high heat. Drizzle poblano peppers with 1 tablespoon olive oil, and grill for 3 or 4 minutes per side. Transfer peppers to a baking sheet or dish, hollow side up.

4. In a small skillet over medium heat, heat remaining 1 tablespoon olive oil. Add garlic and spinach, and cook for about 2 minutes or until spinach is wilted. Season with sea salt and black pepper.

5. In a large bowl, combine quinoa, spinach, remaining ¼ cup chicken broth, and tomato sauce. Spoon equal amounts of quinoa mixture into pepper halves. Top with equal amounts of pepper jack cheese. Broil for 3 to 5 minutes or until cheese is melted and lightly browned in some places. Serve hot.

Variation: If you like, you could add cooked chicken or shredded pork, too. This recipe also works well subbing red, yellow, or green bell peppers for the poblanos. For **Beef and Quinoa Stuffed Chili Peppers with Pepper Jack Cheese,** cook ½ pound lean ground beef and toss with the quinoa, spinach, remaining chicken broth, and tomato sauce.

Roasted Pumpkin with Spicy Jalapeño Quinoa

Jalapeños, cinnamon, honey, pumpkin, and quinoa? Those probably aren't flavors you'd think of for a side dish, but one taste of this delicious dish filled with antioxidants and protein will change your mind.

Yield:	Prep time:	Cook time:	Serving size:
6 cups	20 minutes	1 hour	1 cup
Each serving has:			
217.4 calories	35.9 g carbohydrates	6.7 g fat	4.7 g fiber
6.1 g protein			

1 (4- or 5-lb.) pumpkin	2 cups vegetable broth
2 TB. olive oil	1 medium jalapeño, seeded and minced
1 tsp. ground nutmeg	
1 tsp. ground cinnamon	1 TB. honey
1 cup uncooked quinoa, rinsed and drained	¼ tsp. sea salt
	½ tsp. lemon pepper

1. Preheat the oven to 400°F. Line a baking sheet with parchment paper.

2. Slice off outer rind of pumpkin, cut in half, scoop out seeds and pulp, and cut pumpkin into 2-inch pieces. Place pumpkin pieces on the prepared baking sheet, drizzle with olive oil, and sprinkle with nutmeg and cinnamon. Roast for about 45 minutes or until just fork-tender but still firm and not mushy.

3. Meanwhile, in a large saucepan over medium-high heat, combine quinoa and vegetable broth. Bring to a boil, cover, reduce heat to low, and simmer for 15 minutes or until almost all liquid has been absorbed.

4. Stir in minced jalapeño, honey, sea salt, and lemon pepper. Add roasted pumpkin to quinoa, and toss well to coat. Serve hot.

KEEN ON QUINOA

Quinoa can replace rice in pretty much all rice dishes. Because it's lighter than rice, it can be combined with roasted vegetables, as in this recipe, without the dish being too bulky or heavy.

Delectable Desserts

Believe it or not, quinoa makes delicious desserts. Cooked quinoa and quinoa flour can be used to make crusts for pies and crumbles for cobblers, in cookies, and in so many more delicious dessert recipes. And best of all, these recipes are simple and easy to follow for a delicious dessert every time.

Quinoa's nutty flavor makes it a perfect companion to fruity desserts, ginger, coconut, and even peanut butter and chocolate. It's all about getting comfortable with quinoa flour, and the chapters in Part 7 help you do just that. Now you can make a healthful dessert—and eat it, too!

Crumbles, Cookies, and Bars

In This Chapter

- Creative quinoa crumbles
- Quinoa in cookies? Yes!
- Baking with gluten-free quinoa flour

By now you should realize that quinoa is great in all kinds of foods—even desserts! Both the cooked seed and ground quinoa flour make wonderful desserts.

In this chapter, I share delicious dessert recipes that use quinoa as a topping, in the body of a dessert, or as a crust. Yum!

Flour: The Key Ingredient

One of the most popular baking flours is all-purpose flour, a.k.a. plain flour, which contains the protein gluten. Gluten helps breads and mixes stretch and rise during the baking process. Because quinoa flour is naturally gluten free, it's not ideal for baking unless combined with other leavening agents or gluten-rich flours.

If you're not gluten intolerant, using 50 percent quinoa flour and 50 percent all-purpose flour is generally acceptable for baking, and your finished product likely won't be adversely affected. If you're gluten intolerant, combine quinoa flour with almond flour, buckwheat flour, tapioca starch, and cornstarch, for example, because quinoa flour on its own has a strong flavor and can make baked goods overly crumbly.

Toasting quinoa flour helps mellow out its flavor. Spread it on a baking sheet, and bake it at 200°F to 225°F for about 2 hours. Store in an airtight container in a cool, dry place, or in the refrigerator.

Baked Apples with Quinoa Crumble

Apples are baked with cinnamon, nutmeg, and a little bit of sugar until just tender and topped with a *crumble* of quinoa, oats, lemon zest, brown sugar, and butter.

Yield:	Prep time:	Cook time:	Serving size:
6 baked apples	15 minutes	1 hour, 20 minutes	1 baked apple with 2 tablespoons crumble

Each serving has:			
457.2 calories	93.0 g carbohydrates	17.6 g fat	7.2 g fiber
2.7 g protein			

½ cup Quick-and-Easy Quinoa (recipe in Chapter 1)	8 TB. cold unsalted butter, cut into ½-in. pieces
1 cup gluten-free rolled oats	1 tsp. ground cinnamon
¼ cup quinoa flour	¼ tsp. ground nutmeg
½ cup light brown sugar, lightly packed	½ cup sugar
½ TB. fine grate lemon zest	6 medium to large Granny Smith apples
⅛ tsp. sea salt	1 cup apple juice

1. Preheat the oven to 325°F. Line a baking sheet with parchment paper.

2. In a food processor fitted with a chopping blade, pulse Quick-and-Easy Quinoa, rolled oats, quinoa flour, light brown sugar, lemon zest, and sea salt 3 or 4 times to combine.

3. Add 6 tablespoons unsalted butter, and pulse until butter is evenly distributed throughout and mixture is crumbly. Be careful not to overmix.

4. Spread quinoa crumble mixture on the prepared baking sheet in an even layer. Bake for 10 minutes, stir, and bake for 5 to 10 more minutes or until mixture is lightly browned. Remove from the oven, and set aside.

5. In a small bowl, combine cinnamon, nutmeg, and sugar. Set aside.

6. Core Granny Smith apples ¾ the way down, leaving bottom part of apple intact to hold cinnamon mixture. Remove ½ inch of skin from around top of apples. Fill each apple with cinnamon mixture, and top each apple with 1 teaspoon unsalted butter. Place apples in a 9×13-inch baking dish, and pour in apple juice. Cover with aluminum foil, and bake for about 40 minutes to 1 hour or until apples are tender.

7. Remove apples from the oven, top each apple with 2 tablespoons quinoa crumble, and serve.

DEFINITION

A **crumble** is a baked topping made of sugar, butter or other fat, and flour and crumbled over sweet or savory foods. Here cooked quinoa is added to give more "crumble," while healthier quinoa flour is used in place of all-purpose flour.

🍴 Chef Jessica's Chocolate Strawberry Quinoa Maki

Quinoa pilaf is sweetened with sugar; combined with basil, vanilla, chocolate, and cashews; and wrapped in soy paper in this maki (or roll) recipe by Chef Jessica Obie, corporate management trainee at Hyatt Gainey Ranch (Scottsdale, AZ).

Yield:	Prep time:	Cook time:	.	Serving size:
32 pieces	25 minutes	27 minutes		4 pieces
Each serving has:				
221.1 calories	28.1 g carbohydrates	11.1 g fat		2.1 g fiber
4.0 g protein				

1 cup uncooked quinoa, rinsed and drained

2¼ cups plus 2 TB. water

¼ cup plus 2 TB. sugar

¼ tsp. pure vanilla extract

¼ cup baking chocolate

6 fresh basil leaves

½ cup heavy whipping cream

¼ cup ground cashews

4 sheets soy paper

1 cup fresh chopped strawberries

1. Line a baking sheet with parchment paper.

2. In a medium saucepan over medium heat, combine quinoa and 2 cups water. Bring to a boil, cover, reduce heat to low, and simmer for 15 minutes or until almost all liquid has been absorbed. Remove from heat, uncover, and set aside to cool.

3. In a small saucepan over medium-low heat, combine sugar, remaining $\frac{1}{4}$ cup plus 2 tablespoons water, and vanilla extract. Simmer simple syrup for about 5 minutes or until sugar is dissolved.

4. Gently fold $\frac{1}{2}$ of simple syrup over cooked quinoa. Add additional simple syrup if needed without making quinoa too wet. Spread on the prepared baking sheet to cool. (Refrigerate any remaining simple syrup for up to 1 month.)

5. Place baking chocolate in the top bowl of a double boiler. Fill bottom bowl $\frac{1}{2}$ inch deep with water, and set over medium heat to melt chocolate.

6. In a food processor fitted with a chopping blade or a blender, purée 4 basil leaves with heavy whipping cream. Strain mixture through a fine mesh strainer. Using an electric mixer on medium-high speed, whip strained whipping cream until soft peaks form. Refrigerate until ready to use.

7. Using a paper towel, pat out excess moisture from quinoa. Stir in ground cashews.

8. Microwave remaining 2 basil leaves for 2 minutes to crisp. Crumble into a small bowl, and set aside.

9. Lay 1 piece of soy paper on a flat work surface. Line right and left edges with melted chocolate, and press quinoa on top of chocolate. Allow to cool.

10. Place a thin layer of quinoa on remaining soy paper to cover. Top quinoa with a small drizzle of chocolate, followed by $\frac{1}{4}$ of strawberries. Immediately before rolling, line uncovered end of soy paper with chocolate to help seal roll. Roll soy paper to make a log, as you would a sushi roll. Slice roll into 8 segments. Top segments with a small dollop of whipped cream, and add a small amount of crushed basil leaves before serving.

KEEN ON QUINOA

Quinoa is one of the healthiest items we can eat, … so I wanted to show people that if they are creative, they can make something delicious out of even the healthiest thing.

—Chef Jessica Obie

Chocolate-Chip Quinoa Cookies

Toasting quinoa flour takes away some of its earthy flavor and makes it more palatable for baking. Here toasted quinoa flour is combined with almond milk, molasses, and chocolate chips for a truly delicious cookie.

Yield:	Prep time:	Cook time:	Serving size:
12 cookies	10 minutes	2 hours, 12 minutes	2 cookies

Each serving has:			
379.2 calories	41.2 g carbohydrates	23.6 g fat	3.9 g fiber
5.1 g protein			

1 cup quinoa flour	2 large eggs
2 TB. baking soda	2 TB. molasses
2 TB. cornstarch	$\frac{1}{2}$ cup almond milk
$\frac{1}{4}$ cup sugar	2 TB. pure vanilla extract
$\frac{1}{2}$ cup unsalted butter, softened	$\frac{1}{2}$ cup dark chocolate chips

1. Preheat the oven to 225°F. Line a baking sheet with parchment paper.

2. Spread quinoa flour on the prepared baking sheet, and toast for 2 hours. Remove from the oven, and set aside to cool completely.

3. Increase the oven temperature to 350°F. Retain parchment paper on the baking sheet.

4. Place cooled quinoa flour in a large bowl, and stir in baking soda, cornstarch, and sugar.

5. In a separate large bowl, and using a wooden spoon, beat together unsalted butter, eggs, molasses, almond milk, and vanilla extract. Slowly incorporate quinoa flour mixture into butter mixture, but do not overmix. Stir in dark chocolate chips.

6. Drop batter by tablespoonfuls onto the prepared baking sheet. Bake for 12 minutes or until lightly golden. Cool on a wire rack.

Oatmeal Raisin Quinoa Cookies

Healthy quinoa flour is added to brown sugar, vanilla, honey, cinnamon, oatmeal, raisins, and superfood, walnuts.

Yield:	Prep time:	Cook time:	Serving size:
2 dozen cookies	15 minutes	18 minutes	2 cookies

Each serving has:			
492.5 calories 7.2 g protein	88.2 g carbohydrates	21.0 g fat	4.8 g fiber

1 cup unsalted butter

1¼ cups light brown sugar, firmly packed

2 large eggs

2 tsp. pure vanilla extract

2 TB. honey

1 cup all-purpose flour

1 cup whole-wheat flour

½ tsp. baking soda

1 tsp. sea salt

½ tsp. ground cinnamon

1 cup toasted quinoa flour

2 cups quick-cooking oats

½ cup chopped toasted walnuts

1 cup raisins

1. Preheat the oven to 350°F. Line a baking sheet with parchment paper.

2. In a large bowl, and using an electric mixer on low speed, cream together unsalted butter and light brown sugar. Add eggs, vanilla extract, and honey, and mix well.

3. In a separate large bowl, combine all-purpose flour, whole-wheat flour, baking soda, and sea salt. Stir flour mixture into butter mixture. Stir in toasted quinoa flour, oats, walnuts, and raisins.

4. Drop batter by tablespoonfuls onto the prepared baking sheet. Bake for 18 minutes or until lightly golden brown. Cool on a wire rack.

Lemon Quinoa Cookies

Quinoa flour, almond flour, toasted cooked quinoa, lemon zest, lemon juice, and honey give these cookies a must-have taste. They're good for you, too!

Yield:	Prep time:	Cook time:	Serving size:
24 cookies	15 minutes	18 minutes	2 cookies

Each serving has:			
107.1 calories	22.5 g carbohydrates	0.9 g fat	1.4 g fiber
2.2 g protein			

1 cup Quick-and-Easy Quinoa (recipe in Chapter 1)	1 TB. honey
½ cup almond flour	1 TB. fresh lemon juice
⅓ cup toasted quinoa flour	9 TB. unsalted butter, softened
1 TB. fine lemon zest	1 tsp. baking soda
1 cup sugar	2 TB. boiling water

1. Preheat the oven to 350°F. Line a baking sheet with parchment paper.

2. Evenly spread Quick-and-Easy Quinoa on the prepared baking sheet, and toast for about 15 minutes. Remove from the oven, and let cool.

3. In a large bowl, combine Quick-and-Easy Quinoa, almond flour, toasted quinoa flour, lemon zest, and sugar.

4. In a small saucepan over medium heat, melt honey, lemon juice, and unsalted butter.

5. In a small bowl, combine baking soda and boiling water. Add baking soda mixture to flour mixture, and stir in the melted butter mixture.

6. Roll batter into 24 balls, and place 2 inches apart on the prepared baking sheet. Press balls lightly with a fork to flatten. Bake for 15 to 20 minutes or until dark golden in color. Cool on a wire rack.

KEEN ON QUINOA

Keep these delicious cookies on hand for a quick energy snack on busy days. Cool completely before storing in an airtight container for up to 7 days.

Peanut Butter Quinoa Cookies

Instead of using quinoa flour for the cookie base, cooked quinoa is stirred together with peanut butter for a healthy version of this peanut butter favorite.

Yield:	Prep time:	Cook time:	Serving size:
12 cookies	10 minutes	12 minutes	2 cookies

Each serving has:			
481.0 calories	72.8 g carbohydrates	23.3 g fat	3.3 g fiber
13.9 g protein			

$\frac{1}{2}$ cup all-purpose flour

1 cup Quick-and-Easy Quinoa (recipe in Chapter 1), cooled

1 cup light brown sugar, firmly packed

1 cup creamy peanut butter

1 large egg

$\frac{1}{2}$ TB. molasses

1. Preheat the oven to 350°F. Line a baking sheet with parchment paper.

2. In a medium bowl, stir together all-purpose flour and Quick-and-Easy Quinoa.

3. In a separate medium bowl, combine light brown sugar, peanut butter, egg, and molasses. Add to quinoa mixture, and stir well.

4. Drop batter by tablespoonfuls onto the prepared baking sheet. Bake for about 12 minutes or until lightly golden brown. Cool on a wire rack.

Chocolate Quinoa Nut Bars

Nut lovers rejoice! Nutty quinoa is mixed with walnuts, pecans, hazelnuts, and chocolate for a truly memorable dessert.

Yield:	Prep time:	Cook time:	Serving size:
36 bars	15 minutes	20 minutes	2 bars

Each serving has:			
394.3 calories	37.9 g carbohydrates	27.0 g fat	3.0 g fiber
5.3 g protein			

1 cup unsalted butter, softened	1 tsp. pure vanilla extract
2 cups all-purpose flour	$\frac{1}{2}$ cup chopped hazelnuts
$\frac{1}{4}$ cup sugar	$\frac{1}{2}$ cup chopped walnuts
$\frac{1}{4}$ cup brown sugar, firmly packed	$\frac{1}{2}$ cup chopped pecans
$\frac{1}{4}$ tsp. sea salt	$\frac{1}{2}$ cup dark chocolate chips or chopped dark chocolate
1 (14-oz.) can sweetened condensed milk	$\frac{1}{2}$ cup Quick-and-Easy Quinoa (recipe in Chapter 1)
2 cups semisweet chocolate chips	

1. Preheat the oven to 350°F. Lightly coat a 9×13-inch baking dish with nonstick cooking spray.

2. In a large bowl, and using an electric mixer on medium speed, beat unsalted butter until fluffy. Add all-purpose flour, sugar, brown sugar, and sea salt, and beat again until crumbly.

3. Set aside 1 cup flour mixture. Press remaining flour mixture into the bottom of the prepared baking dish. Bake for 12 minutes or until lightly golden and set.

4. In a medium saucepan over low heat, heat sweetened condensed milk and $1\frac{1}{2}$ cups semisweet chocolate chips, stirring until chocolate chips have melted. Remove from heat, and stir in vanilla extract. Spread mixture over baked crust.

5. In a large bowl, combine hazelnuts, walnuts, pecans, dark chocolate chips, remaining $\frac{1}{2}$ cup semisweet chocolate chips, Quick-and-Easy Quinoa, and remaining flour mixture. Sprinkle nut mixture over chocolate layer. Bake for about 15 to 20 minutes or until set. Cool on a wire rack before slicing into 36 (2-inch) bars.

Variation: Substitute $\frac{1}{2}$ cup butterscotch chips for the dark chocolate or add $\frac{1}{2}$ cup shredded coconut if you love coconut.

Puddings, Pies, and Cobblers

In This Chapter

- Sweet quinoa puddings
- Quinoa piecrusts
- Simple quinoa cobblers

Quinoa is a natural for sweet puddings, pies, and cobblers. And adding a little nutty, earthy flavored quinoa to sweet treats provides fiber, protein, and other nutrients, so you can indulge your sweet tooth nearly guilt-free!

The Scoop on Pie

Most commonly, pies are baked with both a top and bottom pastry crust and filled with fruit fillings. It's perfectly acceptable, however, to skip the top layer and save yourself a few extra calories and carbs.

When making traditional high-gluten flakey piecrust, you use chilled fats like butter and vegetable shortening. If the fat is too warm, your piecrust can turn out tough. Any liquids used should be chilled, too, and used only to moisten the dough, not saturate it.

In this chapter, quinoa flour will be used for a simple pastry dough, and cooked and toasted quinoa will be used to make an easy nonpastry piecrust.

Cobblers Made Simple

The essential difference between a pie and a cobbler is in the crust. Cobblers have no bottom crust and are made by pouring a fruit or savory filling into a baking dish and covering it with a batter, biscuit, or piecrust. Both quinoa flour and cooked quinoa can be mixed with butter, milk, and flavorings for a delicious cobbler topper.

Quinoa Bread Pudding with Golden Raisins and Bourbon Sauce

One of the best uses for day-old bread is to cut it into pieces; toss it with milk, egg, sugar, raisins, and spices; and bake for a delicious bread pudding that's topped with a rich, creamy bourbon sauce.

Yield:	Prep time:	Cook time:	Serving size:
1 (9×13-inch) pudding	45 minutes	1 hour	1 (3¼-inch) square

Each serving has:			
869.1 calories 13.8 g protein	107.6 g carbohydrates	46.8 g fat	1.8 g fiber

4 cups heavy whipping cream

4½ cups whole milk

6 large eggs

1¾ cups plus 2 TB. light brown sugar, firmly packed

1 TB. pure vanilla extract

1 tsp. ground cinnamon

½ tsp. ground nutmeg

1 tsp. fine grate orange zest

¼ tsp. plus ⅛ tsp. salt

½ cup golden raisins

½ cup Quick-and-Easy Quinoa (recipe in Chapter 1)

1 or 2 large day-old French loaves, cut into 1-in. cubes (14 cups)

3 TB. unsalted butter

½ cup sugar

2 TB. cornstarch mixed with 2 TB. water

2 tsp. fine grate lemon zest

¾ cup Kentucky bourbon or other whiskey

1. In a large bowl, whisk together 2 cups heavy whipping cream, 4 cups whole milk, eggs, 1¾ cups light brown sugar, vanilla extract, cinnamon, nutmeg, orange zest, ¼ teaspoon salt, golden raisins, and Quick-and-Easy Quinoa.

2. In a separate large bowl, place bread cubes. Pour heavy whipping cream mixture over bread, and allow to soak for about 45 minutes at room temperature.

3. Preheat the oven to 350°F. Grease a 9×13-inch baking dish with 1 tablespoon unsalted butter.

4. Pour bread mixture into the prepared baking dish, and bake for about 1 hour or until center is set.

5. In a medium saucepan over medium heat, combine remaining 2 cups heavy whipping cream, remaining $\frac{1}{2}$ cup whole milk, and sugar. Whisk in cornstarch mixture, lemon zest, $\frac{1}{4}$ cup Kentucky bourbon, and remaining 2 tablespoons light brown sugar. Bring to a gentle boil, reduce heat to low, and simmer, stirring occasionally, for 5 minutes. Remove from heat

6. Add remaining $\frac{1}{8}$ teaspoon salt, and whisk in remaining 2 tablespoons unsalted butter and remaining $\frac{1}{2}$ cup Kentucky bourbon. Pour over bread pudding, and serve warm.

KEEN ON QUINOA

This recipe is not for the faint of heart, but it is so delicious! If you're not a fan of bourbon, skip the sauce altogether and replace with a dollop of vanilla bean ice cream.

🍳 Fit Chef Katy Clark's Tropical Quinoa Pudding

Coconut water, coconut milk, and ginger are tossed with fresh lime, mango, pomegranate seeds, and quinoa for a flavorful, antioxidant-rich pudding in this recipe by Chef Katy Clark, *The Next Food Network Star* (season 7) contestant, and Mrs. Long Beach 2011.

Yield:	Prep time:	Cook time:	Serving size:
4 cups	10 minutes	20 minutes	1 cup

Each serving has:			
575.4 calories	49.9 g carbohydrates	39.2 g fat	4.2 g fiber
10.9 g protein			

2 cups coconut water	Zest of 1 medium lime
2 cups light coconut milk	Juice of 1 medium lime
1 cup uncooked quinoa, rinsed and drained	1 medium mango, peeled, pitted, and chopped
1 tsp. dried ginger	$\frac{1}{2}$ cup fresh pomegranate seeds

1. In a medium saucepan over medium heat, combine coconut water, light coconut milk, quinoa, ginger, and lime zest. Bring to a boil, cover, reduce heat to low, and simmer for 10 minutes.

2. Uncover and simmer for 5 more minutes. Be sure some liquid remains to cover quinoa. Add lime juice, and stir to combine.

3. Place 1 cup quinoa mixture in a serving bowl, top with chopped mango and pomegranate seeds, and serve.

KEEN ON QUINOA

What's not to love about quinoa? As a mom I am always looking for speedy recipes that will encourage my children to eat more protein. They love this sweet play on dessert, and we make it the old-fashioned way sometimes, with cinnamon and raisins.

—Chef Katy Clark

Simple Quinoa Pastry Piecrust

Bake this tasty gluten-free piecrust made with quinoa flour, fill it with your favorite pie filling, and enjoy your dessert gluten free!

Yield:	Prep time:	Cook time:	Serving size:
1 (9-inch) piecrust	15 minutes	2 hours, 20 minutes	1 (9-inch) piecrust
Each serving has:			
851.8 calories 0.9 g protein	84.7 g carbohydrates	57.7 g fat	3.3 g fiber

¾ cup quinoa flour
¼ cup plus 1 TB. unsalted butter
½ tsp. sea salt

½ tsp. baking powder
2 TB. water

1. Preheat the oven to 225°F. Line a baking sheet with parchment paper.

2. Spread quinoa flour onto the prepared baking sheet, and toast for 2 hours. Remove from the oven, and set aside to cool completely.

3. Increase the oven temperature to 350°F.

4. In a medium saucepan over low heat, melt ¼ cup unsalted butter. When butter has melted, remove from heat and add toasted quinoa flour, salt, and baking powder, and stir to combine. Add remaining 1 tablespoon unsalted butter, and stir until flour is evenly mixed with butter. Add water, and mix until water is evenly combined with flour mixture.

5. Using your fingers, press quinoa dough into the bottom and sides of a 9-inch pie plate or pan. Using a fork, poke about 6 holes in bottom of crust. Bake for about 15 to 20 minutes or until lightly browned. Remove from the oven, and allow to cool completely before adding pie filling.

Easy Quinoa Graham Cracker–Style Piecrust

Cooked quinoa is used in place of graham crackers for another delicious gluten-free crust!

Yield:	Prep time:	Cook time:	Serving size:
1 (9-inch) piecrust	10 minutes	10 minutes	1 piecrust

Each serving has:			
1,413.2 calories 13.0 g protein	128.1 g carbohydrates	97.7 g fat	6.0 g fiber

1 batch Quick-and-Easy Quinoa (recipe in Chapter 1)	½ cup melted unsalted butter ⅓ cup sugar

1. Preheat the oven to 400°F.

2. In a food processor fitted with a chopping blade or a blender, pulse Quick-and-Easy Quinoa 1 or 2 times, but do not overpulse. You don't want quinoa flour, only quinoa crumbs.

3. In a medium bowl, combine quinoa crumbs, melted unsalted butter, and sugar. Mix well and press into the bottom and sides of a 9-inch pie plate or pan.

4. Bake for 10 minutes or until lightly golden. Remove from the oven, and allow to cool before adding filling.

Quinoa Apple Pie with Frozen Yogurt

This healthy, gluten-free apple pie is made with a quinoa pastry crust, fresh crisp apples, cinnamon, and nutmeg and served with low-fat frozen vanilla yogurt.

Yield:	Prep time:	Cook time:	Serving size:
1 (9-inch) pie	20 minutes	1 hour	$\frac{1}{8}$ of pie

Each serving has:			
381.7 calories	71.2 g carbohydrates	16.3 g fat	3.9 g fiber
2.1 g protein			

8 cups peeled, cored, and sliced Granny Smith apples

2 TB. fresh lemon juice

$\frac{3}{4}$ cup sugar

$\frac{1}{4}$ cup light brown sugar, firmly packed

$\frac{1}{4}$ cup toasted quinoa flour

1 tsp. ground cinnamon

$\frac{1}{4}$ tsp. ground nutmeg

1 baked Simple Quinoa Pastry Piecrust (recipe earlier in this chapter)

2 TB. unsalted butter, cut into cubes

1 unbaked Simple Quinoa Pastry Piecrust (recipe earlier in this chapter)

1 large egg yolk

1 TB. low-fat milk

2 cups low-fat vanilla frozen yogurt

1. Preheat the oven to 425°F.

2. In a large bowl, toss together Granny Smith apples and lemon juice.

3. In a small bowl, combine sugar, light brown sugar, quinoa flour, cinnamon, and nutmeg. Pour sugar mixture over apples, and toss well to coat.

4. Pour apples into baked Simple Quinoa Pastry Piecrust, and evenly distribute unsalted butter pieces on top of apples.

5. Top apples with unbaked Simple Quinoa Pastry Piecrust, and secure edges. Using a knife, cut slits in top of crust to vent.

6. In a small bowl, beat together egg yolk and milk. Using a pastry brush, brush egg yolk mixture over top of crust. Bake for 15 minutes, reduce heat to 350°F, and bake for 40 more minutes or until crust is golden and filling is bubbly.

7. Allow to cool for about 5 minutes before slicing into 8 slices and serving with a dollop of low-fat vanilla frozen yogurt.

QUICK FIX

You can use the unbaked pastry crust to make creative apple pie toppings. Use cookie cutters to make themed designs or cut the pastry crust into strips for a lattice.

Southern Pecan Pie with Quinoa Crust

Pecans and sugar top a baked quinoa crust for a gluten-free, slightly healthier version of this American favorite.

Yield:	Prep time:	Cook time:	Serving size:
1 (9-inch) pie	15 minutes	50 minutes	$\frac{1}{8}$ of pie
Each serving has:			
421.3 calories	55.1 g carbohydrates	28.5 g fat	1.6 g fiber
3.8 g protein			

$\frac{1}{4}$ cup unsalted butter	1 tsp. pure vanilla extract
$\frac{1}{2}$ cup light brown sugar, firmly packed	1 cup pecan halves
3 large eggs, beaten	1 baked Simple Quinoa Pastry Piecrust (recipe earlier in this chapter)
$\frac{3}{4}$ cup corn syrup	

1. Preheat the oven to 400°F.

2. In a large bowl, and using a wooden spoon or an electric mixer on low speed, cream unsalted butter and light brown sugar. Stir in eggs, corn syrup, vanilla extract, and pecan halves.

3. Pour pecan mixture into Simple Quinoa Pastry Piecrust. Bake for 10 minutes, reduce heat to 350°F, and bake for 30 to 35 more minutes or until a toothpick inserted comes out clean.

KEEN ON QUINOA

This recipe is adapted from my sister's traditional Southern pecan pie recipe to use a quinoa crust. Thanks, sis!

Key Lime Pie with Quinoa Crust

Tart Key lime juice is mixed with sweetened condensed milk and poured into a healthy, high-fiber quinoa crust. Another delicious gluten-free dessert that's as easy as … well … pie!

Yield:	Prep time:	Cook time:	Serving size:
1 (9-inch) pie	5 minutes	15 minutes	$\frac{1}{8}$ of pie

Each serving has:			
298.3 calories	24.0 g carbohydrates	19.7 g fat	0.8 g fiber
7.6 g protein			

5 large egg yolks, beaten	1 baked Easy Quinoa Graham Cracker–Style Piecrust (recipe earlier in this chapter)
1 (14-oz.) can sweetened condensed milk	
$\frac{1}{2}$ cup Key lime juice	

1. Preheat the oven to 375°F.

2. In a medium bowl, whisk together egg yolks, sweetened condensed milk, and Key lime juice. Pour into baked Easy Quinoa Graham Cracker–Style Piecrust.

3. Bake for 15 minutes. Remove from the oven, and allow to cool completely before slicing into 8 equal slices and serving.

Quinoa Georgia Peach Pie

Fresh peaches are tossed with sugar, lemon juice, a little toasted quinoa flour, brown sugar, butter, and eggs and poured into a tasty gluten-free quinoa crust.

Yield:	Prep time:	Cook time:	Serving size:
1 (9-inch) pie	25 minutes	1 hour	$\frac{1}{8}$ of pie

Each serving has:			
383.3 calories	65.2 g carbohydrates	15.2 g fat	4.0 g fiber
2.8 g protein			

8 large ripe firm peaches	$\frac{1}{4}$ cup plus 1 TB. toasted quinoa flour
$1\frac{1}{2}$ TB. fresh lemon juice	
$\frac{3}{4}$ cup sugar	1 baked Easy Quinoa Graham Cracker–Style Piecrust
$\frac{1}{4}$ cup light brown sugar, firmly packed	2 TB. unsalted butter, thinly sliced
2 large eggs, beaten	

1. Preheat the oven to 400°F.

2. Fill a large bowl with ice water.

3. Bring a large saucepan full of water to a boil. Using a sharp knife, make an X on the bottom of each peach. Place peaches in boiling water for about 30 seconds. Using a slotted spoon, transfer peaches to ice water bath. Drain. Peel peaches, cut into $\frac{3}{4}$-inch wedges, and discard pits.

4. Place peaches in a large bowl, and toss with lemon juice, sugar, light brown sugar, eggs, and toasted quinoa flour. Let rest for 5 minutes.

5. Pour peach mixture into baked Easy Quinoa Graham Cracker–Style Piecrust, and top with unsalted butter slices. Bake for 15 minutes, reduce heat to 350°F, and bake for 40 to 45 more minutes. Cool on a wire rack before slicing into 8 equal slices and serving.

Variation: For a little something extra, serve this pie with the bourbon sauce from the Quinoa Bread Pudding with Golden Raisins and Bourbon Sauce recipe (earlier in this chapter).

Wild Berry Quinoa Cobbler

Sweet and tangy fresh blackberries, blueberries, and raspberries are as rich in anti-oxidants as they are in flavor. Tossed with lemon juice and sugar, these berries are topped with a combo of quinoa, lemon, sugar, and fresh mint.

Yield:	Prep time:	Cook time:	Serving size:
1 (9-inch-square) cobbler	15 minutes	45 minutes	1 (3-inch) square

Each serving has:			
174.0 calories	36.3 g carbohydrates	2.7 g fat	5.6 g fiber
2.7 g protein			

2 cups fresh blackberries	$\frac{1}{2}$ cup almond flour
2 cups fresh blueberries	$\frac{1}{3}$ cup toasted quinoa flour
2 cups fresh raspberries	1 TB. fine lemon zest
2 tsp. fresh lemon juice	1 tsp. baking powder
1 TB. plus $\frac{1}{2}$ cup sugar	$1\frac{1}{4}$ TB. unsalted butter
1 TB. cornstarch or tapioca flour	$\frac{1}{2}$ cup low-fat milk
1 TB. chopped fresh mint leaves	1 tsp. pure vanilla extract
$\frac{1}{4}$ cup Quick-and-Easy Quinoa (recipe in Chapter 1)	

1. Preheat the oven to 400°F.

2. In a large bowl, toss together blackberries, blueberries, and raspberries with lemon juice, 1 tablespoon sugar, cornstarch, and mint leaves. Pour into a 9-inch baking dish, and bake for 15 minutes.

3. In a large bowl, combine Quick-and-Easy Quinoa, almond flour, toasted quinoa flour, lemon zest, remaining $\frac{1}{2}$ cup sugar, and baking powder.

4. Using a pastry cutter, cut in unsalted butter until crumbly. Stir in low-fat milk and vanilla extract. Drop batter by spoonfuls over fruit. Bake for 30 more minutes or until golden brown. Remove from heat, slice into 9 equal squares, and serve.

Variation: Use peaches, plums, apples, or pears or any fresh fruit combination you like.

Cakes, Cupcakes, and Crepes

In This Chapter

- Adding nutrients and texture with quinoa
- Delicious quinoa cakes
- Light and fluffy quinoa crepes

Quinoa flour is a healthier option than white wheat flour, hands down. But before you go replacing all the flours in your pantry with quinoa flour, you need to be aware of a few tricks. As you'll learn in this chapter, mixing quinoa flour with other high-gluten and nongluten flours works best for most cake and cupcake recipes. And when it comes to crepes, quinoa flour makes a delicious and healthy batter that you can then top with fresh fruit topping.

Tips for Perfect Cakes

Although you can use quinoa flour in baked goods, you can't substitute it directly for all-purpose flour. The best blend is no more than 30 percent quinoa flour to 70 percent all-purpose flour.

When baking completely gluten-free items, mix quinoa flour with other naturally gluten-free flours, and use agents like xanthan gum, cornstarch, and tapioca starch to obtain the desired consistency. Add moisture to gluten-free flours and baked goods by using applesauce, orange juice, and jams.

Mix ingredients thoroughly, but be careful not to overmix. Overmixing batter can cause your cake to be tough and dense.

Always put your baked goods in a preheated oven for more even cooking temperature throughout the baking process. Cooking in a nonpreheated oven can result in a drier, flatter baked good.

Don't be afraid to experiment with different flour combinations and ingredients. Just be sure you write down the ingredients and quantities as you go along so you can repeat your perfect cake!

Pineapple Upside-Down Quinoa Cake

Quinoa flour is added to the cake batter to add fiber and other nutrients, and cooked quinoa is used along with pineapple and maraschino cherries.

Yield:	Prep time:	Cook time:	Serving size:
1 (9-inch-square) cake	15 minutes	1 hour	1 square

Each serving has:			
393.7 calories	71.7 g carbohydrates	13.7 g fat	1.3 g fiber
3.4 g protein			

¼ cup unsalted butter

⅔ cup light brown sugar, firmly packed

9 slices canned pineapple in juice, drained

9 maraschino cherries, stems removed

½ cup Quick-and-Easy Quinoa (recipe in Chapter 1)

1 cup all-purpose flour

⅓ cup toasted quinoa flour

1 cup sugar

⅓ cup shortening

1½ tsp. baking powder

½ tsp. sea salt

¾ cup low-fat milk

1 large egg

⅓ cup unsweetened applesauce

1. Preheat the oven to 350°F.

2. In a 9-inch square baking dish, place unsalted butter. Set in the preheating oven to melt.

3. Sprinkle light brown sugar evenly over melted butter. Arrange pineapple slices over brown sugar, and place 1 maraschino cherry in center of each pineapple slice. Sprinkle cooked Quick-and-Easy Quinoa evenly over pineapple slices.

4. In a medium bowl, and using an electric mixer on low speed, beat all-purpose flour, quinoa flour, sugar, shortening, baking powder, sea salt, low-fat milk, egg, and applesauce, scraping down the sides of the bowl as needed. Increase speed to high, and beat for 3 minutes. Pour batter over quinoa pineapple layer.

5. Bake for 50 to 55 minutes or until a toothpick inserted comes out clean.

6. Immediately place a heat-safe serving plate upside down over baking dish. Turn plate and baking dish over. Leave baking dish upside down a few minutes so brown sugar mixture can drizzle over cake. Remove baking dish. Slice cake into 9 equal squares, and serve warm.

KEEN ON QUINOA

Sure, shortening adds fat and sugar adds calories to this dessert, but using quinoa flour and cooked quinoa also adds fiber to help your body process the fat. Pineapple also contains a natural enzyme that helps break down fats and proteins, aiding the body's metabolism. Plus, pineapple is packed with vitamin C, potassium, and fiber.

Triple-Chocolate Torte
with Hazelnut Quinoa

Coffee, cayenne, quinoa, hazelnuts, and chocolate, chocolate, chocolate are at the heart of this chocolate-lover's dream. First, bake the chocolate torte and then generously drizzle with chocolate-covered hazelnuts and quinoa. Heaven!

Yield:	Prep time:	Cook time:	Serving size:
1 (9-inch-round) torte	20 minutes	35 minutes plus 4 hours or overnight rest time	$\frac{1}{16}$ of torte

Each serving has:			
288.7 calories 5.4 g protein	34.5 g carbohydrates	17.3 g fat	2.8 g fiber

1 TB. plus $\frac{1}{2}$ cup unsalted butter	6 large egg yolks
1 TB. plus $\frac{1}{3}$ cup unsweetened cocoa powder	$\frac{1}{2}$ cup sugar
1 (8-oz.) pkg. semisweet chocolate squares, chopped	$\frac{1}{4}$ cup toasted quinoa flour
	$\frac{3}{4}$ cup all-purpose flour
$\frac{1}{2}$ tsp. cayenne	$1\frac{1}{2}$ tsp. pure vanilla extract
1 tsp. instant coffee granules	$\frac{1}{2}$ tsp. sea salt
2 TB. water	1 cup chopped dark chocolate
6 large egg whites	1 tsp. shortening
$\frac{1}{8}$ tsp. cream of tartar	$\frac{1}{2}$ cup chopped hazelnuts
$\frac{1}{2}$ cup confectioners' sugar	$\frac{1}{4}$ cup Quick-and-Easy Quinoa (recipe in Chapter 1)

1. Preheat the oven to 375°F. Lightly coat a 9-inch-round springform pan with 1 tablespoon unsalted butter. Dust the bottom of the pan with 1 tablespoon unsweetened cocoa powder.

2. Place semisweet chocolate squares, remaining $\frac{1}{2}$ cup unsalted butter, and cayenne in the top bowl of a double boiler. Fill bottom bowl $\frac{1}{2}$ inch deep with water, and set over medium heat to melt chocolate and butter.

3. In a small bowl, whisk together instant coffee granules and water. Set aside.

4. In a large bowl, using an electric mixer on high speed, beat egg whites with cream of tartar and confectioners' sugar to stiff peaks. Set aside.

5. In a medium bowl, beat egg yolks and sugar until mixture is thick and lemony in color. Stir in toasted quinoa flour, all-purpose flour, vanilla extract, sea salt, chocolate mixture, coffee mixture, and remaining $1/3$ cup unsweetened cocoa powder. Gently fold beaten egg whites into yolk mixture.

6. Pour batter into the prepared springform pan. Bake for 35 to 40 minutes (center will be slightly soft). Remove from the oven, and set aside to cool. Once cooled, remove cake from the pan (pop the springform pan to open), and transfer cake to a serving plate.

7. Meanwhile, in a medium saucepan over low heat, melt dark chocolate and shortening. Stir in hazelnuts and Quick-and-Easy Quinoa, and spread or drizzle over cooled cake. Let cake rest for 4 hours or overnight before slicing into 16 slices and serving.

Lemon Poppy Seed Quinoa Cupcakes

Poppy seeds, quinoa, buttermilk, and lemons contribute to the deliciousness of these cupcakes, but the real lemon kicker is in the frosting! Butter, sugar, and lemon are spread atop already delicious cupcakes in this surefire favorite for lemon lovers.

Yield:	Prep time:	Cook time:	Serving size:
24 cupcakes	45 minutes	25 minutes	1 cupcake

Each serving has:			
267.3 calories	32.0 g carbohydrates	14.9 g fat	0.4 g fiber
2.5 g protein			

$1/3$ cup poppy seeds

1 cup reduced-fat buttermilk

$1/4$ cup toasted quinoa flour

$1^3/4$ cups all-purpose flour

2 tsp. baking powder

$1/2$ tsp. baking soda

2 TB. Quick-and-Easy Quinoa (recipe in Chapter 1)

$3/4$ cup shortening

$1^1/2$ cups sugar

1 tsp. pure vanilla extract

1 TB. fine grate lemon zest

4 TB. fresh lemon juice

4 large egg whites

2 sticks unsalted butter, softened

$1^1/4$ cups superfine or granulated sugar

2 or 3 drops yellow food coloring

Decorative sprinkles (optional)

1. Preheat the oven to 350°F. Line 24 muffin tins with decorative cupcake liners.

2. In a small bowl, soak poppy seeds in buttermilk for 30 minutes.

3. In a medium bowl, whisk together toasted quinoa flour, all-purpose flour, baking powder, baking soda, and Quick-and-Easy Quinoa.

4. In a large bowl, and using an electric mixer on medium speed, beat shortening and sugar until light and fluffy. Mix in vanilla extract, lemon zest, and 2 tablespoons lemon juice until well combined. Mix in $\frac{1}{2}$ of poppy seed mixture followed by $\frac{1}{2}$ of flour mixture. Repeat with remaining poppy seed and flour mixture.

5. In a separate medium bowl, beat egg whites until soft peaks form. Gently fold egg whites into batter.

6. Fill cupcake liners $\frac{1}{2}$ to $\frac{3}{4}$ full with batter, and bake for 20 to 25 minutes or until a toothpick inserted comes out clean. Allow cupcakes to cool completely on a wire rack.

7. Meanwhile, in a separate large bowl, beat unsalted butter until very soft and smooth. Beat in superfine sugar and remaining 2 tablespoons lemon juice. Stir in yellow food coloring.

8. Spoon icing into a pastry bag fitted with tip or a zipper-lock plastic bag with the corner snipped off. Pipe icing onto cupcakes, and top with decorative sprinkles (if using).

QUICK FIX

Use this delicious icing for more than just cupcakes. Spread on pound cakes, birthday cakes, or any kind of cake. Change the color to suit the occasion by using your food coloring of choice. To ice the perfect cake, use an offset spatula, starting at one side and spreading to the other, working in one direction so you don't tear the cake.

Carrot Quinoa Cupcakes with Cream Cheese Frosting

Cooked quinoa is added to this delicious cupcake recipe adapted from my grandmother's Southern carrot cake. Cream cheese frosting tops off these delicious cupcakes of carrot, cinnamon, and quinoa.

Yield:	Prep time:	Cook time:	Serving size:
24 cupcakes	15 minutes	20 minutes	1 cupcake

Each serving has:			
320.8 calories	26.7 g carbohydrates	22.9 g fat	0.8 g fiber
3.5 g protein			

2 cups grated, peeled fresh carrots	1 tsp. baking powder
5 large eggs	$\frac{1}{2}$ cup Quick-and-Easy Quinoa (recipe in Chapter 1)
$1\frac{1}{2}$ cups canola oil	1 (8-oz.) pkg. cream cheese
2 cups sugar	1 stick unsalted butter, softened
2 cups all-purpose flour	2 cups confectioners' sugar
2 tsp. ground cinnamon	$\frac{1}{4}$ cup finely chopped toasted pecans (optional)
$\frac{1}{2}$ tsp. ground nutmeg	
1 tsp. sea salt	
1 tsp. baking soda	

1. Preheat the oven to 350°F. Line 24 muffin tins with decorative cupcake liners.

2. In a large bowl, and using an electric mixer on medium speed, beat carrots, eggs, and canola oil. Add sugar, all-purpose flour, cinnamon, nutmeg, sea salt, baking soda, baking powder, and Quick-and-Easy Quinoa, and mix well.

3. Fill cupcake liners $\frac{1}{2}$ to $\frac{3}{4}$ full with batter. Bake for about 18 to 20 minutes or until a toothpick inserted comes out clean.

4. Meanwhile, in a separate large bowl, and using an electric mixer on medium speed, cream together cream cheese, unsalted butter, and confectioners' sugar. Spread over cooled cupcakes, and sprinkle each cupcake with $\frac{1}{2}$ teaspoon chopped pecans (if using).

Variation: You can substitute $\frac{1}{2}$ cup quinoa flour for $\frac{1}{2}$ cup all-purpose flour if you like. I used all all-purpose flour because I incorporated $\frac{1}{2}$ cup cooked quinoa and wanted to be sure the cupcakes were moist enough.

Raspberry Cream Quinoa Crepes

A traditional French recipe, crepes are very thin pancakes usually made from wheat flour. Here, toasted quinoa flour combines with soy milk and *grapeseed oil* and is filled with whipped cream, raspberry jam, and fresh raspberries.

Yield:	Prep time:	Cook time:	Serving size:
12 crepes	20 minutes	20 minutes	2 crepes

Each serving has:			
392.9 calories	63.7 g carbohydrates	15.6 g fat	4.2 g fiber
3.8 g protein			

1 cup toasted quinoa flour	$\frac{1}{2}$ TB. fine grate lemon zest
$1\frac{1}{2}$ cups soy milk	$\frac{1}{2}$ cup heavy whipping cream
$\frac{1}{2}$ TB. grapeseed oil	$1\frac{1}{2}$ tsp. confectioners' sugar
$\frac{1}{4}$ tsp. sea salt	1 tsp. pure vanilla extract
3 TB. unsalted butter, cut into 12 pieces	$1\frac{1}{2}$ cups fresh raspberries
1 cup raspberry jam	

1. Preheat the oven to 200°F. Line a baking sheet with parchment paper.

2. In a medium bowl, whisk together toasted quinoa flour, soy milk, grapeseed oil, and sea salt. Let stand for 20 minutes.

3. In a 10-inch nonstick crepe pan or skillet over medium-low heat, melt 1 piece of unsalted butter (or spray skillet with nonstick cooking spray). Ladle $\frac{1}{4}$ cup batter into the skillet, and quickly tilt the pan to form an even coating of batter on the bottom of the pan. Cook for 1 minute or until set and lightly browned. Using a spatula, loosen sides of crepe and flip over. Cook for 1 more minute. Arrange crepes on the prepared baking sheet and place in the oven to keep warm. Repeat with remaining unsalted butter and batter.

4. In a small bowl, combine jam and lemon zest. Set aside.

5. In a large bowl, whip heavy whipping cream until soft peaks form. Add confectioners' sugar and vanilla extract, and continue to whip until stiff peaks form. Gently fold in $\frac{1}{2}$ cup fresh raspberries.

6. To serve, place 1 crepe on a serving plate, and spread with 2 teaspoons jam mixture. Starting at one edge, roll crepes into a tube shape. Top with about 2 heaping tablespoons whipped cream, and finish with a couple fresh raspberries.

DEFINITION

Grapeseed oil is a polyunsaturated oil, meaning it's easier for your body to digest as opposed to saturated oil. Grapeseed oil, made by pressing grape seeds, has a mild nutty flavor and is a light oil great for cooking and vinaigrettes.

Glossary

agave nectar   Sap from the agave (*ah-GAH-vay*) plant, native to southern Mexico. It's used as a natural sweetener, in the same way as honey. It can be substituted for sugar in many recipes, including desserts, sauces, salad dressings, and drinks.

aioli   A garlic mayonnaise traditionally made by puréeing garlic, olive oil, and eggs. There are as many variations as you can imagine.

al dente   Italian for "against the teeth," this term refers to pasta or rice that's neither soft nor hard but just slightly firm against the teeth.

all-purpose flour   Flour that contains only the inner part of the wheat grain. It's suitable for everything from cakes to gravies.

allspice   A spice named for its flavor echoes of several spices (cinnamon, cloves, nutmeg) used in many desserts and in rich marinades and stews.

almond flour   Also referred to as almond meal, almond flour is ground almonds. It's naturally gluten free.

andouille sausage   A sausage made with highly seasoned pork chitterlings and tripe. It's a standard component of many Cajun dishes.

antipasto   A classic Italian-style appetizer that includes an assortment of meats, cheeses, and vegetables such as prosciutto, capicolla, mozzarella, mushrooms, and olives.

arborio rice   A plump Italian rice used for, among other purposes, risotto.

artichoke heart   The center part of the artichoke flower, often found canned in grocery stores.

arugula   A spicy-peppery green with leaves that resemble a dandelion and have a distinctive and very sharp flavor.

bake   To cook in a dry oven. Dry-heat cooking often results in a crisping of the exterior of the food being cooked. Moist-heat cooking, through methods such as steaming, poaching, etc., brings a much different, moist quality to the food.

baking powder   A dry ingredient used to increase volume and lighten or leaven baked goods.

balsamic vinegar   Vinegar produced primarily in Italy from a specific type of grape and aged in wood barrels. It's heavier, darker, and sweeter than most vinegars.

basil   A flavorful, almost sweet, resinous herb delicious with tomatoes and used in all kinds of Italian- or Mediterranean-style dishes.

baste   To keep foods moist during cooking by spooning, brushing, or drizzling with a liquid.

beat   To quickly mix substances.

blanch   To place a food in boiling water for about 1 minute or less to partially cook the exterior and then submerge in or rinse with cool water to halt the cooking.

blend   To completely mix something, usually with a blender or food processor, slower than beating.

boil   To heat a liquid to the point where water is forced to turn into steam, causing the liquid to bubble. To boil something is to insert it into boiling water. A rapid boil is when a lot of bubbles form on the surface of the liquid.

bok choy   A member of the cabbage family with thick stems, crisp texture, and fresh flavor. It's perfect for stir-frying.

broil   To cook in a dry oven under the overhead high-heat element.

broth   *See* stock.

brown   To cook in a skillet, turning, until the food's surface is seared and brown in color, to lock in the juices.

brown rice   A whole-grain rice, including the germ, with a characteristic pale brown or tan color. It's more nutritious and flavorful than white rice.

bruschetta (or **crostini**)   Slices of toasted or grilled bread with garlic and olive oil, often with other toppings.

cake flour   A high-starch, soft, and fine flour used primarily for cakes.

canapé   A bite-size hors d'oeuvre usually served on a small piece of bread or toast.

caper   The flavorful buds of a Mediterranean plant, ranging in size from *nonpareil* (about the size of a small pea) to larger, grape-size caper berries produced in Spain.

caramelize   To cook sugar over low heat until it develops a sweet caramel flavor, or to cook vegetables (especially onions) or meat in butter or oil over low heat until they soften, sweeten, and develop a caramel color.

caraway   A distinctive spicy seed used for bread, pork, cheese, and cabbage dishes. It's known to reduce stomach upset, which is why it's often paired with foods like sauerkraut.

cardamom   An intense, sweet-smelling spice used in baking and coffee and common in Indian cooking.

cayenne   A fiery spice made from hot chile peppers, especially the cayenne chile, a slender, red, and very hot pepper.

ceviche   A seafood dish in which fresh fish or seafood is marinated for several hours in highly acidic lemon or lime juice, tomato, onion, and cilantro. The acid "cooks" the seafood.

chevre   A creamy-salty soft goat cheese. Chevres vary in style from mild and creamy to aged, firm, and flavorful.

chickpea (or **garbanzo bean**)   A yellow-gold, roundish bean used as the base ingredient in hummus. Chickpeas are high in fiber and low in fat.

chile (or **chili**)   Any one of many different "hot" peppers, ranging in intensity from the relatively mild ancho pepper to the blisteringly hot habañero.

chili powder   A warm, rich seasoning blend that includes chile pepper, cumin, garlic, and oregano.

Chinese five-spice powder   A pungent mixture of equal parts cinnamon, cloves, fennel seed, anise, and Szechuan peppercorns.

chive   A member of the onion family, chives grow in bunches of long leaves that resemble tall grass or the green tops of onions and offer a light onion flavor.

chop   To cut into pieces, usually qualified by an adverb such as "*coarsely* chopped" or by a size measurement such as "chopped into $1/2$-inch pieces." "Finely chopped" is much closer to mince.

chutney   A thick condiment often served with Indian curries made with fruits and/ or vegetables with vinegar, sugar, and spices.

cider vinegar   A vinegar produced from apple cider, popular in North America.

cilantro   A member of the parsley family used in Mexican dishes (especially salsa) and some Asian dishes. Use in moderation because the flavor can overwhelm. The seed of the cilantro plant is the spice coriander.

cinnamon   A rich, aromatic spice commonly used in baking or desserts. Cinnamon can also be used for delicious and interesting entrées.

clove   A sweet, strong, almost wintergreen-flavor spice used in baking.

compote   A chilled dish of fresh or dried fruit that's slowly cooked in a sugary syrup made of liquid and spices.

coriander   A rich, warm, spicy seed used in all types of recipes, from African to South American, from entrées to desserts.

cornstarch   A thickener used in baking and food processing. It's the refined starch of the endosperm of the corn kernel and often mixed with cold liquid to make into a paste before adding to a recipe to avoid clumps.

count   In terms of seafood or other foods that come in small sizes, the number of that item that compose 1 pound. For example, 31 to 40 count shrimp are large appetizer shrimp often served with cocktail sauce; 51 to 60 count are much smaller.

couscous   Granular semolina (durum wheat) that's cooked and used in many Mediterranean and North African dishes.

cream   To beat a fat such as butter, often with another ingredient such as sugar, to soften and aerate a batter.

crepe   A thin, pancake-style pastry originating from France. Usually made from wheat flour, crepes are served with a variety of fillings, including fruit and sugary fillings as well as savory fillings with rich sauces.

crimini mushroom   A relative of the white button mushroom that's brown in color and has a richer flavor. The larger, fully grown version is the portobello. *See also* portobello mushroom.

crumble   A baked topping made with sugar, fat, and flour and crumbled over sweet or savory foods.

cumin   A fiery, smoky-tasting spice popular in Middle Eastern and Indian dishes. Cumin is a seed; ground cumin seed is the most common form used in cooking.

curry   Rich, spicy, Indian-style sauces and the dishes prepared with them. A curry uses curry powder as its base seasoning.

curry powder   A ground blend of rich and flavorful spices used as a basis for curry and many other Indian-influenced dishes. Common ingredients include hot pepper, nutmeg, cumin, cinnamon, pepper, and turmeric. Some curry can also be found in paste form.

custard   A cooked mixture of eggs and milk popular as a base for desserts.

dash   A few drops, usually of a liquid, released by a quick shake.

deglaze   To scrape up bits of meat and seasoning left in a pan or skillet after cooking.

devein   To remove the dark vein from the back of a large shrimp with a sharp knife.

dice   To cut into small cubes about $\frac{1}{4}$-inch square.

Dijon mustard   A hearty, spicy mustard made in the style of the Dijon region of France.

dill   An herb perfect for eggs, salmon, cheese dishes, and, of course, vegetables (pickles!).

dollop   A spoonful of something creamy and thick, like sour cream or whipped cream.

double boiler   A set of two pots designed to nest together, one inside the other, and provide consistent, moist heat for foods that need delicate treatment. The bottom pot holds water (not quite touching the bottom of the top pot); the top pot holds the food you want to heat.

dredge   To coat a piece of food on all sides with a dry substance such as flour or cornmeal.

drizzle   To lightly sprinkle drops of a liquid over food, often as the finishing touch to a dish.

edamame   Fresh, plump, pale green soybeans, similar in appearance to lima beans, often served steamed and either shelled or still in their protective pods.

emulsion   A combination of liquid ingredients that do not normally mix well that are beaten together to create a thick liquid, such as a fat or oil with water. Creating emulsions must be done carefully and rapidly to ensure the particles of one ingredient are suspended in the other.

endive   A green that resembles a small, elongated, tightly packed head of romaine lettuce. The thick, crunchy leaves can be broken off and used with dips and spreads.

entrée   The main dish in a meal.

extra-virgin olive oil   *See* olive oil.

extract   A concentrated flavoring derived from foods or plants through evaporation or distillation that imparts a powerful flavor without altering the volume or texture of a dish.

fava bean   A large bean native to parts of Africa and Asia and also popular in Mediterranean cooking. Also known as *broad beans*, fava beans are often immersed in boiling water (blanched) to remove their outer skin. A hearty bean with robust flavor, fava beans provide many nutrients, are low in fat, and are a good source of protein.

fennel   In seed form, a fragrant, licorice-tasting herb. The bulbs have a mild flavor and a celery-like crunch and are used as a vegetable in salads or cooked recipes.

flour   Grains ground into a meal. Wheat is perhaps the most common flour, but oats, rye, buckwheat, soybeans, chickpeas, etc. can also be used. *See also* all-purpose flour; cake flour; whole-wheat flour.

fold   To combine a dense and light mixture with a circular action from the middle of the bowl.

frittata   A skillet-cooked mixture of eggs and other ingredients that's not stirred but is cooked slowly and then either flipped or finished under the broiler.

fry   *See* sauté.

garlic   A member of the onion family, a pungent and flavorful vegetable used in many savory dishes. A garlic bulb contains multiple cloves. Each clove, when chopped, provides about 1 teaspoon of garlic.

ginger   A flavorful root available fresh or dried and ground that adds a pungent, sweet, and spicy quality to a dish.

grapeseed oil   A polyunsaturated oil that's easier for your body to digest as opposed to saturated oil. Grapeseed oil has a mild nut flavor. It's made by pressing grapeseeds and is a light oil great for cooking and vinaigrettes.

Greek yogurt   A strained yogurt that's a good natural source of protein, calcium, and probiotics. Greek yogurt averages 40 percent more protein per ounce than traditional yogurt.

handful   An unscientific measurement, it's the amount of an ingredient you can hold in your hand.

herbes de Provence A seasoning mix of basil, fennel, marjoram, rosemary, sage, and thyme, common in the south of France.

hoisin sauce A sweet Asian condiment similar to ketchup made with soybeans, sesame, chile peppers, and sugar.

hominy Hulled corn. The hulls have been removed by soaking in lye. Hominy is used whole as you would traditional corn kernels in recipes for casseroles, soups, and stews. Ground hominy is the base for grits, tamales, and tortillas.

hors d'oeuvre French for "outside of work" (the "work" being the main meal), an hors d'oeuvre can be any dish served as a starter before a meal.

horseradish A sharp, spicy root that forms the flavor base in condiments such as cocktail sauce and sharp mustards. Prepared horseradish contains vinegar and oil, among other ingredients. Use pure horseradish much more sparingly than the prepared version, or try cutting it with sour cream.

hummus A thick, Middle Eastern spread made of puréed chickpeas, lemon juice, olive oil, garlic, and often tahini.

infusion A liquid in which flavorful ingredients such as herbs have been soaked or steeped to extract their flavor into the liquid.

Italian seasoning A blend of dried herbs, including basil, oregano, rosemary, and thyme.

jicama A juicy, crunchy, sweet, large, round Central American vegetable. If you can't find jicama, try substituting sliced water chestnuts.

julienne A French word meaning "to slice into very thin pieces."

kalamata olive Traditionally from Greece, a medium-small, long black olive with a rich, smoky flavor.

Key lime A very small lime grown primarily in Florida known for its tart taste.

knead To work dough to make it pliable so it holds gas bubbles as it bakes. Kneading is fundamental in the process of making yeast breads.

kosher salt A coarse-grained salt made without any additives or iodine.

lentil A tiny lens-shaped pulse used in European, Middle Eastern, and Indian cuisines.

maki   "Roll" in Japanese, maki refers to any type of sushi roll made with sushi rice, toasted seaweed, and filling.

marinate   To soak meat, seafood, or other food in a seasoned sauce, a marinade, that's high in acid content. The acids break down the muscle of the meat, making it tender and adding flavor.

marjoram   A sweet herb, cousin of and similar to oregano, popular in Greek, Spanish, and Italian dishes.

masa harina   A coarse flour made from ground corn. It's used in many recipes traditional to Mexico, Central America, and South America.

meld   To allow flavors to blend and spread over time. Melding is often why recipes call for overnight refrigeration and is also why some dishes taste better as leftovers.

meringue   A baked mixture of sugar and beaten egg whites, often used as a dessert topping.

mesclun   Mixed salad greens, usually containing lettuce and other assorted greens such as arugula, cress, and endive.

Microplane   The brand name for a specific type of zester or grater. Typically, a Microplane has a rubber handle attached to a long metal shaft with small, sharp metal teeth, perfect for zesting citrus fruits and for grating hard cheeses.

millet   A tiny, round, yellow-colored nutty-flavored grain often used as a replacement for couscous.

mince   To cut into very small pieces, smaller than diced, about $1/8$ inch or smaller.

miso   A fermented, flavorful soybean paste, key in many Japanese dishes.

nutmeg   A sweet, fragrant, musky spice used primarily in baking.

Old Bay Seasoning   A blend of herbs and spices used mainly in seafood dishes.

olive   The fruit of the olive tree commonly grown on all sides of the Mediterranean. Black olives are also called ripe olives. Green olives are immature, although they're also widely eaten. *See also* kalamata olives.

olive oil   A fragrant liquid produced by crushing or pressing olives. Extra-virgin olive oil—the most flavorful and highest quality—is produced from the first pressing of a batch of olives; oil is also produced from later pressings.

oregano   A fragrant, slightly astringent herb used in Greek, Spanish, and Italian dishes.

orzo   A rice-shaped pasta used in Greek cooking.

oxidation   The browning of fruit flesh that happens over time and with exposure to air. Minimize oxidation by rubbing the cut surfaces with lemon juice.

paella   A Spanish dish of rice, shellfish, onion, meats, rich broth, and herbs.

pane toscano   A handmade Italian bread made with no salt. Due to its low salt content, the bread hardens and becomes stale quicker than other breads, making it great for soups and stews.

paprika   A rich, red, warm, earthy spice that lends a rich red color to many dishes.

parboil   To partially cook in boiling water or broth.

parchment paper   A moisture-resistant paper used in baking. It creates a nonstick baking surface and is heat resistant.

parsley   A fresh-tasting green leafy herb, often used as a garnish.

pâté   A savory loaf that contains meats, poultry, or seafood; spices; and often a lot of fat. It's served cold and spread or sliced on crusty bread or crackers.

pesto   A thick spread or sauce made with fresh basil leaves, garlic, olive oil, pine nuts, and Parmesan cheese.

pilaf   A rice dish in which the rice is browned in butter or oil and then cooked in a flavorful liquid such as a broth, often with the addition of meats or vegetables. The rice absorbs the broth, resulting in a savory dish.

pinch   An unscientific measurement for the amount of an ingredient—typically, a dry, granular substance such as an herb or seasoning—you can hold between your finger and thumb.

pine nut   A nut that's rich (high in fat), flavorful, and a bit pine-y. Pine nuts are a traditional ingredient in pesto and add a hearty crunch to many other recipes.

pita bread   A flat, hollow wheat bread often used for sandwiches or sliced pizza style. They're terrific soft with dips or baked or broiled as a vehicle for other ingredients.

poach   To cook a food in simmering liquid such as water, wine, or broth.

polenta   A mush made from cornmeal that can be eaten hot with butter or cooked until firm and cut into squares.

porcini mushroom   A rich and flavorful mushroom used in rice and Italian-style dishes.

portobello mushroom   A mature and larger form of the smaller crimini mushroom. Brown, chewy, and flavorful, portobellos are often served as whole caps, grilled, or as thin sautéed slices. *See also* crimini mushrooms.

preheat   To turn on an oven, broiler, or other cooking appliance in advance of cooking so the temperature will be at the desired level when the assembled dish is ready for cooking.

prosciutto   A dry, salt-cured ham that originated in Italy.

purée   To reduce a food to a thick, creamy texture, typically using a blender or food processor.

quinoa   A nutty-flavored seed that's high in protein, fiber, and minerals.

reduce   To boil or simmer a broth or sauce to remove some of the water content, resulting in more concentrated flavor and color.

reserve   To hold a specified ingredient for another use later in the recipe.

rice vinegar   Vinegar produced from fermented rice or rice wine, popular in Asian-style dishes. (It's not the same thing as rice wine vinegar.)

risotto   A popular Italian rice dish made by browning arborio rice in butter or oil and then slowly adding liquid to cook the rice, resulting in a creamy texture.

roast   To cook something uncovered in an oven, usually without additional liquid.

rosemary   A pungent, sweet herb used with chicken, pork, fish, and especially lamb. A little goes a long way.

roux   A mixture of butter or another fat and flour used to thicken sauces and soups.

saffron   An expensive spice made from the stamens of crocus flowers. Saffron lends a dramatic yellow color and distinctive flavor to a dish. Use only tiny amounts.

sage   An herb with a musty yet fruity, lemon-rind scent and "sunny" flavor.

sauté   To pan-cook over lower heat than what's used for frying.

savory   A popular herb with a fresh, woody taste. Can also describe the flavor of food.

scald   To heat milk just until it's about to boil and then remove it from heat. Scalding milk helps prevent it from souring.

scant   An ingredient measurement directive not to add any extra, perhaps even leaving the measurement a tad short.

sear   To quickly brown the exterior of a food, especially meat, over high heat.

sesame oil   An oil made from pressing sesame seeds. It's tasteless if clear and aromatic and flavorful if brown.

shallot   A member of the onion family that grows in a bulb somewhat like garlic but has a milder onion flavor. When a recipe calls for shallot, use the entire bulb.

shellfish   A broad range of seafood, including clams, mussels, oysters, crabs, shrimp, and lobster.

shiitake mushroom   A large, dark brown mushroom with a hearty, meaty flavor. It can be used fresh or dried, grilled, as a component in other recipes, and as a flavoring source for broth.

short-grain rice   A starchy rice popular in Asian-style dishes because it readily clumps, making it perfect for eating with chopsticks.

simmer   To boil gently so the liquid barely bubbles.

skillet (also **frying pan**)   A generally heavy, flat-bottomed, metal pan with a handle designed to cook food over heat on a stovetop or campfire.

skim   To remove fat or other material from the top of liquid.

steam   To suspend a food over boiling water and allow the heat of the steam (water vapor) to cook the food. This quick-cooking method preserves a food's flavor and texture.

steep   To let sit in hot water, as in steeping tea in hot water for 10 minutes.

stew   To slowly cook pieces of food submerged in a liquid. Also, a dish prepared by this method.

stir-fry   To cook small pieces of food in a wok or skillet over high heat, moving and turning the food quickly to cook all sides.

stock   A flavorful broth made by cooking meats and/or vegetables with seasonings until the liquid absorbs these flavors. The liquid is strained and the solids are discarded. Stock can be eaten alone or used as a base for soups, stews, etc.

strata   A savory bread pudding made with eggs and cheese.

superfood   A food that gives you the most nutritional power per serving, often loaded with high fiber, minerals, vitamins, and properties that aid in the prevention of a variety of health problems.

tahini   A paste made from sesame seeds; used to flavor many Middle Eastern recipes.

tamari   A type of soy sauce primarily used for cooking because of its darker and richer consistency and flavor. Regular soy sauce is primarily used as a dipping sauce, although it can be used in cooking.

tamarind   A sweet, pungent, flavorful fruit used in Indian-style sauces and curries.

tamarind paste   Ground pulp from the tamarind fruit. It's sour in flavor and used primarily in Indian and Thai cuisines, but is also found in Asian, Latin American, and Mediterranean dishes.

tapas   A Spanish term meaning "small plates" that describes individual-size appetizers and snacks served cold or warm.

tapenade   A thick, chunky spread made from savory ingredients such as olives, lemon juice, and anchovies.

tarragon   A sweet, rich-smelling herb perfect with seafood, vegetables (especially asparagus), chicken, and pork.

tempeh   An Indonesian food made by culturing and fermenting soybeans into a cake, sometimes mixed with grains or vegetables. It's high in protein and fiber.

temper   To mix ingredients of differing temperatures.

teriyaki   A Japanese-style sauce composed of soy sauce, rice wine, ginger, and sugar that works well with seafood as well as most meats.

thyme   A minty, zesty herb.

tofu   A cheeselike substance made from soybeans and soy milk.

tomatillo   A small, round fruit with a distinctive spicy flavor, often found in south-of-the-border dishes. To use, remove the papery outer skin, rinse off any sticky residue, and chop like a tomato.

turmeric   A spicy, pungent yellow root used in many dishes, especially Indian cuisine, for color and flavor. Turmeric is the source of the yellow color in many prepared mustards.

tzatziki   A Greek dip traditionally made with Greek yogurt, cucumbers, garlic, and mint.

umeboshi vinegar   A Japanese vinegar made with umeboshi plums, sea salt, and perilla leaves. The red vinegar is light, citrusy, and usually very salty.

veal   Meat from a calf, generally characterized by its mild flavor and tenderness.

vegetable steamer   An insert with tiny holes in the bottom designed to fit on or in another pot to hold food to be steamed above boiling water. *See also* steam.

venison   Deer meat.

vinegar   An acidic liquid widely used as a dressing and seasoning, often made from fermented grapes, apples, or rice. *See also* balsamic vinegar; cider vinegar; rice vinegar; white vinegar; wine vinegar.

wasabi   Japanese horseradish, a fiery, pungent condiment used with many Japanese-style dishes. It's most often sold as a powder to which you add water to create a paste.

water chestnut   A tuber popular in many Asian dishes. It's white, crunchy, and juicy, and holds its texture whether cool or hot.

whisk   To rapidly mix, introducing air to the mixture.

white mushroom   A button mushroom. When fresh, white mushrooms have an earthy smell and an appealing soft crunch.

white vinegar   The most common type of vinegar, produced from grain.

whole grain   A grain derived from the seeds of grasses, including rice, oats, rye, wheat, wild rice, quinoa, barley, buckwheat, bulgur, corn, millet, amaranth, and sorghum.

whole-wheat flour   Wheat flour that contains the entire grain.

wild rice   Not a rice at all, this is actually a grass. It has a rich, nutty flavor and serves as a nutritious side dish.

wine vinegar   Vinegar produced from red or white wine.

yeast   Tiny fungi that, when mixed with water, sugar, flour, and heat, release carbon dioxide bubbles, which, in turn, cause the bread to rise.

zest   Small slivers of peel, usually from a citrus fruit such as a lemon, lime, or orange.

Resources

Quinoa, quinoa flour, and other quinoa-related products are making their way into health food and even grocery stores all over the country. If you can't find the quinoa ingredient you want where you live, here are some online sources that might help.

Arrowhead Mills
arrowheadmills.com
Log on to find quinoa and other delicious products.

Barry Farm Foods
barryfarm.com
Barry Farm Foods sells quinoa, red quinoa, quinoa flour, and more.

Bob's Red Mill
bobsredmill.com
Organic quinoa and quinoa flour are available here.

Northern Quinoa Corporation
quinoa.com
Log on here for various quinoa products.

NutsOnline
nutsonline.com
The site sells organic quinoa in 1-pound bags for $3.99 and 5-pound bags for $19.35 (plus shipping).

The Quinoa Corporation
quinoa.net
The Quinoa Corporation produces Ancient Harvest quinoa and other quinoa-based products.

Contributing Chefs

A huge thanks to the many celebrated, talented, and creative chefs who contributed quinoa recipes to the book. Their contributions demonstrate that varied backgrounds, ages, and culinary training and experience can come together to celebrate a common ingredient. May you enjoy their professional recipes and visit their respective restaurants to taste their quinoa dishes firsthand.

Chef Chris Barnett, executive chef, Sherbourne (Los Angeles, CA)   Chef Chris Barnett has been cooking since age 14 and is currently the executive chef at Sherbourne in Los Angeles, which offers alfresco dining with comfort foods such as a roving mashed potato cart with three types of potatoes and toppings from basil to truffle oil. *Recipes: Roasted Salmon, Quinoa, Fennel, Radish, and Blood Orange Salad (Chapter 17); Quinoa Veggie Burger by Chef Chris Barnett (Chapter 15); and Wild Arugula Quinoa Salad with Lemon Vinaigrette (Chapter 14)*

Chef Katy Clark, contestant, *The Next Food Network Star* (season 7)   Fit Chef Katy Clark is a food and fitness lifestyle coach, chef, Mrs. Long Beach 2011, and energetic mother of three. After raising her children in Kunming, China, for 6 years, where she owned Silver Spoon Café, she moved back to Long Beach and opened The Dessert Lady Catering Company and LOOK! I Can Cook, a children's cooking company. Fit Chef Katy inspires "Healthy choices. Healthy you." *Recipe: Fit Chef Katy Clark's Tropical Quinoa Pudding (Chapter 23)*

Chef Brendan Collins, executive chef/owner, Waterloo and City (Culver City, CA) and Larry's Venice Beach (Venice Beach, CA)   At age 15, Brendan Collins quit school to follow his culinary dreams. By 17, he had his first job at a Michelin two-star restaurant, Le Gravroche in London. He continued to hone his skills at some of London's top gastronomic temples, including Café Royal, The Heights, and Pied et Terre, before moving on to The Calls Grill in Leeds, where under his direction, the restaurant earned the prestigious Michelin Bib Gourmand in 1999. After working with the Harvey Nichols Group at Oxo Tower, Collins garnered one

Michelin star at Quo Vadis, working with celebrity chef Marco Pierre White, and then was wooed to Los Angeles by famed Chef Josiah Citrin to serve as Chef de Cuisine of Citrin's Melisse Restaurant in Santa Monica. The restaurant received a Mobile Four Star Rating and was among the first California dining destinations to be awarded a coveted Michelin two-star rating. Chef Collins opened Mesa in Orange County, California, followed by Anisette with Alain Giraud, and then became executive chef of The Hall at Palihouse. Currently, Chef Collins is executive chef and proprietor at Waterloo & City, Culver City, Executive Chef Larry's Venice Beach, and is consulting for The Palihouse in its latest culinary venture. *Recipe: Quinoa and Lobster Thermidor (Chapter 18)*

Chef Mark Ellman, executive chef, Honu (Maui, HI) and executive chef and owner, Mala (Wailea, HI)   Chef Mark Ellman began his culinary career at age 13 in Los Angeles and later launched Can't Rock 'n' Roll, But Sure Can Cook catering with his wife, Judy, feeding rock stars along the California coast. Later, they opened Avalon in Lahaina, Maui, where Chef Ellman became known as one of the original 12 Hawaii Regional Chefs. Ellman, along with Roy Yamaguchi, Sam Choy, Peter Merriman, and Alan Wong, founded Hawaiian Regional Cuisine. He has been featured on *Emeril* and *The Today Show*, among others. Currently, Chef Ellman and Judy own and operate Mala Ocean Tavern, 2007 'Ilima Award winner for Best Maui Restaurant by *The Honolulu Advertiser*, and Penne Pasta Café in Lahaina, Maui. *Recipe: Quinoa Lentil Burger (Chapter 15)*

Denice Fladeboe, executive producer and cohost of *Bikini Lifestyles* on AM 790 KABC, and cofounder, Pink Bikini Productions, LLC   Denice Fladeboe is the executive producer and cohost of *Bikini Lifestyles* on AM 790 KABC; cofounder of Pink Bikini Productions, LLC; and president of Fladeboe Automotive Group of Irvine. *Recipes: Chicken and Rice Confetti Soup (Chapter 10) and Pork Chops with a Quinoa Twist (Chapter 17)*

Kevin Fortun, owner, Desert Sage Restaurant (La Quinta, CA)   Kevin Fortun is creator, owner, and founder of Fortun's Finishing Touch Sauces, an innovative line of 12 gourmet restaurant–quality finishing sauces available in retail food chains. A proven trendsetter in the food business, he's known for developing Stockpot Soups, which he sold to Campbell's Soup. *Recipe: Grilled Halibut with Quinoa, Asparagus, Spinach, and Fortun's Lemon Dill Caper Wine Sauces (Chapter 18)*

Chef Jon Gibson, executive chef, The Beachcomber Café (Newport Beach, CA)   Chef Jon Gibson has been a driving force in California coastal cuisine in Orange and Los Angeles counties. Classically culinary trained at Le Cordon Bleu, Pasadena, Chef Gibson worked alongside Cat Cora and Guy Fieri at the 2006 LA

Food and Wine Festival with two-star Michelin chef Edouard Loubet, and has
appeared at Taste of Newport, KTLA, and *Orange County Register*'s "Cooking with
Cathy Thomas." *Recipe: Chef Jon Gibson's Quinoa Palermo Salad (Chapter 7)*

Chef Lee Gross, executive chef, M Café (Los Angeles, CA)   Chef Gross has
served macrobiotic cuisine at M Café for the last six years, working with Chef
Tachibe and Chaya Restaurant Group. After receiving a degree from Johnson &
Wales University in Providence, Rhode Island, in 1996, Chef Gross worked with a
number of acclaimed chefs and restaurants, including Philippe Jeanty at Domaine
Chandon in Napa Valley, Daniel Bruce at the Boston Harbor Hotel, and Providence's
Al Forno. Chef Gross is a private chef and caterer specializing in macrobiotic cuisine.
Recipe: M Café's Scarlet Quinoa Salad (Chapter 14)

Chef Katsu Hanamure, executive chef, Osaka (Hollywood, CA)   Chef Katsu
Hanamure is a renowned Japanese sushi chef trained by Chef Nobu Matsuhisa at the
famed Matsuhisa in Los Angeles and currently serves as executive chef at Osaka in
Hollywood. *Recipe: Ceviche Nikkei (Chapter 12)*

Chef Elizabeth Howes, owner and chef, Saffron Lane (San Francisco, CA)   As
a chef, freelance food writer, and photographer, Chef Howes loves to create seasonal,
style-driven recipes and photos. She has appeared on the Food Network, has been
featured in the James Beard Foundation publication *JBF Notes*, and is a regular
contributor to Gojee.com and *Edible Marin & Wine Country* magazine. Her work
has been published on Shape.com, SFGate.com, and SlowFoodMarin.com, among
others. Learn more at saffronlane.com/blog. *Recipe: Farmers' Market Quinoa Salad
with Pistachio-Lemon Vinaigrette (Chapter 7)*

**Chef Ashley James, executive chef, Four Seasons Los Angeles at Beverly Hills
(Beverly Hills, CA)**   Executive Chef Ashley James has 24 years' experience at
some of the world's finest restaurants. As executive chef of Four Seasons Hotel Los
Angeles at Beverly Hills, Chef Ashley serves Hollywood's A-list. Recently, Chef
Ashley created the "World of Plates" menu at Windows Lounge, featuring a variety
of appetizers from Asia, Europe, North America, and South America. Chef James
was executive chef at the Four Seasons Hotel, Buenos Aires, when the restaurant
Le Mistral was named the number-one restaurant in the country. He was executive
sous chef at Four Seasons Resort, Punta Mita, Mexico, where he was part of the
hotel's preopening team. He began his career with Four Seasons as chef de cuisine at
Maxims de Paris at the Regent Singapore. He graduated from Staffordshire College
of Food and Domestic Arts in England, was named Young Chef of the Year (under
24) in France in 1992, and is a member of L'Académie Culinaire de France. *Recipe:
Achiote Roasted Red Snapper with Quinoa and Avocado Cilantro Crema (Chapter 18)*

Hailey Kehoe, owner, Culinartist Catering (San Francisco, CA)   Hailey Kehoe, age 16, is currently a culinary sophomore at Johnson and Wales University in Providence, Rhode Island. Hailey was recognized in the Bay Area as a Rising Star Chef in the *Almanac Newspaper* for her very specialized, gluten-free catering business, Culinartist, which she launched at the age of 16. Hailey specializes in developing recipes for her celiac and gluten-free clients, putting together five-course, gluten-free dinner parties for customers such as former Williams-Sonoma vice president Beverly Stern. *Recipe: Quinoa Carbonara with Fresh Spring Peas, Topped with a Quail Eggs (Chapter 14)*

Chef Brock Kleweno, executive chef, Yamashiro Restaurant (Hollywood, CA)   After graduating from the University of Washington with a bachelor's degree in marketing, Chef Brock Kleweno headed to culinary school at Le Cordon Bleu in Pasadena. Kleweno's first restaurant job was at Balboa Steakhouse, working his way through the kitchen. In 2004, Kleweno became sous chef at Yamashiro Restaurant, where he was promoted to executive chef in 2009. In 2010, he took on the additional role of food and beverage director. Today, Chef Kleweno can be found creating innovative dishes in Yamashiro's kitchen and is a regular at the Yamashiro Farmers' Market, where he serves the famed tacos from his new eatery, Komida. *Recipe: Quinoa Paillard (Chapter 21)*

Chef Manfred Lassahn, senior executive chef, Hyatt Regency Century Plaza (Los Angeles, CA)   Chef Lassahn is the former executive chef for Hyatt properties, including Hyatt Regency Long Beach, Valencia, Huntington Beach Resort, and was selected to participate in the annual "Masters of Food and Wine" in Carmel, California. *Recipe: Red Beet Quinoa and Zucchini Noodle (Chapter 15)*

Chef James McDonald, executive chef/owner, I'o Restaurant, Pacific'o Restaurant, The Feast at Lele, Aina Gourmet Market, O'o Farm (Lahaina, Maui, HA)   A James Beard–award nominee, Chef James was voted "Maui's Best Chef" by the readers of the *Maui News* and *Maui Time* newspapers and was a 2009 *Chef Magazine* "Chef of the Year" finalist. His cuisine and restaurants have garnered rave reviews from *Bon Appétit*, *Travel and Leisure*, and *The New Yorker*, to name a few. *Gourmet* magazine voted his two restaurants in the top 10 in the United States for "farm to table" dining. He is the only recipient of the Distinguished Restaurants of North America (DiRoNA) distinction on Maui. In addition, his restaurants are the only in the state to own and operate a farm, the 8-acre O'o Farm in upcountry Maui, where they grow their own produce. *Recipe: Chef James McDonald's Quinoa Super Salad (Chapter 7)*

Chef Jessica Obie, corporate management trainee, training for Sous Chef at Hyatt Gainey Ranch (Scottsdale, AZ)   Jessica Obie is a culinary corporate management trainee (CMT) at Hyatt Gainey Ranch. While in this position, she has partnered with local schools to develop nutritional programs, helped redesign a healthier employee cafeteria menu, and teaches nutritional classes for health-conscious groups. Prior to Hyatt Gainey Ranch, she was a Cook II in the Grand Met Restaurant at the Grand Hyatt DFW, where she assisted the executive chef during the Epicurean Studio cooking classes. She has also studied at Le Cordon Bleu in Dallas. Upon finishing her CMT training, Chef Jessica will begin her new position as sous chef for Hyatt Gainey Ranch. *Recipe: Chef Jessica's Chocolate Strawberry Quinoa Maki (Chapter 22)*

Chef Keith Otter, executive chef, Desert Sage Restaurant (La Quinta, CA) Chef Keith Otter, graduate of the California Culinary Academy in San Francisco, began his culinary career at Pascal's in Newport Beach, California. His career has been enlightened by renowned chefs Julian Serrano of award-winning Masa's San Francisco and Chef Joachim Splichal of Patina Los Angeles. Chef Otter is joined at Desert Sage by General Manager Sam Fugate; together, they form a food and wine team that spans more than 20 years. Both Chef Keith and Sam came to Desert Sage after partnering in Otter's Restaurant in Sun Valley, Idaho. *Recipe: Grilled Halibut with Quinoa, Asparagus, Spinach and Fortun's Lemon Dill Caper Wine Sauces (Chapter 18)*

Chef Serena Palumbo, finalist, *The Next Food Network Star* (season 6)   Born and raised in Salerno, Italy, Chef Palumbo moved to New York in 2004 to study for her Master's of law and had to adapt to a much smaller kitchen in her Manhattan apartment. In 2008, with her husband, Kurt, she decided to create a series of instructional webisodes called *Cooking in Manhattan*, with the goal of teaching viewers to prepare great food within the confines of a small urban kitchen. *Cooking in Manhattan* led to appearances on Food2, CNN, and BBC, and earned her a spot as one of the finalists on *The Next Food Network Star* (season 6). *Recipe: Quinoa "Pasta" and Lentils (Chapter 15)*

Chef Bruno Serato, executive chef and owner, Anaheim White House (Anaheim, CA)   Voted one of the 2011 Top 10 Heroes of the World by CNN due to his work through Caterina's Club, which was founded by his mother in 2005, Executive Chef Bruno Serato is an Italian immigrant who moved to Orange County, California, in 1987 and took over Anaheim White House, which now features steak and seafood with northern Italian cuisine. His award-winning excellence and signature entrées have brought fine dining to Orange County. Chef Bruno's philosophy is simple: to treat each and every one of his patrons as a distinguished guest in his home. Every night, he and his Anaheim White House team serve dinners to children in the "Motel Kid" program through the Boys and Girls Club of Anaheim. They've served more than 350,000 dinners to date. *Recipe: Tilapia over Quinoa (Chapter 18)*

Chef Randal St. Clair, executive chef, Mohawk Bend (Los Angeles, CA)   Chef Randal St. Clair is the executive chef of Mohawk Bend, a restaurant known for its craft beer and vegan dishes. Before heading the kitchen at Mohawk Bend, Chef St. Clair worked on organic farms. A veteran of the Beverly Hills Farmers' Market, Chef St. Clair's menu at Mohawk Bend is mostly vegetarian—more than half of it vegan—with an emphasis on California produce and products. *Recipe: Mohawk Bend's Breakfast Quinoa (Chapter 3)*

Chef Giselle Wellman, executive chef, Petrossian Boutique and Restaurant (West Hollywood, CA)   After graduating from Le Cordon Bleu Academie d'Art Culinaire in Mexico City, Chef Wellman worked in stellar kitchens, including Jack's La Jolla, Jean Georges NYC, Mario Batali's Del Posto, and Thomas Keller's Bouchon. Wellman brings her expertise with pasta and seafood to Petrossian caviar–accented dishes. "There's a rustic, home-style element to the food, combined with my knowledge from my fine-dining background and my continuous learning of all the different ways I can utilize caviar in my dishes," she says. *Recipe: Poached Salmon with Cucumber and Tomato Quinoa Salad (Chapter 18)*

Index